C000005494

ATLAS OF TOWN PLANS
NORTHERN ENGLAND & SCOTLAND

Published by the Automobile Association
Fanum House, Basingstoke, Hants RG21 2EA

Route Planning Map

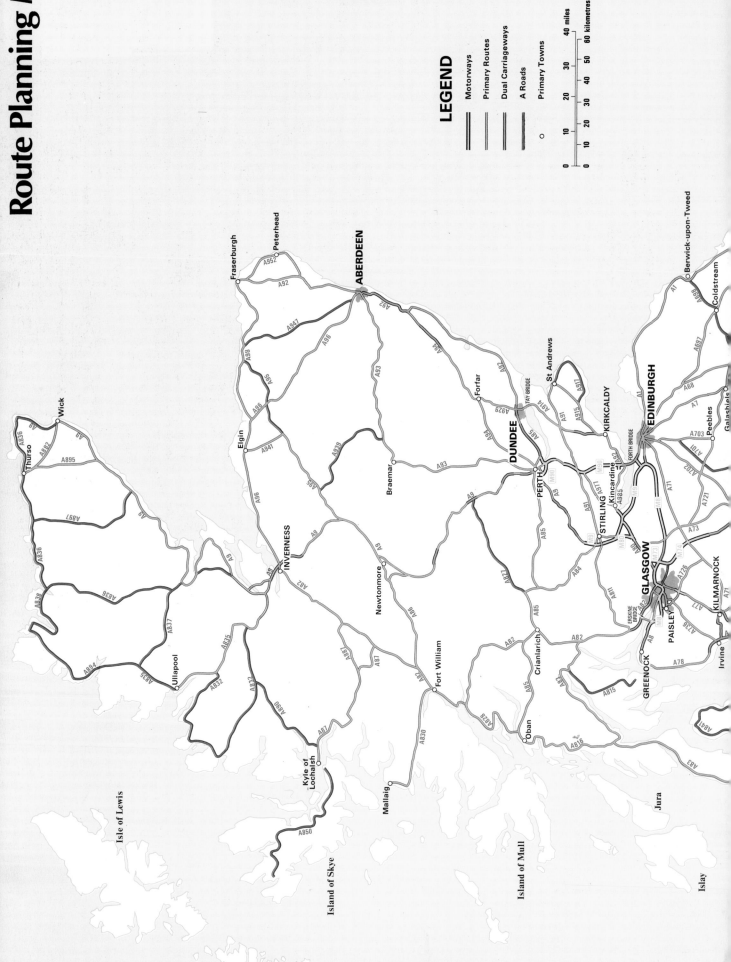

Isle of Lewis

Wick

Thurso
A836
A882
A895
A9
A897
A838
A9
A836
A837
Ullapool
A835
A832
A894
A835
A832
A830
A87
Kyle of Lochalsh
A850
Mallaig
A851
A830

Island of Skye

INVERNESS
A9
A82
A96
A95
Elgin
A941
A96
A98
A95
A96
A947
Fraserburgh
A952
Peterhead
A92

ABERDEEN
A92
A93

A939
Braemar
A93
A94
A90
A9

Newtonmore
A86
A9
A889

Fort William
A82
A828
Oban
A85
A816
A819
Crianlarich
A82
A85
A84
A821
A9
A822

Forfar
A92
St Andrews
TAY BRIDGE
A929
A914
DUNDEE
PERTH
A90
A85
A9
A91
A915
KIRKCALDY
A977
Kincardine
M90
STIRLING
A985
FORTH BRIDGE
EDINBURGH
A9
M9
M80
M876
A80
GLASGOW
ERSKINE BRIDGE
M8
M77
PAISLEY
A737
A726
A78
KILMARNOCK
A71
A77
Irvine
A841
A83
GREENOCK
A8
A815
A814

Island of Mull

Jura

Islay

Berwick-upon-Tweed
A1
Coldstream
A698
A697
A68
A7
Peebles
A703
A701
A702
A72
Galashiels
A721
A73
A71

A83

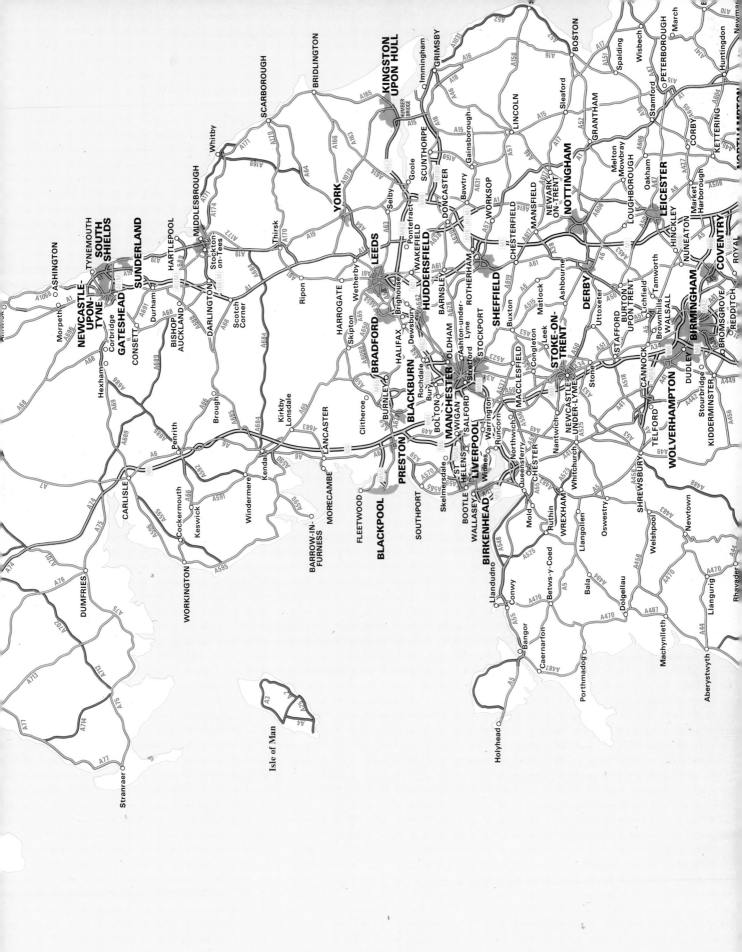

Stone is the key to the look of landscape and townscape in
Scotland and Northern England. Even in the boom times of the 19th
century, when buildings appeared almost as quickly as
mushrooms, it was nearly always stone – most often local stone –
that was used, giving a sense of unity with place. Our age, the age of
concrete, steel and glass, has imposed alien and intrusive materials
on some of these towns, but most retain some at least of their
original character. A handful of examples illustrates how rich the
northern townscapes can be – York, with a visible continuity of
occupation since Roman times; Edinburgh, with one of the finest
town designs in Europe; Stockton-on-Tees, rich in industrial history;
and Aberdeen, with a granite face given new glamour by the riches
of oil. Stone has created dramatic scenery, including Britain's
mountain ranges – these are landscapes still wild, still wayward
and quite unlike the streets which are built from them.

There are 123 town plans in this book, ranging from huge industrial
cities to quiet seaside resorts. Location plans and town descriptions
are included, and street indexes make the town plans themselves
practical and easy to use.

Produced by the Cartographic Department
Publishing Division of the Automobile Association

The contents of this book are believed correct at the time of printing. Nevertheless, the publisher can
accept no responsibility for errors or omissions, or for changes in the details given.

© The Automobile Association 1986

Published by the Automobile Association, Fanum House, Basingstoke, Hampshire RG21 2EA

Printed and bound in Spain by Graficromo SA, Spain

ISBN 0 86145 369 7

AA Ref 57671

Northern England and Scotland

AREA MAPS ARE INDICATED IN BOLD.

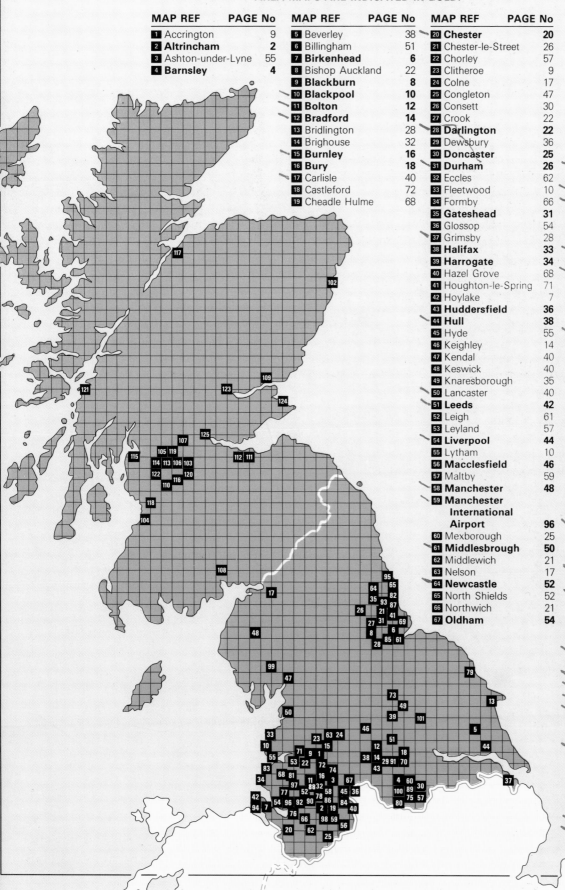

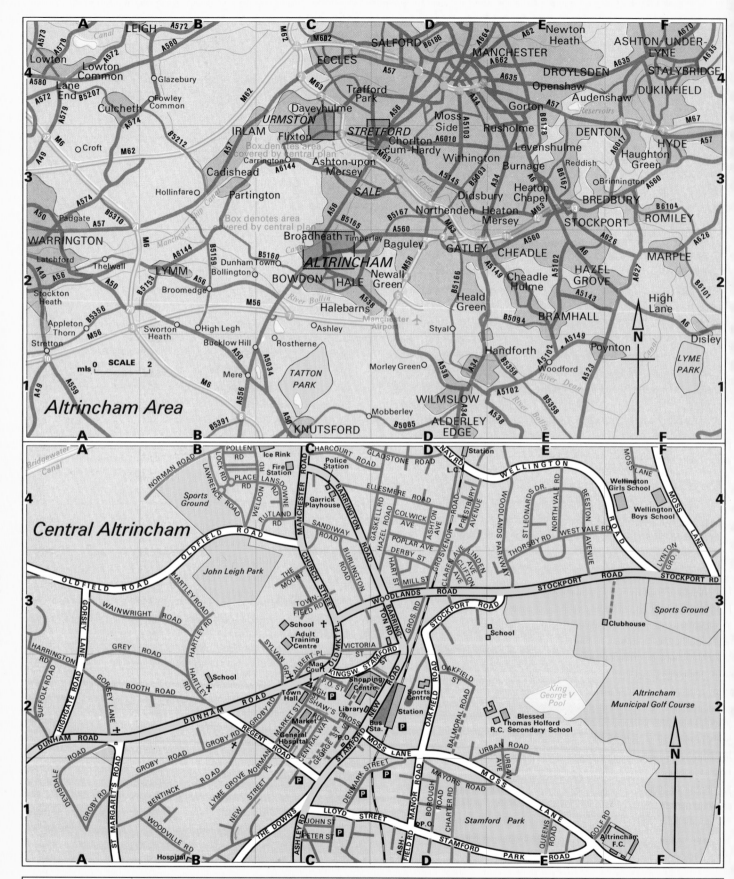

Altrincham

Bonnie Prince Charlie's troops gathered in Altrincham's Old Market Place during the '45 rebellion, to demand lodgings — and Altrincham is still much in demand today as a residential area. Conveniently close to Manchester, it also has good shops, a modern sports centre, a golf course and an ice rink. Not so very long ago it stood in an agricultural district, but the coming of the

railways sparked off the town's development, and it first became a cotton producing town, and later a centre for light industry.

Urmston's Davyhulme Park is one of the most attractive in the area. The town grew with the opening of the Manchester Ship Canal, and the establishment of the Trafford Park industrial estate has brought further development.

Stretford has a chilling reminder of the past in the 'Great Stone' or 'plague stone' which

stands at the entrance to Gorse Hill Park. The two holes in its surface were once filled with disinfectant to purify coins which had been handled by plague victims. Stretford itself used to be a centre for the making of woollen goods, but the opening up of a way to the sea by the linking of the Bridgewater Canal and the Manchester Ship Canal began its years of greatest growth. Today it has one of the biggest shopping centres in the borough, and a modern sports centre.

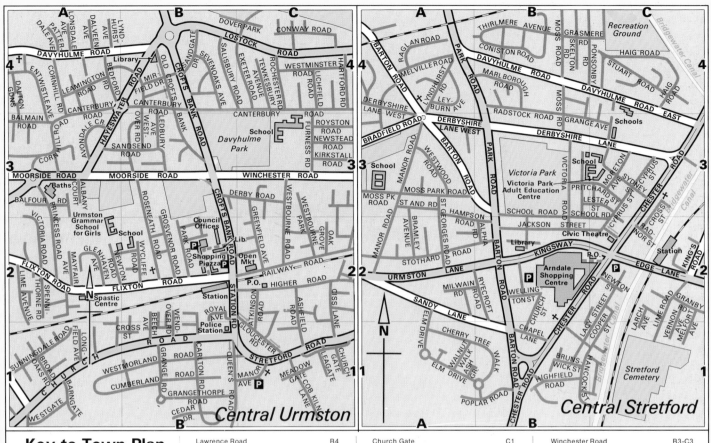

Central Urmston

Central Stretford

Key to Town Plan and Area Plan

Town Plan
AA Recommended roads
Other roads
Restricted roads
Buildings of interest   Cinema
Churches
Car Parks
Parks and open spaces
One way streets

Area Plan
A roads
B roads
Locations   Ibsley ○
Urban area

STREET INDEX

Altrincham

Albert Place	C2
Ashfield Road	D1
Ashley Road	C1
Ashton Avenue	D4
Balmoral Road	D2
Barrington Road	C4-C3-D3
Beeston Avenue	E3-E4
Bentinck Road	A1-B1-B2
Booth Road	A2-B2
Borough Road	D1
Burlington Road	C3-C4
Central Way	C1-C2
Charter Road	D1
Church Street	C3-C4
Clarendon Avenue	D3
Clifton Avenue	D3
Colwick Avenue	D4
Cross Street	C2
Denmark Street	C1-D1
Derby Street	D3
Devisdale Road	A1-A2
Dunham Road	A1-A2-B2-C2
Ellesmere Road	C4-D4
Gaskell Road	C4-D4
George Street	C1-C2
Gladstone Road	C4-D4
Golf Road	E1-F1
Gorsey Lane	A2-A3
Grey Road	A2-A3-A2-B2
Groby Road	A1-B1-B2-C2
Grosvenor Road	D3-D4
Harcourt Road	C4-D4
Harrington Road	A2-A3
Hartley Road	B2-B3
Hart Street	D3
Hazel Road	D3-D4
Highgate Road	A2
High Street	C2
John Street	C1
Kingsway	C2
Landsdowne Road	C4
Lawrence Road	B4
Linden Avenue	D3
Lloyd Street	C1-D1
Lock Road	B4
Lyme Grove	B1
Lynton Grove	F3-F4
Manchester Road	C4
Manor Road	D1
Market Street	C2
Mayors Road	D1-E1
Mill Street	D3
Moss Lane	C2-D2-D1-E1-F1
Moss Lane	F3-F4
Navigation Road	D4
New Street	B1-C1-C2
Norman Place	B1-C1-C2
Norman Road	B4
North Vale Road	E4
Oakfield Road	D2-D3
Oakfield Street	D2
Oldfield Road	A3-B3-B4-C4
Old Market Place	C2-C3
Peter Street	C1
Place Road	B4
Pollen Road	B4
Poplar Avenue	D4
Post Office Street	C2
Prestbury Avenue	D4
Queens Road	E1
Regent Road	E1
Rutland Road	C4
St Leonards Drive	E4
St Margaret's Road	A1-A2
Sandiway Road	C4
Shaw's Road	C2
Stockport Road	D3-E3-F3
Stamford Park Road	D1-E1
Stamford New Road	C1-C2-D2-D3
Stamford Street	C2-D2-D3
Suffolk Road	A2
Sylvan Grove	C2-C3
The Downs	B1-C1
The Mount	C3
Thorsby Road	E3-E4
Townfield Road	C3
Urban Avenue	E1-E2
Urban Road	D1-D2-E2
Victoria Street	C3-D3
Wainwright Road	A3-B3
Weldon Road	B4-C4
Wellington Road	D4-E4-F4-F3
West Vale Road	E4-F4
Woodlands Parkway	E3-E4
Woodlands Road	C3-D3-E3
Woodville Road	B1

Urmston

Albany Court	A3
Ashfield Road	C1-C2
Atkinson Road	C1-C2
Avondale Crescent	A3
Balfour Road	A3
Balmain Road	A3
Barngate	A1
Bedford Road	A4
Beech Avenue	B1-B2
Broadoaks Road	A1
Canterbury Road	A3-A4-B4-C4
Carlton Road	B1
Cedar Drive	B1
Church Gate	C1
Church Road	A1-B1
Ciss Lane	C1-C2
Cob Kiln Lane	C1
Conway Road	C4
Cornhill Road	A3-A4
Crofts Bank Road	B2-B3-B4
Cross Street	A1-B1
Cumberland Road	A1-B1
Dalton Gardens	A3-A4
Dalveen Avenue	A4
Davyhulme Road	A4-B4
Derby Road	B3-C3
Dover Park	B4-C4
Entwistle Avenue	A3-A4
Exeter Road	B4-C4
Flixton Road	A2-B2
Furness Road	C3
Glenhaven Avenue	A2
Gloucester Road	C1-C2
Grange Road	B1
Grangethorpe Road	B1
Grosvenor Road	B2-B3
Greenfield Avenue	C2-C3
Hartford Road	C4
Hayeswater Road	A3-A4-B4
Higher Road	B2-C2
Kirkstall Road	C3
Leagate	C1
Leamington Road	A4
Ledbury Avenue	B3-B4
Lichfield Road	C4
Lime Avenue	A1-A2
Longfield Avenue	A1
Lonsdale Avenue	A4
Lostock Road	B4-C4
Lyndhurst Avenue	A4
Manor Avenue	B1-C1
Mayfair Avenue	A2
Meadow Gate	C1
Mirfield Drive	B4
Moorside Road	A3-B3
Newstead Road	C3
Newton Road	A2
Oak Grove	C2
Old Crofts Bank	B3-B4
Park Road	B2
Patterdale Avenue	A4
Princess Road	A2-A3
Queen's Road	B1
Railway Road	B2-C2
Rochester Road	C4
Roseneath Road	B2-B3
Royal Avenue	B2
Royston Road	C3
Salisbury Road	B4-C4
Sandgate Drive	B4
Sandsend Road	A3-B3
Sevenoaks Avenue	B4
Spennithorne Road	A2
Station Road	B1-B2
Stretford Road	B1-C1
Sunningdale Road	A1
Tewkesbury Avenue	C4
Victoria Road	A2-A3
Wendover Road	B1-B2
Westbourne Park	C2-C3
Westbourne Road	C2-C3
Westgate	A1
Westminster Road	C4
Westmorland Road	A1-B1-C1
Westover Road	B3-B4
Winchester Road	B3-C3

Stretford

Alpha Road	B2
Ash Grove	A1
Barton Road	A4-A3-B3-B2-B1
Bradfield Road	A3
Bramley Avenue	A2-A3
Brunswick Street	B1
Chapel Lane	B1
Cherry Tree Walk	A1-B1
Chester Road	B1-B2-C2-C3-C4
Church Street	B1-B2
Coniston Road	B4
Cooper Street	C1-C2
Cross Street	C2-C3
Cyprus Street	C2-C3
Davyhulme Road	A4-B4
Davyhulme Road East	B4-C4-C3
Derbyshire Lane	B3-C3
Derbyshire Lane West	A4-A3-B3
Edge Lane	C2
Elm Drive	A1-A2
Granby Road	C2
Grange Avenue	B3-C3
Grasmere Road	B4-C4
Haig Road	C4
Hampson Road	A3-A2-B2
Hancock Street	B1-C2
Highfield Road	B1
Jackson Street	B2-C2
King's Road	C2
Kingsway	B2-C2
Lacy Street	B1-C1-C2
Larch Avenue	C1-C2
Lester Street	B3-C3
Leyburn Avenue	A4
Lime Road	C1-C2
Lyndhurst Road	A4
Manor Road	A2-A3
Marlborough Road	B4
Melfort Avenue	C1-C2
Melville Road	A4
Milwain Road	A2-B2
Moreton Avenue	C3
Moss Road	B3-B4
Moss Park Road	A3
Newton Street	C2
Park Road	A4-B4-B3
Ponsonby Road	B4-C4
Poplar Road	A1-B1
Pritchard Street	B3-C3
Rador Street	C2
Radstock Road	B3-B4
Raglan Road	A4
Ryecroft Road	A2-B2
St Andrew's Road	A3
St Georges Road	A2-A3
Sandy Lane	A2-B2-B1
School Road	B3-B2-C2
Skelton Road	B4
Stothard Road	A2-B2
Stuart Road	C4
Sydney Street	C3
Thirlmere Avenue	B4
Urmston Lane	A2-B2
Vernon Avenue	C1-C2
Victoria Road	B2-B3
Walnut Walk	A1
Wellington Street	B2
Westwood Road	A3

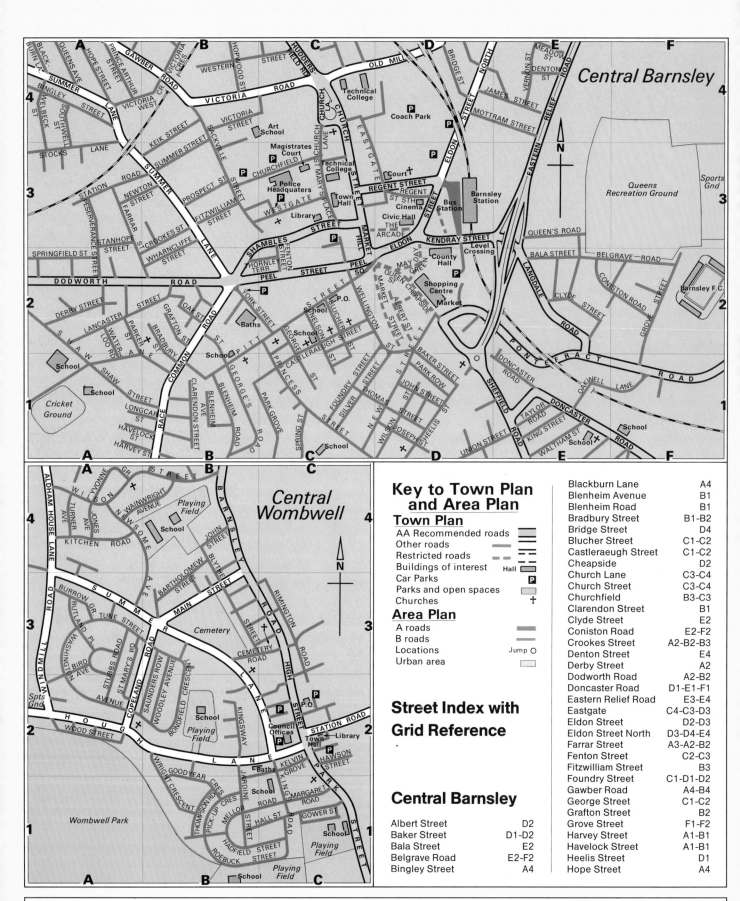

Key to Town Plan and Area Plan

Town Plan

AA Recommended roads	
Other roads	
Restricted roads	
Buildings of interest	Hall
Car Parks	P
Parks and open spaces	
Churches	†

Area Plan

A roads	
B roads	
Locations	Jump O
Urban area	

Street Index with Grid Reference

Central Barnsley

Barnsley

Amongst the claims to fame of Barnsley must be numbered the local football club — at present in the Second Division of the Canon League. Started in 1887, it achieved fame in the early part of the present century by reaching the FA Cup Final twice, and by winning the trophy in 1911/1912. Barnsley lies in the midst of a coalmining district, and the Yorkshire area of the National Union of Mineworkers has its headquarters in a Victorian building which is one of the many impressive features of the town. Other landmarks are the modern development of the Metropolitan Centre with its new market hall, and the tower which stands in Locke Park (on the south-eastern edge of town) which has a public viewing gallery. Leisure is catered for in the town's four sports centres, and in Worsbrough Country Park. This lies to the south and has a reservoir — popular with both fishermen and wildlife. A working 17th-century watermill which is now a museum can also be seen here, and just north of the town centre are the remains of Monk Bretton Priory, founded in the 12th century.

Wombwell is an area of new industries, which have arrived to replace its declining local collieries. A popular place to live, it has good shops and extensive open spaces in Wombwell Park, to the south-west of the town centre.

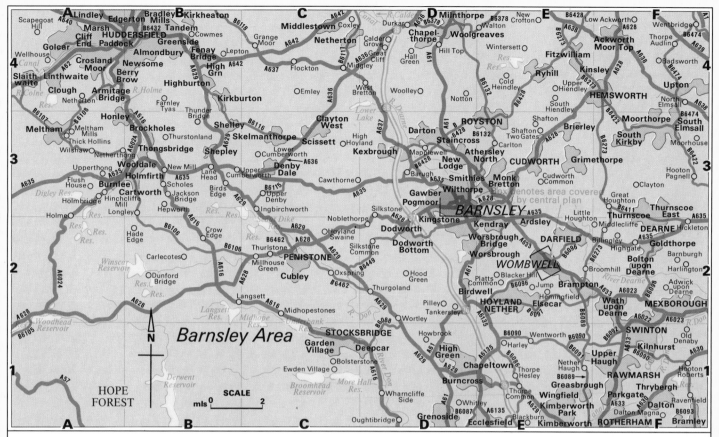

Barnsley Area

HOPE FOREST

SCALE
mls 0 _____ 2

Hopwood Street	B4	Queens Avenue	A4	Westgate	B3-C3	
Huddersfield Road	C4	Race Common Road	B1-B2	Wharncliffe Street	B2-B3	
James Street	D4-E4	Regent Street	C3-D3	Wilson Street	D1	
John Street	D1	Regent Street South	D3	York Street	B2-C2	
Joseph Street	D1	St George's Road	B1-B2			
Keik Street	B3-B4	St Mary's Place	C3			
Kendray Street	D3-E3	Sackville Street	B4-B3-C3			
King Street	E1	Shambles Street	B2-B3-C3			
Lancaster Street	A2-B2	Shaw Lane	A2-A1-B1			
Langdale Road	E2	Shaw Street	A1-B1			
Longcar Street	A1-B1	Sheffield Road	D1-E1			
Market Hill	C2-C3	Silver Street	C1-D1-D2			
Market Street	C2-D2	Southwell Street	A3-A4			
May Day Green	D2-D3	Spring Street	C1			
Meadow Street	E4	Springfield Street	A2			
Mottram Street	D4-E4	Stanhope Street	A3			
Nelson Street	C1-C2	Station Road	A3-B3			
New Street	C1-D1-D2	Stocks Lane	A3-A4			
Newton Street	A3-B3	Summer Lane	A4-A3-B3-B2			
Oak Street	B2	Summer Street	B3-B4			
Oakwell Lane	E1-F1	The Arcade	C3-D3			
Old Mill	C4-D4	Taylor Road	E1			
Park Grove	B1-C1	Thomas Street	C1-D1			
Park Row	D1	Thornley Terrace	B2-C2			
Parker Street	A2	Union Street	D1-E1			
Peel Square	C2	Vernon Street	E4			
Peel Street	B2-C2	Victoria Crescent	B4			
Pitt Street	B1-B2-C2	Victoria Crescent West	A4-B4			
Pontefract Road	E2-E1-F1	Victoria Road	B4-C4			
Perserverance Street	A2-A3	Victoria Street	B4-C4			
Prince Arthur Street	A4	Walterloo Road	A1-A2			
Princess Street	C1-C2	Waltham Street	E1			
Prospect Street	B3	Welbeck Street	A3-A4			
Queen Street	D2	Wellington Street	C2-D2			
Queen's Road	E3	Western Street	B4-C4			

Central Wombwell

Aldham House Lane	A4	Margaret Road	C1
Bartholomew Street	B3-B4	Mellor Road	B1-C1
Barnsley Road	B4-B3-C3	Newsome Avenue	A3-A4-B4-B3
Bird Avenue	A3	Park Street	C1-C2
Blythe Street	B3-B4	Pick-Up Crescent	B1
Bondfield Crescent	B2-B3	Rimington Road	C2-C3
Burrow Grove	A3	Roebuck Street	B1-C1
Cemetery Road	B3-C3	Rutland Place	A3
Copeland Road	A2-A3-B3-B2	St Mary's Road	A2-A3
Goodyear Crescent	B1-B2	Saunders Row	A2-B2-B3
Gower Street	C1	Station Road	C2
Hadfield Street	B1-C1	Stubbs Road	A2-A3
Hall Street	B1-C1	Summer Lane	A4-A3-B3-B2-C2
Hawson Street	C2	Thompson Road	B1
High Street	C2-C3	Tune Street	A3-B3
Hough Lane	A2-B2-C2	Turner Avenue	A4
Jardine Street	B1-B2	Wainwright Avenue	A4-B4
John Street	B4	Washington Avenue	A2-A3
Jones Avenue	A4	Wilson Street	A4-B4
Kelvin Grove	C2	Windmill Road	A2-A3
Kings Road	C1-C2	Wood Street	A2
Kingsway	B2	Woodley Avenue	B2-B3
Kitchen Road	A4	Wright Crescent	B1-B2
Main Street	B3-B4	Yvonne Grove	A4

BARNSLEY
Opened by HRH the Prince of Wales on 14 December 1933 and built at a cost of £188,000, the magnificent four-storey Town Hall has a 145ft tower of Portland stone, and is one of the town's most impressive sights.

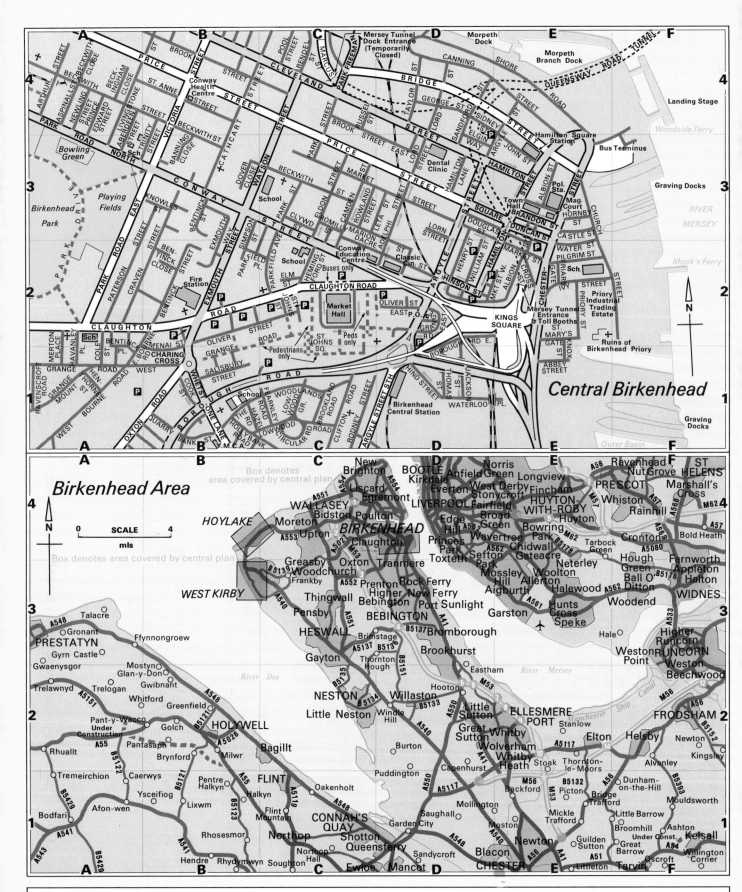

Birkenhead

You can take the famous 'ferry across the Mersey' to reach this largest town on the Wirral Peninsula, but it also connected to Liverpool by bridges and the Mersey Tunnel. The town grew up around the Merseyside docks to become an important ship-building centre, and a number of engineering firms are still located here. Amongst Birkenhead's places of history are the remains of

a 12th-century Benedictine Priory at Monks Ferry, and the Williamson Art Gallery and Museum, which stages regular art exhibitions and also houses the Wirral Maritime Museum.

West Kirby is a place for walking and water. Lying on the estuary of the River Dee, it is well known for its Marine Lake, where boating and sailing can be enjoyed, while just offshore is the wildlife of the Hilbre Islands (accessible only to permit holders). Several pleasant parks can be

found in the town, and to the south, the Wirral Way Country Park incorporates the 12 miles of the Wirral Way footpath.

Hoylake's Windswept and world famous, the Royal Liverpool Golf Course stretches its length along the coast between Hoylake and West Kirby. Numerous parks and gardens are another attraction of this former fishing village, which lies at the north-west corner of the Wirral Peninsula and enjoys an extensive seafront.

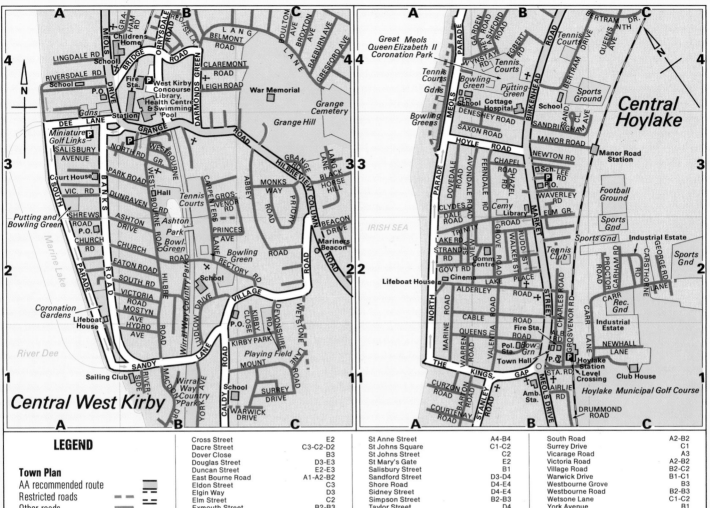

Central West Kirby

Central Hoylake

IRISH SEA

River Dee

Marine Lake

Hoylake Municipal Golf Course

LEGEND

Town Plan

AA recommended route	
Restricted roads	
Other roads	
Buildings of interest	Theatre ▣
Car parks	℗
Parks and open spaces	
One way streets	←

Area Plan

A roads	
B roads	
Locations	Littleney ○
Urban area	

Street Index with Grid Reference

Birkenhead

Abbey Street	E1
Aberdeen Street	A3-A4
Adelphi Street	D2-D3
Albion Street	E3
Argyle Street	D2-D3-E3-E4
Argyle Street South	C1-D1
Arthur Street	A4
Aspinall Street	A4
Banning Close	B3
Beckingham Close	A4
Beckwith Close	A4
Beckwith Street	A4-B4-B3, C3
Bentinck Close	B2
Bentinck Place	A1-A2
Bentinck Street	B2-B3
Borough Road	B1-C1-D1
Borough Road East	D1-D2-E2
Brandon Street	E3
Bridge Street	C4-D4-E4-E3
Brook Street	B4-C4
Brook Street East	C4-C3-D3
Brookland Road	C1
Camden Street	C3
Canning Street	D4-E4
Castle Street	E3
Cathcart Street	B3-B4
Charing Cross	B1
Chester Street	E2-E3
Church Street	E3-E2-F2
Circular Road	C1
Claughton Road	A2-B2-C2-D2
Cleveland Street	B4-C4-D4-D3
Clifton Road	C1
Clywd Street	C3
Cook Street	B1
Cole Street	A1-A2
Conway Street	B3-C3-C2
Craven Street	A2-B2-B3
Cross Street	E2
Dacre Street	C3-C2-D2
Dover Close	B3
Douglas Street	D3-E3
Duncan Street	E2-E3
East Bourne Road	A1-A2-B2
Eldon Street	C3
Elgin Way	D3
Elm Street	C2
Exmouth Street	B2-B3
Exmouth Way	B2-B3
Fearnley Road	C1
Friars Gate	E2
George Street	D4
Grange Mount	A1
Grange Road	B1-B2-C2
Grange Road East	D2
Grange Road West	A1-B1
Hamilton Road	D3
Hamilton Square	D3-E3
Hamilton Street	D2-E2-E3
Havanley Place	A1-A2
Hazel Road	B1
Hemingford Street	C2
Henry Street	D2-D3
Henthorne Street	A1
Hind Street	D1
Hinson Street	D2
Hollybank Road	B1-C1
Hornby Street	E3
Ivy Street	E2
Jackson Street	D1
John Street	E3
Knowles Street	B3
Knox Street	E1-E2
Leta Street	C3-D3
Livingstone Street	A3-A4-B4
Lord Street	D3-D4
Lorn Street	D3
Lowwood Green	C1
Lowwood Road	B1-C1
Marcus Street	C4
Marion Street	C3-D3-D2
Market Street	C3-D3-E3-E2
Market Street West	D2-E2
Menai Street	B1
Merton Place	A1-A2
Newling Street	A4
Oliver Street	B2-C2
Oliver Street East	D2
Oxton Road	A1-B1
Park Freeman	C4
Park Road East	A2-A3-B3
Park Road North	A4-A3-B3
Park Street	C3-C4
Parkfield Avenue	C2-C3
Parkfield Place	B2-C2
Paterson Street	A2-A3-B3
Pilgrim Street	E2
Pool Street	C4
Price Street	A4-B4-C4-C3-D3
Priory Street	E2
Prince Edward Street	A4
Quarry Bank Street	B1
Queensway Road Tunnel	C4-D4-E4-F4, E2-E3, D3-D4
Ravenscroft Road	A1
Rendel Street	C4
Rodney Street	C1
Romilly Street	C3
Rowland Street	C3
Russel Street	C4

St Anne Street	A4-B4
St Johns Square	C1-C2
St Johns Street	C2
St Mary's Gate	E2
Salisbury Street	B1
Sandford Street	D3-D4
Shore Road	D4-E4
Sidney Street	D4-E4
Simpson Street	B2-B3
Taylor Street	D4
The Woodlands	B1-C1
Thomas Street	D1
Trinity Street	A3-B3-B4
Victoria Street	B3-B4
Waterloo Place	D1-E1
Water Street	E2
Watson Street	B3-C3-C4
West Bourne Road	A1
Whetstone Lane	B1
William Street	D2

West Kirby

Abbey Road	C2-C3
Ashton Drive	A3-A2-B2
Banks Road	A3-A2-A1-B1
Beacon Drive	C2
Belmont Road	B4-C4
Black Horse Hill	C3
Boulton Avenue	C4
Bridge Road	A4-B4
Broxton Avenue	C4
Caldy Road	B1
Carpenters Lane	B2-B3
Church Road	A2-B2
Claremont Road	B4-C4
Darmonds Green	B3-B4
Dee Lane	A3
Devonshire Road	C1-C2
Dunraven Road	A3-B3
Eaton Road	A2-B2
Graham Road	A4-B4
Grange Road	B3-C3
Gresford Avenue	C4
Grosvenor Road	B3
Hilbre Road	B1-B2
Hilbreview Column Road	C2-C3
Hydro Avenue	B1
Kirby Close	C1-C2
Kirby Park	B1-C1
Lang Lane	B4-C4
Leigh Road	B4-C4
Lingdale Road	A4
Ludlow Drive	B1-B2
Macdona Drive	B1
Meols Drive	A4
Monks Way	C3
Mostyn Avenue	B2
Mount Road	B1-C1
North Road	A3-B3
Orrysdale Road	B4
Park Road	A3-B3
Princes Avenue	B2-C2
Priory Road	C2-C3
Raeburn Avenue	C4
Rectory Road	B2-C2
Red House Lane	B4
Riversdale Road	A4
Riverside	B1
Salisbury Avenue	A3
Sandy Lane	A1-B1
Shrewsbury Road	A2-A3
South Parade	A1-A2-A3

South Road	A2-B2
Surrey Drive	C1
Vicarage Road	A3
Victoria Road	A2-B2
Village Road	B2-C2
Warwick Drive	B1-C1
Westbourne Grove	B3
Westbourne Road	B2-B3
Wetsone Lane	C1-C2
York Avenue	B1

Hoylake

Airlie Road	B1
Albion Road	B1
Alderley Road	A2-B2
Ashford Road	B4
Avondale Road	B2-B3
Barton Road	A1
Bertram Drive	B4-C4
Bertram Drive North	C4
Birkenhead Road	B3-B4
Cable Road	A2-B2
Carham Road	C2
Carr Lane	C1-C2
Carsthorne Road	C2
Chapel Road	B3
Charles Road	B1-B2
Clydesdale Road	A3
Courtenay Road	A1
Curzon Road	A1
Deneshay Road	A4-B4-B3
Dovedale Road	A3
Drummond Road	B1
Egbert Road	B4
Elm Grove	B3
Ferndale Road	B3
Garden Hay Road	B4
George Road	C2
Government Road	A2
Grove Road	B2
Grosvenor Road	B1-B2
Hazel Road	B3
Hoyle Road	A3-B3
Lake Place	B2
Lake Road	A2
Lee Road	B3
Manor Road	B2
Marine Road	A1-A2
Market Street	B1-B2-B3
Meols Drive	B1
Meols Parade	A3-A4
Newhall Lane	C1
Newton Road	B3
North Parade	A1-A2-A3
Proctor Road	C2
Queens Avenue	C4
Queens Road	A1-B1
Rudd Road	B2
Sandringham Avenue	B3-C3
Sandringham Close	B3
Saxon Road	A2
Sea View	A2
Stanley Road	B1
Station Road	B1
Strand Road	A2
The Kings Gap	A1-B1
Trinity Road	A2-B2-B3
Valentia Road	B1-B2
Walker Road	B2
Warren Road	A1
Waverley Road	B3
Wynstay Road	A4-B4

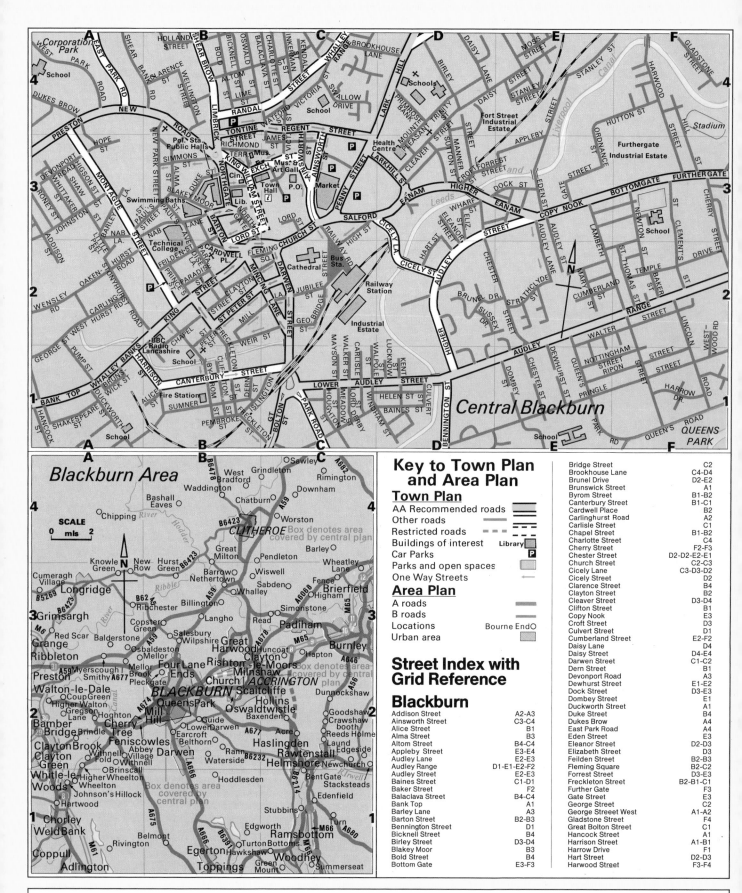

Key to Town Plan and Area Plan

Town Plan
- AA Recommended roads
- Other roads
- Restricted roads
- Buildings of interest — Library
- Car Parks — P
- Parks and open spaces
- One Way Streets

Area Plan
- A roads
- B roads
- Locations — Bourne End ○
- Urban area

Street Index with Grid Reference

Blackburn

Addison Street	A2-A3
Ainsworth Street	C3-C4
Alice Street	B1
Alma Street	B3
Altom Street	B4-C4
Appleby Street	E3-E4
Audley Lane	E2-E3
Audley Range	D1-E1-E2-F2
Audley Street	E2-E3
Baines Street	C1-D1
Baker Street	F2
Balaclava Street	B4-C4
Bank Top	A1
Barley Lane	A3
Barton Street	B2-B3
Bennington Street	D1
Bicknell Street	B4
Birley Street	D3-D4
Blakey Moor	B3
Bold Street	B4
Bottom Gate	E3-F3
Bridge Street	C2
Brookhouse Lane	C4-D4
Brunel Drive	D2-E2
Brunswick Street	A1
Byrom Street	B1-B3
Canterbury Street	B1-C1
Cardwell Place	B2
Carlinghurst Road	A2
Carlisle Street	C1
Chapel Street	B1-B2
Charlotte Street	C4
Cherry Street	F2-F3
Chester Street	D2-D2-E2-E1
Church Street	C2-C3
Cicely Lane	C3-D3-D2
Cicely Street	D2
Clarence Street	B4
Clayton Street	B2
Cleaver Street	D3-D4
Clifton Street	B1
Copy Nook	E3
Croft Street	D3
Culvert Street	D1
Cumberland Street	E2-F2
Daisy Lane	D4
Daisy Street	D4-E4
Darwen Street	C1-C2
Dern Street	B1
Devonport Road	A3
Dewhurst Street	E1-E2
Dock Street	D3-E3
Dombey Street	E1
Duckworth Street	A1
Duke Street	B4
Dukes Brow	A4
East Park Road	A4
Eden Street	E3
Eleanor Street	D2-D3
Elizabeth Street	D3
Feilden Street	B2-B3
Fleming Square	B2-C2
Forrest Street	D3-E3
Freckleton Street	B2-B1-C1
Further Gate	F3
Gate Street	E3
George Street	C2
George Streeet West	A1-A2
Gladstone Street	F4
Great Bolton Street	C1
Hancock Street	A1
Harrison Street	A1-B1
Harrow Drive	F1
Hart Street	D2-D3
Harwood Street	F3-F4

Blackburn

The glittering heights of championship rollerskating at the Starskate roller rink are a far cry from Blackburn's 'workshop of England' image — an image it is doing its best to change. Once the weaving centre of the world but no longer even predominantly a textile town, it has seen the redevelopment of its old industrial areas while the entire town centre is being converted into a traffic-free shopping precinct. But memories of an older Blackburn can still be seen outside the centre, and some of the stone-built terraces have been declared conservation areas. Blackburn Cathedral is an interesting mixture of old and new: it was built up around the 19th-century church which is now its nave.

Clitheroe is overlooked by a record-breaking castle keep — not only is it the smallest keep in England but it is also one of Lancashire's oldest stone structures. Little else remains of the castle, which dates back to the 12th century and was a Royalist stronghold in the Civil War. This is a very old industrial town, but one with a pleasantly rural atmosphere. St Mary Magdalene's Church is noted for its twisted spire.

Accrington's fame was built on cotton and bricks: noted for their hardness, the smooth red bricks produced in the town spread its name throughout Victorian Britain.

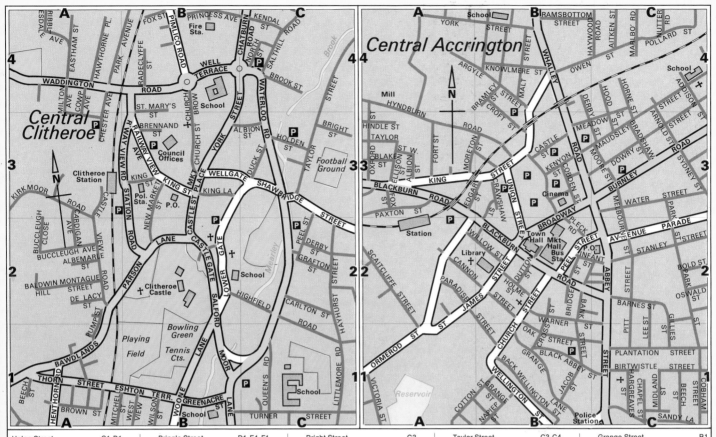

Clitheroe index (columns)

Helen Street	C1-D1
High Street	C2-C3
Higher Audley Street	D1-D2-D3-E3
Higher Eanam	D3-E3
Higson Street	A3
Hill Street	F3-F4
Holland Street	B4
Hope Street	A3
Houghton Street	C1
Hutton Street	E4-F4
Inkerman Street	C4
Islington	B1-C1
James Street	C3
Johnston Street	A3
Jubilee Street	C2
Kendal Street	C4
Kent Street	D1
King Street	B2
King William Street	B3-C3
Lambeth Street	E3-E2-F2-F1
Lark Hill	C4-D4
Larkhill Street	C3-D3
Limbrick	B3-B4
Lime Street	B4
Lincoln Road	F1-F2
Little Peel Street	A2-A3
Lord Street	B2-B3, C3
Lord Derby Street	C1
Lower Audley Street	C1-D1
Lucknow Street	D1
Manner Sutton Street	D3-D4
Mary Street	E2
Mayson Street	C1
Meadow Street	C1
Mill Lane	B2-C2
Mincing Lane	B2-C2
Montague Street	A4-A3-A2-B2
Mount Pleasant	D3-D4
Moss Street	E4
Nab Lane	A3-B3
Newton Street	F2-F3
New Park Street	B3-B4
Northgate	B3
Nottingham Street	E1-F1-F2
Oakenhurst Road	A2
Ordnance Street	E3-E4
Oswald Street	B2
Paradise Lane	B2
Paradise Street	B2
Pembroke Street	B1
Penny Street	C3
Park Road	C1
Preston New Road	A3-A4-B4-B3
Primrose Bank	D4
Prince's Street	B2

Pringle Street	D1-E1-F1
Pump Street	A1-A2
Queen's Road	F1
Queen's Park Road	E2-E1-F1
Railway Road	C2-C3
Randal Street	B4-C4
Regent Street	C3-C4
Richmond Terrace	B3-C3
Ripon Street	E1-F1
Roney Street	E1
St Clement's Street	F2-F3
St Paul's Avenue	B2-B3
St Paul's Street	B1-B3
St Peter Street	B1-B2
St Thomas Street	F2
Salford Eanam	C3-D3
Shakespeare Street	A1
Shaw Street	A3
Shear Bank Road	A4-B4
Shear Brow	B4
Simmon Street	B3
Stanley Street	E4-F4
Stonyhurst Road	A2-B2
Strathclyde Street	E2
Sumner Street	B1
Sussex Drive	D2-E2
Swallow Drive	C4
Temple Drive	F2
Tontine Street	B3-B4
Trinity Street	D4
Victoria Street	C3-C4
Walker Street	C1
Walpole Street	C1
Walter Street	E2-F2
Watford Street	C4
Weir Street	B2-C2
Wellington Street	B4
Wensley Road	A2
West Park Road	A4
Westwood Road	F1-F2
Whalley Banks	A1-A2-B2
Whalley Range	C4
Wharf Street	D3
Whittaker Street	A3
Windham Street	C1-D1

Clitheroe

Albemarle Street	A2
Albion Street	B3-C3
Baldwin Hill	A2
Bawdlands	A1-A2
Beech Street	A1
Brennand Street	B3

Bright Street	C3
Brook Street	C4
Brown Street	A1
Buccleugh Avenue	A2
Buccleugh Close	A2
Cardigan Avenue	A2-A3
Carlton Street	C2
Castle Gate	B2
Castle Street	B2-B3
Castle View Road	A2-A3
Chatburn Road	B4-C4
Chester Avenue	A3-A4
Church Brow	B3-B4
Church Street	B3
Cowper Avenue	A3-A4
De Lacy Street	A2
Derby Street	C2
Duck Street	C3
Eastham Street	A4
Eshton Terrace	A1-B1
Fox Street	B4
Grafton Street	C2
Greenacre Street	B1
Hawthorne Place	A4
Hayhurst Street	C1-C2
Henthorn Road	A1
Highfield Road	B2-C2-C1
Kendal Street	C4
King Lane	B3
King Street	B3
Kirkmoor Road	A3
Littlemore Road	C1
Lower Gate	B2-B3
Market Place	B3
Milton Avenue	A3-A4
Mitchell Street	A1
Montague Street	A2
New Market Street	B2-B3
North Street	C4
Peel Street	C2-C3
Park Avenue	A4-B4
Parson Lane	A2-B2
Pimlico Road	B4
Princess Avenue	B4-C4
Pump Street	A1-A2
Queen's Road	C1
Radcyclyffe Street	B4
Railway View Avenue	B3
Railway View Road	A3-B3
Ribblesdale Avenue	A4
St Mary's Street	B3-B4
Salford Moor Lane	B1-B2
Salthill Road	C4
Shawbridge Street	C2-C3
Station Road	B2-B3

Taylor Street	C3-C4
Thorn Street	A1
Turner Street	B1-C1
Waddington Road	A4-B4
Waterloo Road	C3-C4
Wellgate	B3-C3
Well Terrace	B4
West View	B1
Wilson Street	B1
Woone Lane	B1
York Road	B3-B4-C4

Accrington

Abbey Street	C1-C2-C3
Addison Street	C3-C4
Aitken Street	C4
Albion Street	A3
Argyle Street	A4-B4
Arnold Street	C3-C4
Avenue Parade	C2-C3
Back Wellington Street	B1
Bank Street	B1-B2
Barnes Street	C2
Beech Street	C1
Birtwistle Street	C1
Black Abbey Street	B1-C1
Blackburn Road	A3-A2-B2-C2
Blake Street	A3
Bradshaw Street	C3
Bramley Street	B4
Bridge Street	B2
Broadway	B2-B3
Bold Street	C2
Burnley Road	C3
Cannon Street	A2-B2
Castle Street	B3
Chapel Street	C1
Church Street	B1-B2
Cobden Street	B3
Cobham Street	C1
Cotton Street	A1-B1
Crawshaw Street	B2-B3
Croft Street	B3-B4
Cross Street	B1-B2
Derby Street	B4-B3-C3
Dowry Street	B3-C3-C4
Dutton Street	B2
Edgar Street	A3-B3
Ellison Street	A2-A3
Fort Street	A3
Fox Street	A3
Gillies Street	C1-C2
Grange Lane	B1

Grange Street	B1
Hargreaves Street	C1
Haywood Road	C4
Hindle Street	A3
Holme Street	B2
Hood Street	C3-C4
Horne Street	C3-C4
Hyndburn Road	A4-A3-B3
Infant Street	B2-C2
Jacob Street	B1
Kenyon Street	B3
King Street	A3-B3
Knowlmere Street	B4
Lee Street	C1-C2
Malt Street	B4
Marlborough Road	C4
Maudsley Street	B3-C3-C4
Meadow Street	B3-C3-C4
Melbourne Street	C2-C3
Midland Street	C1
Moore Street	C3
Napier Street	B1
Nutter Road	C4
Oak Street	B2-B1-C1
Ormerod Street	A1
Oswald Street	C2
Owen Street	B4-C4
Oxford Street	A3-A4
Paradise Street	A2-B2-B1
Park Street	C1-C2-C3
Paxton Street	A3
Peel Street	B2-C2
Pitt Street	C1-C2
Plantation Street	C1
Pleck Road	B2
Pollard Street	C2
St James Street	A1-A2-B2
Sandy Lane	C4
Scaitcliffe Street	A1-A2
Stanley Street	C2
Sydney Street	C3
Taylor Street West	A3
Union Street	B2-B3
Victoria Street	A1
Warner Street	B2-C2-C1
Water Street	C3
Wellington Street	B1
Whalley Road	B4-B3-C3
Willow Street	A2-B2
York Street	A4-B4

BLACKBURN

A central sanctuary and altar allow everyone to see the service at the Cathedral, which has a Gothic revival church of Longridge stone for its nave. A church has stood on this site since at least the 10th century.

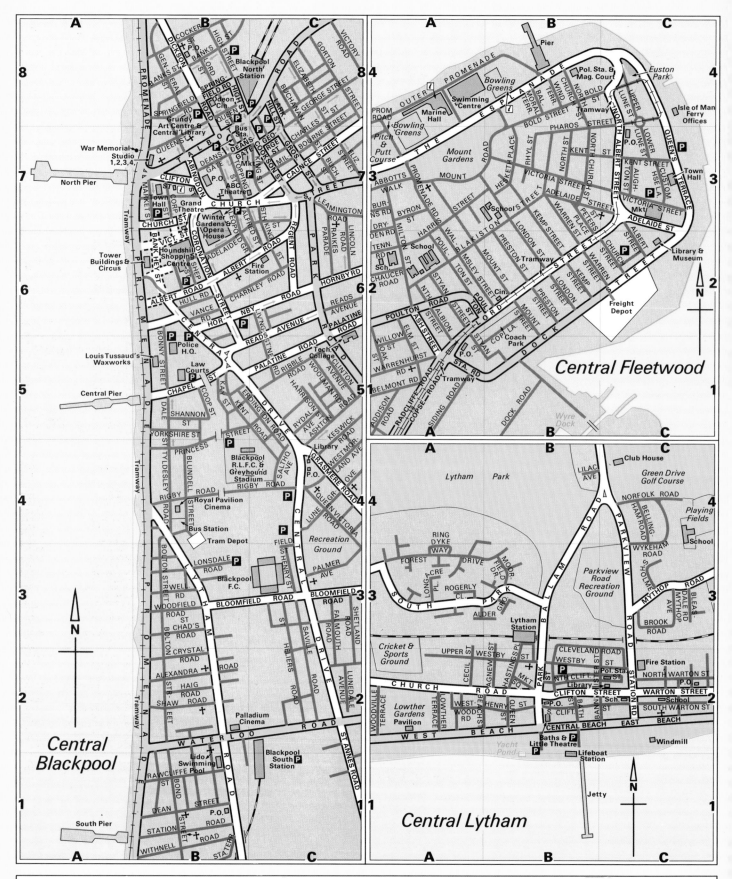

Central Blackpool

Central Fleetwood

Central Lytham

Blackpool

No seaside resort is regarded with greater affection than Blackpool. It is still the place where millions of North Country folk spend their holidays; its famous illuminations draw visitors from all over the world. It provides every conceivable kind of traditional holiday entertainment, and in greater abundance than any other seaside resort in Britain. The famous tower – built in the 1890s as a replica of the Eiffel Tower – the three piers, seven miles of promenade, five miles of illuminations, countless guesthouses, huge numbers of pubs, shops, restaurants and cafes play host to eight million visitors a year.

At the base of the tower is a huge entertainment complex that includes a ballroom, a circus and an aquarium. Other 19th-century landmarks are North Pier and Central Pier, the great Winter Gardens and Opera House and the famous trams that still run along the promenade – the only electric trams still operating in Britain. The most glittering part of modern Blackpool is the famous Golden Mile, packed with amusements, novelty shops and snack stalls. Every autumn it becomes part of the country's most extravagant light show – the illuminations – when the promenade is ablaze with neon representations of anything and everything from moon rockets to the Muppets. Autumn is also the time when Blackpool is a traditional venue for political party conferences.

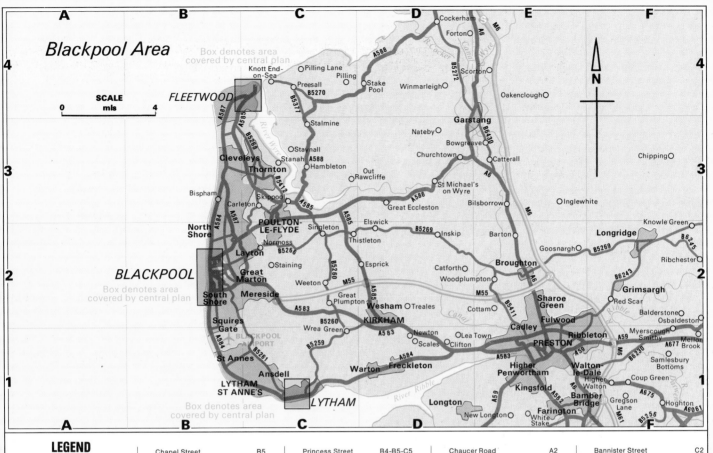

Blackpool Area

FLEETWOOD

BLACKPOOL

Box denotes area covered by central plan

SCALE
mils
0   4

N

LEGEND

Town Plan
AA recommended route
Restricted roads
Other roads
Buildings of interest School
Car parks P
Parks and open spaces
One way streets

Area Plan
A roads
B roads
Locations Wrea Green ○
Urban area

Street Index with Grid Reference

Blackpool

Abingdon Street	B7
Adelaide Street	B6-B7-C7
Albert Road	B6-C6
Alexandra Road	B2
Alfred Street	B7-C7-C6
Ashton Road	C4-C5
Bank Hey Streets	B6-B7
Banks Street	B8
Bloomfield Road	B3-C3
Blundell Street	B4
Bolton Street	B2-B3-B4
Bond Street	B1-B2
Bonny Street	B5-B6
Buchanan Street	C7-C8
Caunce Street	C7-C8
Central Drive	B6-B5-C5-C4-C3-C2
Chapel Street	B5
Charles Street	C7-C8
Charnley Road	B6-C6
Church Street	B7-C7
Clifton Street	B7
Clinton Avenue	C5
Cocker Street	B8
Cookson Street	B8-B7-C7
Coop Street	B5
Coronation Street	B5-B6-B7
Corporation Street	B7
Crystal Road	B2
Dale Street	B4-B5
Deansgate	B7-C7
Dean Street	B1
Dickson Road	B7-B8
Erdington Road	B5-C5-C4
Elizabeth Street	C7-C8
Falmouth Road	C2-C3
Field Street	C3
General Street	B8
George Street	C7-C8
Gorton Street	C8
Grasmere Road	C4
Grosvenor Street	C7
Haig Road	B2
Harrison Street	C5
Henry Street	C3
High Street	B8
Hornby Road	B6-C6
Hull Road	B6
Kay Street	B5
Kent Road	B5-C5-C4
Keswick Road	C4-C5
King Street	C7
Larkhill Street	C8
Leamington Road	C7
Leopold Grove	B7-B6-C6
Lincoln Road	C6-C7
Livingstone Road	C5-C6
Lonsdale Road	B3
Lord Street	B8
Lunedale Avenue	C2
Lune Grove	C4
Lytham Road	B1-B2-B3-B4
Market Street	B7
Milbourne Street	C7-C8
Osbourne Road	B1
Palatine Road	B5-C5-C6
Palmer Avenue	C3
Park Road	C5-C6-C7
Princess Parade	A7-A8-B8-B7
Princess Street	B4-B5-C5
Promenade	B1-B2-B3-B4-B5-B6-A6-A7-B7-B8
Queen Street	B7-B8
Queen Victoria Road	C3-C4
Raikes Parade	C6-C7
Rawcliffe Street	B1
Reads Avenue	B5-C5-C6
Regent Road	C6-C7
Ribble Road	C5
Rigby Road	B4-C4
Rydal Avenue	C5
St Annes Road	C1-C2
St Chad's Road	B3
St Heliers Road	C2-C3
Salthouse Avenue	C4
Saville Road	C2-C3
Shannon Street	B5
Shaw Road	B2
Sheppard Street	B6
Shetland Road	C2-C3
South King Street	C6-C7
Springfield Road	B8
Station Road	B1
Station Terrace	B1
Talbot Road	B7-B8-C8
Topping Street	B7
Tyldesley Road	B4
Vance Road	B6
Victoria Street	B6
Victory Road	C8
Waterloo Road	B2-C2
Wellington Road	B3
Westmorland Avenue	C4
Woodfield Road	B3
Woolman Road	C5
Yorkshire Street	B5

Fleetwood

Abbotts Walk	A3
Adelaide Street	B3-C3-C2
Addison Road	A1
Albert Street	C2-C3
Ash Street	A1-A2
Aughton Street	C3
Balmoral Terrace	B4
Belmont Road	A1
Blakiston Street	A2-B2-B3
Bold Street	B4-C4
Burns Road	A3
Byron Street	A3
Chaucer Road	A2
Church Street	C2
Cop Lane	A1-B1-B2
Copse Road	A1
Custom House Lane	A1
Dock Road	B1
Dock Street	B1-B2-C2
Dryder Road	A2-A3
Elm Street	A1-A2
Harris Street	A2-A3-B3
Hesketh Place	B3
Kemp Street	B2-B3
Kent Street	B3-C3
London Street	B2-B3
Lord Street	A1-A2-B2-C2-C3
Lower Lune Street	C3
Milton Street	A2-A3
Mount Road	A3-B3
Mount Street	A2-B2
North Albert Street	C3-C4
North Albion Street	A1-A2
North Church Street	B3-B4
North Street	B3
Oak Street	A1-A2
Outer Promenade	A4-B4
Pharos Street	B3-C3-C4
Poulton Road	A2
Poulton Street	A2
Preston Street	B2
Promenade Road	A3-A4
Queen's Terrace	C3-C4
Radcliffe Road	A1
Rhyl Street	B3
St Peters Place	B2-B3
Siding Road	A1
Station Road	A1
Styan Street	A2-A1-B1
Tennyson Road	A2
The Esplanade	A3-A4-B4
Upper Lune Street	C4
Victoria Street	B3-C3
Walmsley Street	A3-A2-B2
Warrenhurst Road	A1
Warren Street	B3-B2-C2
Willow Road	A1
Windsor Terrace	B4

Lytham

Agnew Street	B2-B3
Alder Grove	A3-B3
Ballam Road	B2-B3-B4-C4
Bannister Street	C2
Bath Street	B2
Beach Street	B2
Bellingham Road	C4
Bleasdale Road	C3
Brook Road	C3
Cecil Street	A2-A3
Central Beach	B2-C2
Church Road	A2-B2
Cleveland Road	B3-C3
Clifton Street	B2-C2
East Beach	C2
Forest Drive	A3-B3
Hastings Place	B2
Henry Street	B2
Lilac Avenue	B4
Longacre Place	A3
Lowther Terrace	A2
Market Square	B2
Moorfield Drive	B3
Mythop Avenue	C3
Mythop Road	C3
Norfolk Road	B2
North Clifton Street	B2-C2
North Warton Street	C2
Park Street	B2
Parkview Road	C2-C3-C4
Queen Street	B2
Ring Dyke Way	A3
Rogerly Close	A3
South Clifton Street	B2-C2
Southolme	C3
South Park	A3-B3
South Warton Street	C2
Station Road	C2
Upper Westby Street	A2-B2
Warton Street	C2
West Beach	A2-B2
Westby Street	B2-C2
Westwood Road	A2
Woodville Terrace	A2
Wykeham Road	C3-C4

BLACKPOOL
Three piers, seven miles of promenade packed with entertainments galore and seemingly endless sandy beaches spread out beneath Blackpool's unmistakable tower which stands 518ft high in Britain's busiest and biggest holiday resort.

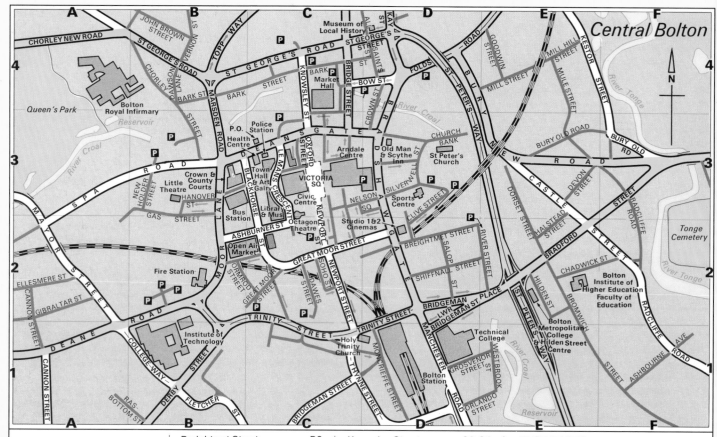

Central Bolton

Key to Town Plan and Area Plan

Town Plan
A.A. Recommended roads
Other roads
Restricted roads
Buildings of interest   Theatre
Car Parks
Parks and open spaces
One way streets

Area Plan
A roads
B roads
Locations   Summers O
Urban area

Street Index with Grid Reference

Central Bolton

All Saints Street	C4-D4
Ashbourne Avenue	F1
Ashburner Street	B2-C2
Bark Street	B4-C4
Blackhorse Street	B3-C3-C2
Bow Street	C4-D4
Bradford Street	E2-E3-F3
Bradshawgate	D2-D3-D4

Breightmet Street	D2
Bridge Street	C3-C4
Bridgeman Place	D2-E2
Bridgeman Street	C1
Bromwich Street	E2-E1-F1
Bury New Road	D4-E4-E3-F3
Bury Old Road	E3-E4
Cannon Street	A1-A2
Castle Street	E3-E2-F2
Chadwick Street	E2-F2
Chorley New Road	A4
Chorley Street	B3-B4
Church Bank	D3
Clive Street	D2-D3
College Way	A1-B1
Crown Street	D3-D4
Dawes Street	C2
Dawson Lane	B4
Deane Road	A1-B1-B2
Deansgate	B3-C3-D3
Derby Street	B1
Devon Street	E3
Dorset Street	E2-E3
Ellesmere Street	A2
Fletcher Street	B1-C1
Folds Road	D4-E4
Gas Street	B3
Gibraltar Street	A2
Goodwin Street	E4
Great Moor Street	C2-D2
Grosvenor Street	D1-E1
Halstead Street	E2-E3
Hanover Street	B3
Hilden Street	E2
John Brown Street	B4
Kay Street	D4
Kestor Street	E4-F4-F3

Knowsley Street	C3-C4
Le Mans Crescent	C2-C3
Lower Bridgeman Street	D1-D2
Manchester Road	D1-D2
Marsden Road	B3-B4
Mayor Street	A2-A3
Mill Street	E4
Mill Hill Street	E4
Moncrieffe Street	D1
Moor Lane	B2-B3
Mule Street	E3-E4
Nelson Square	C3-D3
New Holder Street	B3
Newport Street	C1-C2-C3
Orlando Street	D1-E1
Ormrod Street	B2-C2
Radcliffe Road	F1-F2-F3
Rashbottom Street	A1-B1
River Street	D2-E2
St George's Road	A4-B4-C4
St George's Street	C4-D4
St Peter's Way	D4-D3-E3-E2-E1
Salop Street	D2
Shiffnall Street	D2
Silverwell Street	D3
Soho Street	C1-C2
Spa Road	A2-A3-B3
Trinity Street	B2-C2-C1-D1-D2
Vernon Street	B4
Victoria Square	C2-C3
West Brook Street	E1

BOLTON

public buildings and places of interest

Civic Centre (Town Hall and Tourist Information Centre)	**C3**
Institute of Technology	**B1**
Library and Museum	**C2-C3**
Market Hall	**C4**
New Octagon Theatre	**C3**
Old Man and Scythe Inn	**D3**

An historic old inn, where Lord Derby, executed in 1651, is said to have spent his last night

Technical College	**D1**

Situated in Tonge Moor Road, 1m north-east of the town centre, is the Textile Machinery Museum containing Arkwright's water frame of 1768, Crompton's spinning mule (1799) and Hargreave's original spinning jenny.

2m north, is Hall i'the'Wood, a picturesque, 16th-century, half-timbered house, now a museum. It is associated with William Crompton, 2m north-west is Smithils Hall, a half-timbered 15th-century and later house, noted for its old hall. It is now a museum.

Bolton

This was one of Lancashire's great cotton centres, and a fitting birthplace for revolutioniser of the textile industry Samuel Crompton, whose invention the 'spinning mule' is on display at the Tonge Moor Textile Machinery Museum. Born in 1753, Crompton lived in the picturesque 15th-century house Hall I' Th' Wood, which lies to the north of the town at Firwood Fold.

The town boasts another celebrated son in William Hesketh Lever, born in 1851, who not only founded Lever Brothers (later the giant Unilever Group), but also invented Sunlight Soap. Lever, who became Lord Leverhulme, gave Bolton a school, a church and a park.

Bolton today has become more concerned with engineering than with the textiles for which it was famous, but reminders of the past live on in the town's older monuments. The Victorian Town

Hall and Civic Centre stand prominently amidst the 20th-century development in the middle of town, and nearby is The Old Man and Scythe, a medieval inn. Lord Derby spent his last night here before he was executed by Cromwell in retaliation for a massacre by the Royalists in the Civil War. Popular with both locals and outsiders is Bolton's Octagon Theatre, and another attraction for some is Bolton Wanderers Football Club, providing league football at Burnden Park.

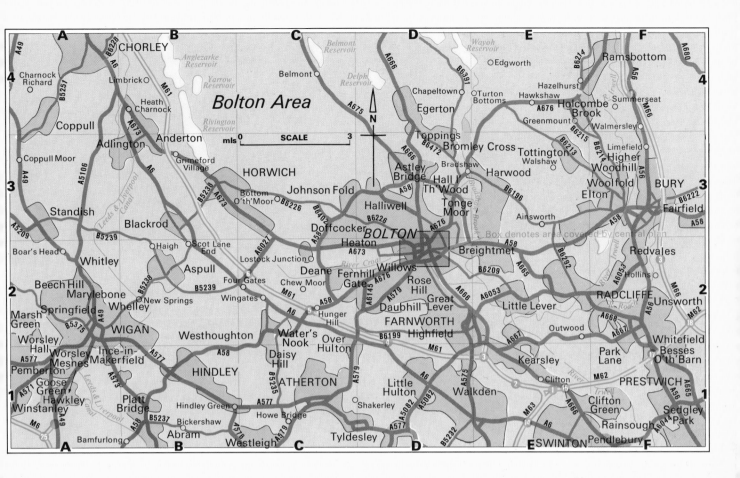

Spinning gold — the machines that made a landscape

It was called a mule because it was a hybrid of two existing machines — and together with a handful of other inventions, it transformed forever the face of northern England. Not overnight and not singlehanded: without the workers and a huge, insatiable demand for cotton, the spinning mule and other 18th-century innovations would have sunk without trace. But coming as they did, when they did, they shaped irrevocably the towns of the industrial north — and most of were the inspiration of local men.

In 1733, **Bury's** John Kay thought up the flying shuttle for faster handloom weaving. Meeting the demand it created for faster spinning of yarn, James Hargreaves of **Blackburn** brought out the 1763 spinning jenny, named after his wife and able to spin six threads at once. Mechanisation came in 1769 with **Preston**-born Richard Arkwright's water-powered spinning frame, and improving on both frame and jenny came the 1770s spinning mule, which could spin fine, strong threads 400 at a time. The frame and the mule took spinning out of the home and into mills — often sited in remote parts of the Pennines to be near water power and probably to keep out radical influences.

For the handloom weavers this was a golden age — but two developments were to make them some of the most pitiable victims of industrialisation. Steam power became the great driving force of the

factories when James Watt of **Greenock** added a separate condenser to the steam engine in the 1770s and turned it for the first time into a really effective tool. And in the 1780's the power loom was invented, by Melton Mowbray clergyman Edmund Cartwright who had never even seen the hand driven variety.

Steam needed coal; the new factories needed space, and they moved down from the Pennine streams to the canals and coalfields. And so began the explosive growth of towns like **Manchester,** king of them all, **Burnley, Bolton, Wigan, Rochdale, Oldham** and **Blackburn** — the once-mighty textile centres of the world.

Samuel Crompton's spinning mule made a fortune for the mill owners of Manchester and Bolton — but the inventor gained only a meagre £60, and died a poor and embittered man.

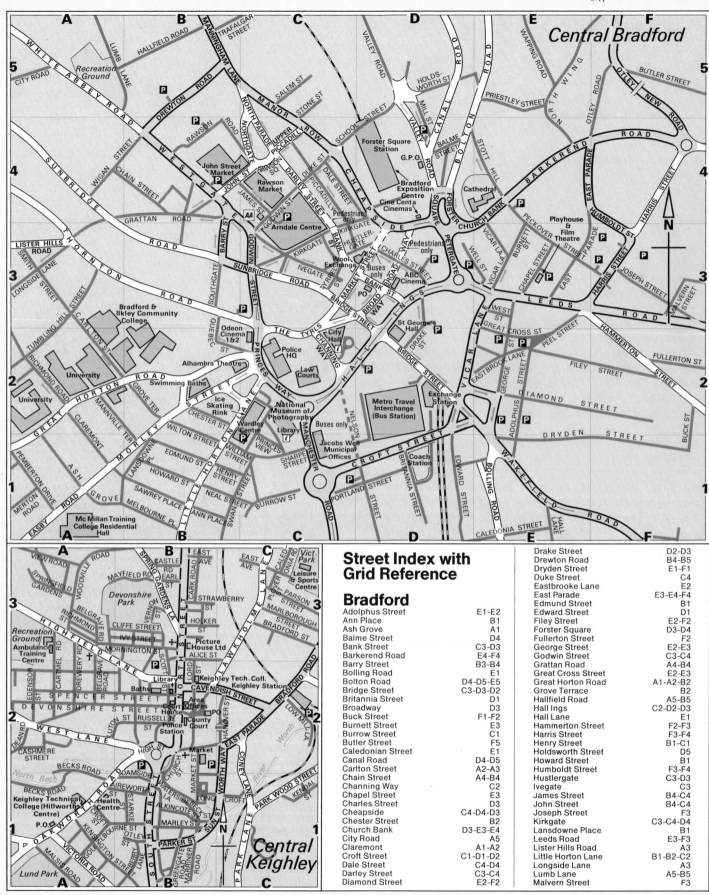

Street Index with Grid Reference

Bradford

Adolphus Street	E1-E2
Ann Place	B1
Ash Grove	A1
Balme Street	D4
Bank Street	C3-D3
Barkerend Road	E4-F4
Barry Street	B3-B4
Bolling Road	E1
Bolton Road	D4-D5-E5
Bridge Street	C3-D3-D2
Britannia Street	D1
Broadway	D3
Buck Street	F1-F2
Burnett Street	E3
Burrow Street	C1
Butler Street	F5
Caledonian Street	E1
Canal Road	D4-D5
Carlton Street	A2-A3
Chain Street	A4-B4
Channing Way	C2
Chapel Street	E3
Charles Street	D3
Cheapside	C4-D4-D3
Chester Street	B2
Church Bank	D3-E3-E4
City Road	A5
Claremont	A1-A2
Croft Street	C1-D1-D2
Dale Street	C4-D4
Darley Street	C3-C4
Diamond Street	E2-F2
Drake Street	D2-D3
Drewton Road	B4-B5
Dryden Street	E1-F1
Duke Street	C4
Eastbrooke Lane	E2
East Parade	E3-E4-F4
Edmund Street	B1
Edward Street	D1
Filey Street	E2-F2
Forster Square	D3-D4
Fullerton Street	F2
George Street	E2-E3
Godwin Street	C3-C4
Grattan Road	A4-B4
Great Cross Street	E2-E3
Great Horton Road	A1-A2-B2
Grove Terrace	B2
Hallfield Road	A5-B5
Hall Ings	C2-D2-D3
Hall Lane	E1
Hammerton Street	F2-F3
Harris Street	F3-F4
Henry Street	B1-C1
Holdsworth Street	D5
Howard Street	B1
Humboldt Street	F3-F4
Hustlergate	C3-D3
Ivegate	C3
James Street	B4-C4
John Street	B4-C4
Joseph Street	F3
Kirkgate	C3-C4-D4
Lansdowne Place	B1
Leeds Road	E3-F3
Lister Hills Road	A3
Little Horton Lane	B1-B2-C2
Longside Lane	A3
Lumb Lane	A5-B5
Malvern Street	F3

Bradford

Wool and Bradford are almost synonymous, such was its importance in the 19th century as a central market after the Industrial Revolution brought steam power to the trade. Like many small market towns that exploded into industrial cities almost overnight, Bradford's architecture is a mish-mash of grand civic buildings, factories and crowded housing. Among the former, the Wool Exchange is impressive, with its ornate tower adorned with stone busts of 13 famous men, and the massive town hall, also topped by a tower, 200ft high. Few traces remain of the town's past but one obvious exception is the cathedral. Set on a rise, its detailed carvings – particularly the 20 angels that support the nave roof – catch the eye.

Bradford boasts several parks – notably Lister Park where there is a boating lake, an open-air swimming pool, a botanical garden and a scented garden for the blind – and Bowling Park, on the other side of town. Cartwright Hall, named after the inventor of the power loom, stands in Lister Park. It now houses Bradford's permanent art collection.

Keighley The Brontë sisters used to walk from Haworth to this pleasant 19th-century town for their shopping sprees. Nowadays, the restored Keighley and Worth Valley Railway is a great attraction and passengers can travel to Oxenhope.

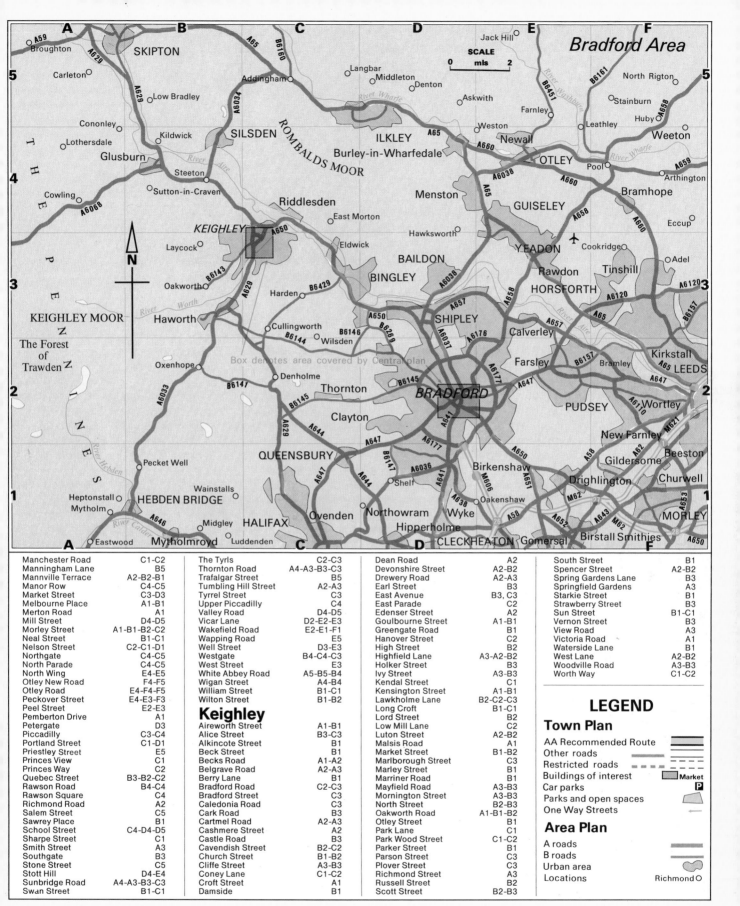

Bradford Area

SCALE 0 mls 2

Bradford

Manchester Road	C1-C2	The Tyrls	C2-C3	Dean Road	A2	South Street	B1
Manningham Lane	B5	Thornton Road	A4-A3-B3-C3	Devonshire Street	A2-B2	Spencer Street	A2-B2
Mannville Terrace	A2-B2-B1	Trafalgar Street	B5	Drewery Road	A2-A3	Spring Gardens Lane	B3
Manor Row	C4-C5	Tumbling Hill Street	A2-A3	Earl Street	B3	Springfield Gardens	A3
Market Street	C3-D3	Tyrrel Street	C3	East Avenue	B3, C3	Starkie Street	B1
Melbourne Place	A1-B1	Upper Piccadilly	C4	East Parade	C2	Strawberry Street	B3
Merton Road	A1	Valley Road	D4-D5	Edenser Street	A2	Sun Street	B1-C1
Mill Street	D4-D5	Vicar Lane	D2-E2-E3	Goulbourne Street	A1-B1	Vernon Street	B3
Morley Street	A1-B1-B2-C2	Wakefield Road	E2-E1-F1	Greengate Road	B1	View Road	A3
Neal Street	B1-C1	Wapping Road	E5	Hanover Street	C2	Victoria Road	A1
Nelson Street	C2-C1-D1	Well Street	D3-E3	High Street	B2	Waterside Lane	B1
Northgate	C4-C5	Westgate	B4-C4-C3	Highfield Lane	A3-A2-B2	West Lane	A2-B2
North Parade	C4-C5	West Street	B1	Holker Street	B3	Woodville Road	A3-B3
North Wing	E4-E5	White Abbey Road	A5-B5-B4	Ivy Street	A3-B3	Worth Way	C1-C2
Otley New Road	F4-F5	Wigan Street	A4-B4	Kendal Street	C1		
Otley Road	E4-F4-F5	William Street	B1-C1	Kensington Street	A1-B1		
Peckover Street	E4-E3-F3	Wilton Street	B1-B2	Lawkholme Lane	B2-C2-C3		
Peel Street	E2-E3			Long Croft	B1-C1		
Pemberton Drive	A1	**Keighley**		Lord Street	B2		
Petergate	D3	Aireworth Street	A1-B1	Low Mill Lane	C2		
Piccadilly	C3-C4	Alice Street	B3-C3	Luton Street	A2-B2		
Portland Street	C1-D1	Alkincote Street	B1	Malsis Road	A1		
Priestley Street	E5	Beck Street	B1	Market Street	B1-B2		
Princes View	C1	Becks Road	A1-A2	Marlborough Street	C3		
Princes Way	C2	Belgrave Road	A2-A3	Marley Street	B1		
Quebec Street	B3-B2-C2	Berry Lane	B1	Marriner Road	B1		
Rawson Road	B4-C4	Bradford Road	C2-C3	Mayfield Road	A3-B3		
Rawson Square	C4	Bradford Street	C3	Mornington Street	A3-B3		
Richmond Road	A2	Caledonia Road	C3	North Street	B2-B3		
Salem Street	C5	Cark Road	B3	Oakworth Road	A1-B1-B2		
Sawrey Place	B1	Cartmel Road	A2-A3	Otley Street	B1		
School Street	C4-D4-D5	Cashmere Street	A2	Park Lane	C1		
Sharpe Street	C1	Castle Road	B3	Park Wood Street	C1-C2		
Smith Street	A3	Cavendish Street	B2-C2	Parker Street	B1		
Southgate	B3	Church Street	B1-B2	Parson Street	C3		
Stone Street	C5	Cliffe Street	A3-B3	Plover Street	C3		
Stott Hill	D4-E4	Coney Lane	C1-C2	Richmond Street	A3		
Sunbridge Road	A4-A3-B3-C3	Croft Street	A1	Russell Street	B2		
Swan Street	B1-C1	Damside	B1	Scott Street	B2-B3		

LEGEND

Town Plan

AA Recommended Route	≡≡≡
Other roads	≡≡≡
Restricted roads	- - -
Buildings of interest	**Market**
Car parks	P
Parks and open spaces	
One Way Streets	←

Area Plan

A roads	≡≡
B roads	≡≡
Urban area	
Locations	Richmond O

BRADFORD
St George's, built with the profits of the wool trade, is one of Bradford's imposing Victorian buildings. It is once again being used for the purpose for which it was intended – a concert hall – and has exceptionally good acoustics.

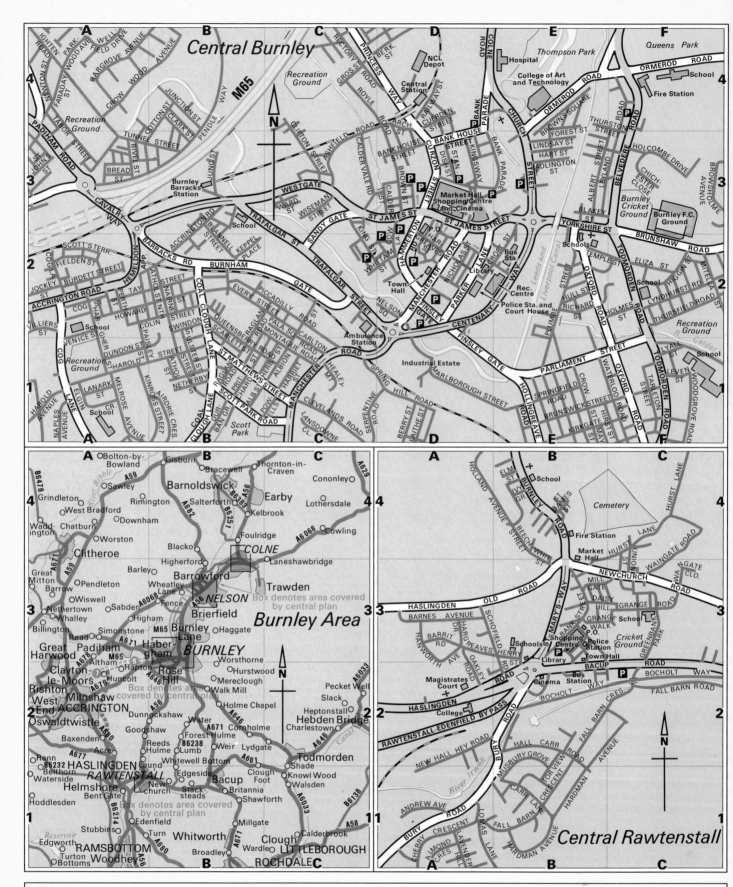

Burnley

International fame was brought to Burnley in the 1960s by its local football team, which can still be seen playing at Turf Moor. An old mill town lying in a bend of the Leeds and Liverpool Canal, Burnley's prosperity is reflected in the fine new developments it has seen, particularly since the opening of the M65. Half a mile south-east of the town stands Towneley Hall, a restored house dating back to the 14th century, which houses an art gallery and museum with an interesting local history collection.

Rawtenstall has made its name in the manufacture of felt, and now enjoys the luxury of an artificial ski-slope in Haslingden Old Road among its many good sports facilities.

Nelson was named after a pub, called Nelson's Inn (in honour of the hero of Trafalgar). It once stood alone here, but a burgeoning cotton town sprang up around it during the 19th century, and eventually took its name. Not far off looms the dark mass of Pendle Hill — the notorious haunt of Lancashire witches.

Colne's 18th-century wool trading prosperity is remembered in the fine Cloth Hall, which dates from this period. With a past traceable back to Roman times, Colne is also the site of the British in India Museum, which stands in Sun Street and can be visited at weekends in summer.

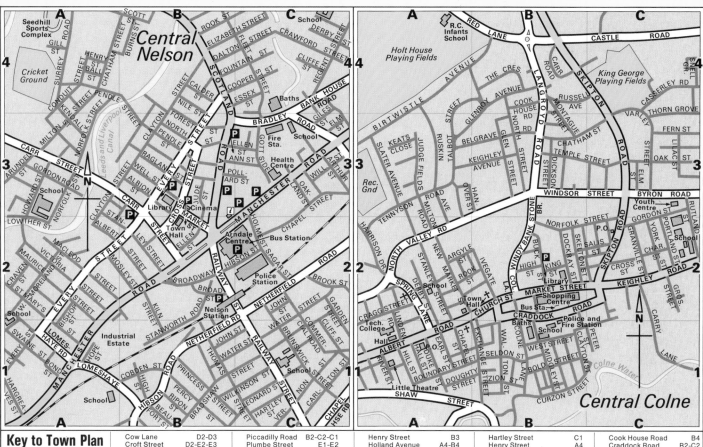

Key to Town Plan and Area Plan

Town Plan

AA Recommended roads
Other roads
Restricted roads
Buildings of interest   Mill
One way street
Car Parks   P
Parks and open spaces

Area Plan

A roads
B roads
Locations   Hawkshaw O
Urban area

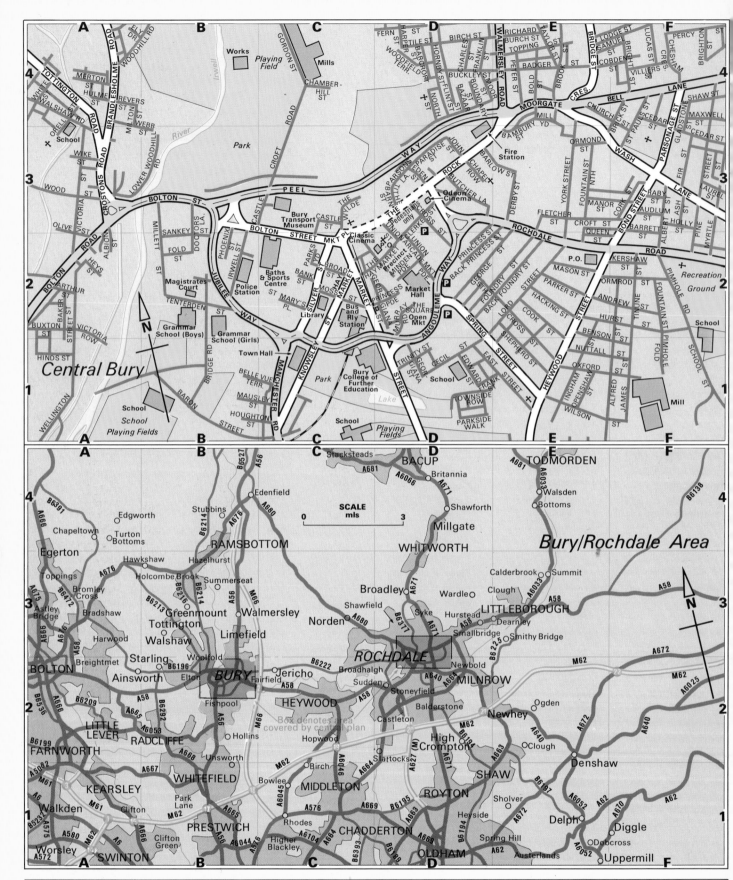

Central Bury

Bury/Rochdale Area

SCALE
mls

0   3

Box denotes area
covered by central plan

Bury / Rochdale

Bury has been celebrated for its black pudding for over a century, and this special delicacy is still an important attraction of Bury Market. The market has been chartered since 1440 and nearby is Bury's oldest building — the Two Tubs, said to have been built around two giant oak trees in the reign of Charles II. Celebrated sons of Bury include 'flying shuttle' inventor John Kay who was born here. His invention helped to transform 18th-century weaving, and the town remembers him by the John Kay Gardens, where his statue stands.

Rochdale Gracie Fields came from Rochdale — a town which saw dramatic changes in the early 19th century. This was when the textile mills arrived and brought with them a whole new lifestyle for local people. They rose to the challenge with innovations like the now worldwide co-operative movement, the brainchild of the 'Rochdale Pioneers' whose original shop has become a museum in the Toad Lane Conservation Area. More radical ideas came from Rochdale-born John Bright, campaigner for the repeal of the Corn Laws in 1846. His statue is one of many in the town, which also has the unusual Lancashire Dialect Writers Memorial. The town centre is dominated by a magnificent Victorian Gothic Town Hall, set in parks and gardens with the medieval Parish Church of St Chad nearby.

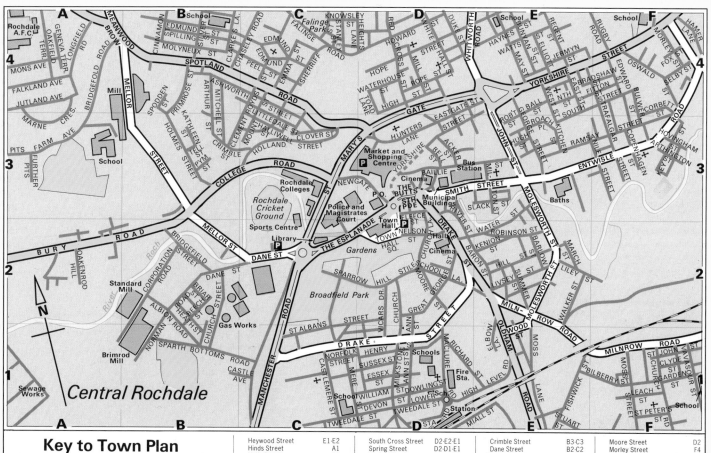

Central Rochdale

Key to Town Plan and Area Plan

Town Plan

AA Recommended roads	
Restricted roads	
Other roads	
Buildings of interest	
Car parks	P
Churches	+
Parks and open spaces	
Hospital	

Area Plan

A roads	
B roads	
Locations	Bottoms○
Urban area	

Street Index with Grid Reference

Bury

Albert Street	F2-F3
Albion Street	A2-A3
Alfred Street	E1-F1-F2
Andrew Street	E2-F2
Angouleme Way	D1-D2
Ash Street	A2
Arthur Street	F3
Audlum Street	F3
Back Foundry Street	D2-E2
Back Princess Street	D2-E2-E3
Badger Street	E4
Baker Street	A2
Bambury Street	E3-E4
Bank Street	C2
Barcroft Street	D4
Barlow Street	D3-E3
Baron Street	B1-C1
Barrett Street	F2-F3
Bazaar Street	D4
Bell Lane	E4-F4
Belle Vue Terrace	B1-C1
Benson Street	E2-E1-F1
Birch Street	D4
Bold Street	E4
Bolton Road	A2-A3
Bolton Street	A3-B3-C3-C2
Bond Street	F2-F3
Boundary Street	D4
Brandlesholme Road	A3-A4
Brick Street	E3-F3-F4
Bridge Road	B1-B2
Bridge Street	E4
Bright Street	F4
Brighton Street	F4
Broad Street	C2
Brook Street	E4
Buckley Street	D4-E4
Butcher Lane	D3
Buxton Street	A2
Castle Street	C3
Castle Croft Road	B3-C3-C4
Cecil Street	D1
Cedar Street	F3-F4
Chamberhill Street	C4
Chapel Row	D3
Charles Street	D4
Chesham Crescent	F4
Church Street	E4-F4-F3
Clerke Street	D2-D3
Cobden Street	E4-F4
Cook Street	E2
Cork Street	F3
Croft Street	E3-F3
Cross Street	D2-D3
Crostons Road	A3
Derby Street	E3
Doctors Lane	B2-B3
East Street	D1-E1
Eden Street	D3
Edward Street	D1
Ely Drive	A4
Fern Street	D4
Fir Street	F3
Fletcher Street	E3
Flint Street	D4
Fold Street	B2
Foundry Street	D2-E2
Fountain Street	F2
Fountain Street North	E3
Frank Street	D1-E1
Franklin Street	D4
George Street	D2-E2
Georgiana Street	C2-D2
Georgiana Street	D1
Gladstone Street	F3-F4
Gordon Street	C4
Hacking Street	E2
Harper Street	D4
Haymarket	C2
Heys Street	A2
Heywood Street	E1-E2
Hinds Street	A1
Holly Street	F3
Hornby Street	D4
Houghton Street	B1-C1
Hulme Street	A4
Hurst Street	E2-F2
Ingham Street	E1-E2
Irwell Street	B2
James Street	F1
John Street	D3
Jubilee Way	B3-B2-C2
Kershaw Street	F2
Knowsley Street	C1-C2
Laurel Street	F3
Lodge Street	E4-F4
Lord Street	D2-E2
Lower Woodhill Road	A3-B3
Lucas Street	D4
Manchester Road	C1
Manor Street	E3-F3
Market Parade	D2
Market Place	C2-C3
Market Street	C2-D2-D1
Mason Street	E2
Mausley Street	B1-C1
Maxwell Street	F4
Merton Street	A4
Mill Yard	E4
Millett Street	B2-B3
Milton Street	A4
Minden Parade	D2
Moor Street	D4
Moorgate Crescent	E4
Moss Street	C2
Murray Road	D2
Myrtle Street	F2-F3
North Street	D4
Nuttall Street	E1-F1
Olive Street	A2-A3
Openshaw Street	E1
Orell Street	A3-A4
Ormond Street	E3
Ormrod Street	E2-F2
Oxford Street	E1-F1
Paradise Street	D3
Parker Street	E2
Parks Yard	C2
Parkside Walk	D1
Parsonage Street	F3-F4
Parsons Lane	D3
Peel Way	B3-C3-D3-D4-E4
Percy Street	F4
Peter Street	E3
Phoenix Street	B2-B3
Pimhole Fold	F1-F2
Pimhole Road	F2
Pine Street	F2-F3
Princess Parade	D2
Princess Street	D2-D3
Queen Street	E2
Raby Street	F3
Revers Street	A4
Richard Burch Street	F3
Rochdale Road	D3-E3-E2-E2
St Mary's Place	C2
St Pauls Street	F3-F4
Samuel Street	E4-F4
Sankey Street	B2
School Street	F1-F2
Shaw Street	F4
Shepherd Street	E1-E2
Silver Street	C2

Rochdale

Acker Street	D3
Albion Road	B1-B2
Ann Street	D1-D2
Arthington Street	F3
Arthur Street	B3-B4
Ashworth Street	B4-C4-C3
Baillie Street	D3-E3
Ball Street	E4
Barlow Street	E2
Baron Street	D2-E2
Beech Street	B2
Bell Street	D3
Bilberry Street	E1-F1
Bradshaw Street	E4-F4
Briar Street	B2
Bridgefield Street	B2
Bridgefold Road	A3-A4
Bulwer Street	F3-F4
Bunyan Street	E2
Bury Road	A2-B2-B3
Castle Avenue	B1-C1
Castlemere Street	C1
Chaseley Road	B4-C4
Church Lane	D2-D3
Church Road	F1
Church Stile	D1-D2
Church Street	B1-B2
Cinnamon Street	B4
Clarke's Lane	B4
Clement Royds Street	B3-C3-C4
Clover Street	C3
Clyde Street	F1
College Road	B3-C3
Copenhagen Street	F3
Corbett Street	F4
Corporation Road	A1-B1-B2
Crimble Street	B3-C3
Dane Street	B2-C2
Devon Street	D1
Dowling Street	D4
Drake Street	C1-D1-D2-E2
Duke Street	D4
East Street	E4
Eastgate Street	D3-D4-E4
Edmund Street	B4-C4
Edward Street	F4
Elbow Lane	E1-E2
Elliott Street	E4
Emma Street	C4
Entwisle Road	E3-F3-F4
Essex Street	D1
Falinge Road	C4
Falkland Avenue	A4
Fishwick Street	E1
Fitton Street	E4-F4
Fleece Street	D3
Fox Street	F4
Further Pits	A3
Garden Street	F1
Geneva Terrace	A4
George Street	E3-E4
Great George Street	D2
Halliwell Street	C3
Hamer Lane	F4
Haynes Street	E4
Heath Street	B1-B2
Heights Lane	C4
Henry Street	D1
High Street	D4
High Level Road	D1-E1
Hill Street	E2
Holland Street	C3
Holmes Street	B3
Hope Street	D4
Hovingham Street	F3
Howard Street	D4
Hugh Street	E3
Hunters Lane	D3
Jermyn Street	C2-D2
John Street	E3
Jutland Avenue	A4
Kathleen Street	B3
Kenion Street	E2
Key Street	F3
Kitchen Street	E3
Knowsley Street	C4
Leach Street	F1
Liley Street	E2-F2
Littledale Street	C3-C4
Livsey Street	E2
Longfield Road	A4
Lower Tweedale Street	D1
Maclure Road	D1
Manchester Road	C1-C2
March Street	E2
Marne Crescent	A3-A4
May Street	D4
Meanwood Brow	A4-B4
Mellor Street	C2-B2-B3-B4-A4
Mere Street	C1-D1
Miall Street	D1-E1
Milkstone Road	D1
Mill Street	E2
Milnrow Road	E2-E1-F1
Milton Street	E2
Mitchell Street	B3-B4
Molesworth Street	E2-E3
Molyneux Street	B3
Mons Avenue	A4
Moore Street	D2
Morley Street	F4
Moss Lane	E1
Moss Street	F1
Mount Street	C3-C4
Nelson Street	D2
Newgate	C3-D3
Nile Street	E3-F3
Norfolk Street	C1
Norman Road	B1-B2
North Street	E4
Oakenrod Hill	A2
Oakfield Terrace	A4
Oldham Road	E1-E2
Oswald Street	F4
Peel Street	C4
Pilling Street	B4
Pits Farm Avenue	A3
Primrose Street	B4
Pym Street	B3
Ramsay Street	E3-F3
Red Cross Street	D4
Regent Street	E4
Richard Street	D1-E1
River Street	D2-D3
Roach Place	E3
Robert Street	E3
Robinson Street	E2
Rope Street	D4
Rugby Road	E4-F4
St Albans Street	C1-C2-D2
St John Street	D1
St Mary's Gate	C2-C3-D3-D4
St Peter's Street	F1
School Lane	D2
Selby Street	F4
Sherriff Street	C4
Silver Street	B4
Slack Street	D3-E3
Smith Street	D3-E3
South Parade	D3
South Street	E3-E4-F4
Sparrow Hill	C2-D2
Spodden Street	B4
Spotland Road	B4-C4-C3-D3
Stanley Street	C4
Station Road	D1
Stuart Street	E1
Summer Street	E2
Sussex Street	C1-D1
Tell Street	B3
The Butts	D3
The Esplanade	C2-D2-D3
Toad Lane	D4
Town Hall Square	D2
Trafalgar Street	F3-F4
Tweedale Street	C1-D1
Vavasour Street	F1
Vicars Drive	D1-D2
Walker Street	E4
Water Street	D2-E2-E3
Waterhouse Street	D4
Watts Street	E4
West Street	E3-E4
Whitehall Street	D4
Whitworth Road	D4
William Street	C1-D1
Wood Street	E1-E2
Yorkshire Street	D3-E3-E4-F4

South Cross Street	D2-E2-E1
Spring Street	D2-D1-E1
Taylor Street	E4
Tenterden Street	B2
The Haymarket	C2-D2
The Rock	C3-D3-E3-E4
The Square	D2
The Wylde	C3
Tile Street	D4
Tinune Street	F2
Tithe Barn Street	D3
Topping Street	E4
Tottington Road	A3-A4
Townside Row	D1
Trinity Street	D1
Union Arcade	D2
Union Street	D2-D3
Victoria Row	A1-A2
Victoria Street	A2-A3
Villiers Street	F4
Walmersley Road	E4
Walshaw Road	A3-A4
Wash Lane	E4-E3-F3
Webb Street	A3-B3
Wellington Street	A1-A2
White Street	A4
Wike Street	A3
Wilson Street	E1-F1
Wood Street	A3
Woodfield Terrace	D4
Woodhill Road	A4-B4
York Street	E3

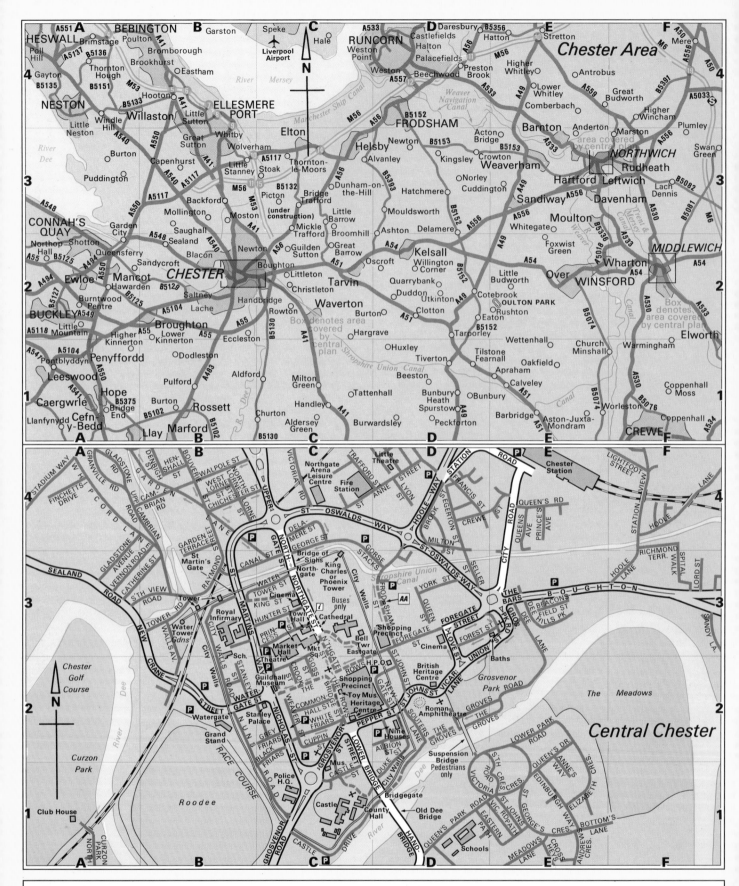

Chester

Chester is the only English city to have preserved the complete circuit of its Roman and medieval walls. On the west side, the top of the walls is now at pavement level, but on the other three sides the walk along the ramparts is remarkable. Two of the old watchtowers contain small museums: the Water Tower, built to protect the old river port, displays relics of medieval Chester; King Charles's

Tower, from which Charles I watched the defeat of the Royalist army at the Battle of Rowton Moor in 1645, portrays Chester's role in the Civil War.

Looking down from the top of the Eastgate, crowned with the ornate and gaily-coloured Jubilee Clock erected in 1897, the view down the main street, the old Roman *Via Principalis*, reveals a dazzling display of the black-and-white timbered buildings for which Chester is famous. One of these, Providence House, bears the inscription

'God's Providence is Mine Inheritance', carved in thanks for sparing the survivors of the plague of 1647 that ravaged the city.

On either side of Eastgate, Watergate and Bridge Street are the Rows, a feature unique to Chester, and dating back at least to the 13th century. These covered galleries of shops, raised up at first-floor level, protected pedestrians from weather and traffic. Chester's magnificent cathedral has beautifully carved choir stalls.

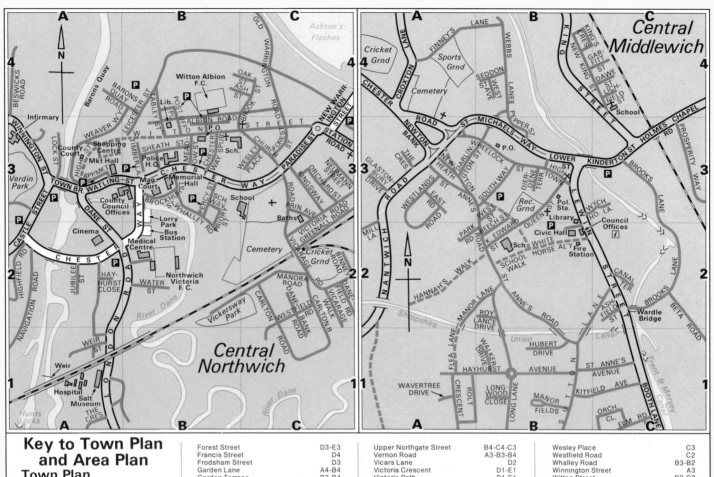

Key to Town Plan and Area Plan

Town Plan
AA Recommended roads
Other roads
Restricted roads
Buildings of interest — College
One Way Streets
Car Parks — P
Parks and open spaces
Churches — +

Area Plan
A roads
B roads
Locations — Duddon O
Urban area

Street Index with Grid Reference

Chester

Albion Street	D2
Andrews Crescent	E1
Anne's Way	E2-E1
Beaconsfield Street	E3
Black Friars	C1-C2
Bottom's Lane	E1-F1
Boughton	E3-F3
Bouverie Street	B4
Bridge Street	C2
Brook Street	D4
Cambrian Road	A4-B4
Canal Street	B3-C3
Castle Drive	C1
Castle Street	C1
Catherine Street	A3-B3
Chichester Street	B4-C4
City Road	E3-E4
City Walls Road	B3-B2
Commonhall Street	C2
Crewe Street	D4-E4
Crook Street	C2
Cross Heys	E1
Cuppin Street	C2
Curzon Park North	A1
Dee Hills Park	E3
Dee Lane	E3
Delamere Street	C4
Denbigh Street	B4
Duke Street	D1-D2
Eastern Path	D1-E1
Edinburgh Way	E1
Egerton Street	D4
Elizabeth Crescent	E1-E2
Finchetts Drive	A4
Foregate Street	D3

Forest Street	D3-E3
Francis Street	D4
Frodsham Street	D3
Garden Lane	A4-B4
Garden Terrace	B3-B4
George Street	C3-C4
Gladstone Avenue	A3-A4
Gladstone Road	A4
Gorse Stacks	C4-C3-D3
Goss Street	C2
Granville Road	A4
Grey Friars	C2
Grosvenor Park Road	E3
Grosvenor Road	C1
Grosvenor Street	C1-C2
Groves Road	D2-E2
Handbridge	D1
Henshall Street	B4
Hoole Lane	F3-F4
Hoole Way	D4
Hunter Street	B3-C3
King Street	B3-C3
Lightfoot Street	E4-F4
Lord Street	F3
Lorne Street	B4
Lower Bridge Street	C2-C1-D1
Lower Park Road	D2-E2
Love Street	D3
Lyon Street	D4
Meadows Lane	E1
Milton Street	D4
New Crane Street	A3-B3-B2
Newgate Street	D2
Nicholas Street	C2-C1
Northgate Street	C3-C2
North Lorne Street	B4
Nuns Road	B2-B1-C1
Pepper Street	C2-D2
Princess Street	C3
Prince's Avenue	E4
Queens Avenue	E4
Queen's Drive	E1-E2
Queen's Park Road	D1-E1
Queen's Road	E4
Queen Street	D3
Raymond Street	B3-B4
Richmond Terrace	F4
St Anne Street	C4-D4
St George's Crescent	E1
St Johns Road	E1
St Johns Street	D2
St John Street	D3-D2
St Martins Way	B4-B3-C3-B2-C2
St Oswalds Way	C4-D4-D3
Sealand Road	A3
Seller Street	D3
Souters Lane	D2
South Crescent Road	D2-E2-E1
South View Road	A3-B3
Spital Walk	F4-F3
Stadium Way	A4
Stanley Street	B2
Station Road	D4-E4
Station View	F4
The Bars	E3
The Groves	D2-E2
The Rows	C2
Tower Road	B3
Trafford Street	C4-D4
Union Street	D2-D3-E3
Upper Cambrian Road	A4-B4-B3

Upper Northgate Street	B4-C4-C3
Vernon Road	A3-B3-B4
Vicars Lane	D2
Victoria Crescent	D1-E1
Victoria Path	D1-E1
Victoria Road	C4
Walls Avenue	B3-B2
Walpole Street	B4
Watergate Street	B2-C2
Water Tower Street	B3-C3
Weaver Street	C2
West Lorne Street	B4
White Friars	C2
Whipcord Lane	A4-B4
York Street	D3

Northwich

Albion Road	B3
Apple Market	A3
Ash Street	B4-C4
Barons Quay Road	A4-B4
Beswicks Road	A4
Binney Road	C2
Brockhurst Street	B3
Brook Street	B3-C3-C4
Carlton Road	C2-C1
Castle Street	A2-A3
Chester Way	A2-B2-B3-C3
Chester Way Spur	B3
Church Road	C3
Danebank Road	C2-C1
Danefield Road	C2
Dane Street	A3-A2
Forest Street	C3
Greenall Road	C2-C3
Hayhurst Close	A2
Highfield Road	A2
High Street	A3
Jubilee Street	A2
Kingsway	C3
Leicester Street	B3-B4
Lock Street	A3
London Road	A1-A2-B2
Manora Road	C2
Meadow Street	B3
Navigation Road	A1-A2
Neumann Street	C3
New Warrington Street	C3-C4
Oak Street	B4-C4
Old Warrington Road	C4-C3
Orchard Street	C3
Paradise Street	C3
Percy Street	B3
Post Office Place	B4-B3
Princes Avenue	C3
Priory Street	B2-B3
School Way	B3
Sheath Street	B3
Station Road	C3
The Crescent	A1
Tabley Street	B4-B3
Timber Lane	B3
Town Bridge	A3
Vicarage Road	C2
Vicarage Walk	C2
Victoria Road	C2-C3
Water Street	B3
Watling Street	A3-B3
Weaver Way	A3-B3-B4
Weir Street	A1

Wesley Place	C3
Westfield Road	C2
Whalley Road	B3-B2
Winnington Street	A3
Witton Street	B3-C3

Middlewich

Ashfield Street	C2
Beech Street	B2-B3
Beta Road	C2-C1
Booth Lane	C1
Brooks Lane	C3-C2
Canal Terrace	C2
Chester Road	A4-A3
Croxton Lane	A4
Darlington Street	A3-B3
Dawe Street	C4
Dierdene Terrace	B3
East Road	A3
Elm Road	C1
Finney's Lane	A4-B4
Flea Lane	A1
Garfitt Street	B4-C4
Glastonbury Drive	A3
Hannah's Walk	A2-B2
Hayhurst Avenue	A1-B1
High Town	B3
Holmes Chapel Road	C3-C4
Hubert Drive	B1
Kinderton Street	B3-C3
King Edward Street	B2
King's Crescent	B4-C4
King Street	B4-C4-C3
Kitfield Avenue	B1-C1
Lewin Street	B3-B2-C2-C1
Lichfield Street	C4
Long Lane	B1
Longwood Close	B2
Manor Fields	B1
Manor Lane	A2-B2
Mill Lane	A2
Nantwich Road	A1-A2-A3
New King Street	B4-C4
Newton Bank	A4-A3
Newton Heath	A3
Orchard Close	C1
Park Road	A2-B2
Pepper Street	B4-B3
Prosperity Way	C3
Queen Street	B2-B3
Rolt Crescent	A1-B1
Roy Lance Drive	B2
St Anne's Avenue	B1-C1
St Anne's Road	A3-B3-B2-B1
St Michaels Way	A3-B3
School Walk	B2
Seddon Street	B4
Southway	B3
Sutton Lane	B1-B2-C2
The Crescent	A3
Walker Drive	B1
Wavertree Drive	A1
Webbs Lane	B4
West Avenue	B4
Westlands Road	A3-A2
West Street	B3
Wheelock Street	A3-B3
White Horse Alley	B2
Wych House Lane	B3-C3

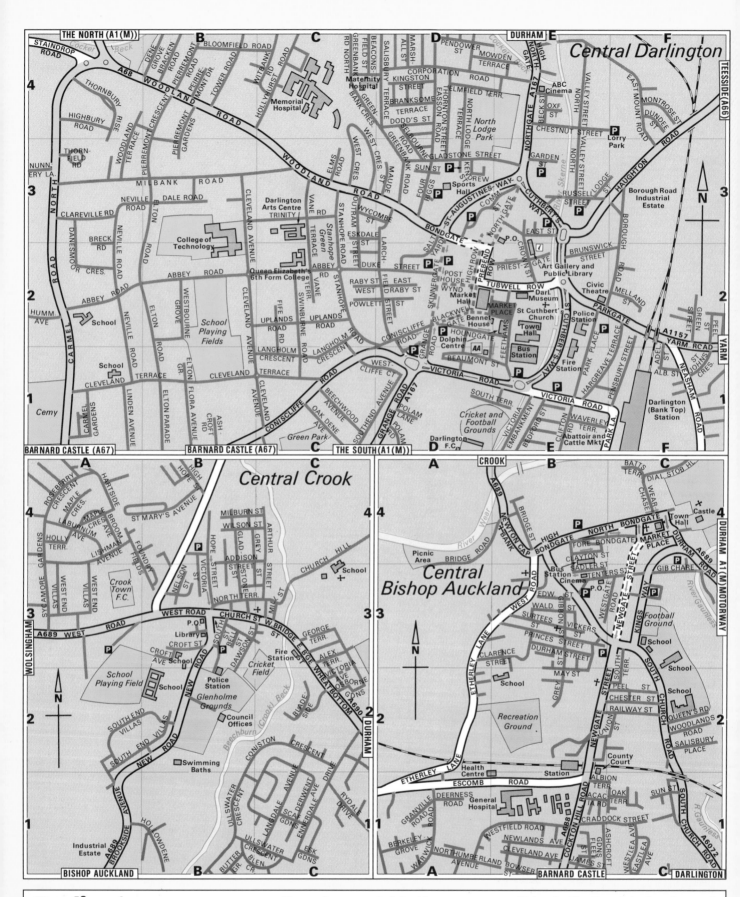

Darlington

Railways and Darlington have gone together since 1825, when George Stephenson's *Locomotion*, the world's first public steam train, passed through on its historic journey from Witton Park to Stockton-on-Tees. The *Locomotion* is now on show with other rolling stock at the Darlington Railway Museum. Appropriately, this is at North Road Station, which is one of the country's earliest.

The town became a major industrial centre during the industrial revolution, and a number of Georgian houses can be seen in the Market Square area. Bennet House, a former merchant's residence, is used by community service organisations, and it stands side by side with the new Dolphin Centre, the most recent addition to the town's leisure facilities. The Parish Church of St Cuthbert is 12th-century, and the Edwardian style of the 1907 Civic Theatre has been carefully preserved.

Bishop Auckland's castle has been the seat of the Bishops of Durham since the 12th century, and stands in an extensive park which is now owned by the local council.

Crook lies between the twin peaks of Mount Pleasant and Dowfold Hill, and has the unusual feature of the 'Blue Stone' or 'Devil's Stone'. Preserved in the Market Place, the stone is thought to have come from Borrowdale in the Lake District, during the Ice Age.

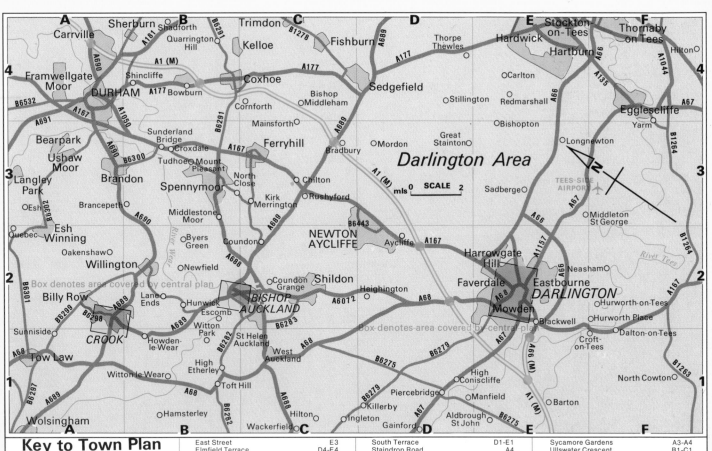

Key to Town Plan and Area Plan

Town Plan

AA Recommended roads
Restricted roads
Other roads
Buildings of interest   Town Hall ▣
AA Centre   AA
Car Parks   P
Parks and open spaces
Churches   †

Area Plan

A roads
B roads
Locations   Mount Pleasant ○
Urban area

Street Index with Grid Reference

Darlington

Abbey Road	A2-B2-C2
Adelaide Street	F1-F2
Albert Street	F1
Ashcroft Road	B1
Beaconsfield Street	C4
Beaumont Street	D1-E1
Beck Street	E4
Bedford Street	E1
Beechwood Avenue	C1
Blackwellgate	
Bloomfield Road	B4-C4
Bondgate	D2-D3
Borough Road	E2-F2-F3
Bracken Road	B4
Branksome Terrace	D4
Breck Road	A2
Brunswick Street	E2-F2
Carmel Gardens	A1
Carmel Road North	A1-A2-A3-A4
Chestnut Street	E4
Clareville Road	A3
Cleveland Avenue	B3-B2-B1-C1
Cleveland Terrace	A1-B1-C1
Clifton Road	E1
Commercial Street	D3-E3
Coniscliffe Road	B1-C1-D1-D2
Corporation Road	D4-E4
Crown Street	E2-E3
Cuthbert's Way	E3
Dale Road	B3
Danesmoor Crescent	A2-A3
Dene Grove	B4
Dodd's Street	D4
Duke Street	C2-D2
Dundee Street	F4
Easson Road	D3-D4
East Mount Road	E4-F4-F3
East Raby Street	D2
East Street	E3
Elmfield Terrace	D4-E4
Elms Road	C3
Elton Grove	B1
Elton Parade	B1
Elton Road	B1-B2-A2-B2-B3
Eskdale Street	C3-D3
Fife Road	C1-C2
Feethams	E1-E2
Flora Avenue	B1
Four Riggs	D3
Garden Street	E3
Gladstone Street	D3-E3
Grange Road	C1-D1-D2
Greenbank Crescent	C4-D4
Greenbank Road	D3-D4
Greenbank Road North	C4
Green Street	F2
Hargreave Terrace	E1-F1-F2
Haughton Road	E3-F3-F4
Highbury Road	A4
High Northgate	E4
High Row	D2
Hollyhurst Road	B4-C4
Houndgate	D2-E2
Hummersknott Avenue	A2
Kendrew Street	D3
Kingston Street	D4
Langholm Crescent	B1-C1-C2
Larchfield Street	D2-D3
Linden Avenue	A1
Lodge Street	E3-F3
Market Place	D2-E2
Marshall Street	D4
Maude Street	D3
Melland Street	F2
Milbank Road	A3-B3-C3
Montrose Street	F4
Mowden Terrace	D4-E4
Neasham Road	F1-F2
Neville Road	A1-A2-A3-B3
Northgate	D2-D3-E3-E4-E4
North Lodge Terrace	D3-D4
Nunnery Lane	A3
Oak Dene Avenue	C1
Outram Street	C2-C3
Oxford Street	E4
Parkgate	E2-F2
Park Lane	E1-F1
Park Place	E1-E2
Peel Street	F2
Pendower Street	D4
Pensbury Street	F1-F2
Pierremont Crescent	B3-B4
Pierremont Drive	B4
Pierremont Gardens	B3-B4
Pierremont Road	B4
Polam Lane	D1
Polam Road	D1
Post House Wynd	D2-E2
Powlett Street	C2-D2
Prebend Row	D2-E2
Priestgate	D2-E2
Raby Street West	C2-D2
Russell Street	E3
St Augustines Way	D3-E3
St Cuthbert's Way	E1-E2
St Johns Crescent	F1
Salisbury Terrace	D4
Salt Yard	D2-D3
Selbourne Road	D3-D4
Skinnergate	D2-D3
Southend Avenue	C1-D1
South Terrace	D1-E1
Staindrop Road	A4
Stanhope Road	C3-C2-D2
Swinburne Road	C1-C2
Sun Street	D3
Thornbury Rise	A3-A4
Thornfield Road	A3
Thornton Street	D3-D4
Tower Road	B4
Trinity Road	B3-C3
Tubwell Row	D2-E2
Uplands Road	B2-C2
Valley Street North	E3-E4
Vane Terrace	C2-C3
Victoria Embankment	E1
Victoria Road	E1
Victoria Road	D1-E1
Waverley Terrace	E1
Westbourne Grove	B2
Westcliffe Court	C1-D1
West Crescent	C3-C4
Witbank Road	C4
Woodland Road	A4-B4-C4-C3-D3
Woodland Terrace	A3-A4
Wycombe Street	C3-D3
Yarm Road	F1-F2

Crook

Addison Street	B4-C4
Alexandra Terrace	C3
Arthur Street	C3-C4
Bell Street	B3
Bladeside	C2
Blencathra Crescent	B1-C1
Brookside Avenue	A1
Broom Avenue	A4
Buttermere Grove	B1
Church Hill	C3-C4
Church Street	B3-C3
Coniston Crescent	B1-B2-C2
Croft Avenue	B3
Croft Street	B3
Dawson Street	B2-B3-C3
Derwent Avenue	C1-C2
East Bridge Street	C3
Ennerdale Drive	C1-C2
Esk Gardens	C1
Foundry Fields	A4-A3-B3
George Terrace	C3
Gladstone Street	B3-B4
Grey Street	B3-B4
Hartside	A4
High Hope Street	B4
Hollowdene	A1-B1
Holly Terrace	A4
Hope Street	B3-B4
Laburnum Avenue	A4
Langdale Avenue	C1-C2
Lishman Avenue	A4
Maple Crescent	A4
Milburn Street	B4-C4
Mill Street	C3
Nelson Street	B3
New Road	A2-B2-B3
North Terrace	B3-C3
Osborne Gardens	C2
Roseberry Crescent	A4
Rydale Drive	C1
St Mary's Avenue	A4-B4
Scafell Gardens	C1
Southend Villas	A2-B2
South Street	B3

Bishop Auckland

Acacia Road	B1-C1
Albion Terrace	B1-C1
Ashcroft Gardens	B1
Batts Terrace	C4
Berkeley Grove	A1
Bowser Street	B3
Bridge Road	A3-A4-B4
Bridge Street	B4
Chester Street	B2-C2
Clarence Street	A3-B3
Clayton Street	B4
Cleveland Avenue	B1
Cockton Hill Road	B1-B2
Craddock Street	B1-C1
Deerness Road	A1
Dial Stob Hill	C4
Durham Road	C3-C4
Durham Street	B3
Eastlea Avenue	C1
Edward Street	B3
Escomb Road	A1-B1
Etherley Lane	A1-A2-A3-B3
Fleet Street	B1
Fore Bondgate	B4-C4
Gib Chare	C3
Gibbon Street	B3
Granvill Road	A1
Grey Street	B2-B3
High Bondgate	B4
James Street	B1
Kings Way	C3
Market Place	C4
May Street	B2-B3
Newgate Street	B2-C2-C3-C4
Newlands Avenue	B1
Newton Cap Bank	B4
North Bondgate	B4-C4
Northumberland Avenue	A1-B1
Oak Terrace	C1
Peel Street	C2
Princes Street	B3
Queen's Road	C2
Railway Street	B2-C2
Sadler Street	B3
Salisbury Place	
South Church Road	C1-C2-C3
South Terrace	C2-C3
Sun Street	C1
Surtees Street	B3
Tenters Street	B3-C3
Union Street	B2-C2
Vickers Street	B3
Waldon Street	B3
Warwick Road	A1
Wearchase	C4
Westfield Road	A1-B1
Westgate Road	B3-C3
Westlea Avenue	B1
West Road	B3-B4
Woodlands Road	C2

(Darlington, continued column)

Sycamore Gardens	A3-A4
Ullswater Crescent	B1-C1
Victoria Avenue	C2-C3
Victoria Street	B3-B4
West Bridge Street	C3
West End Villas	A3
West Road	A3-B3
Wheatbottom	C2-C3
Wilson Street	B4-C4

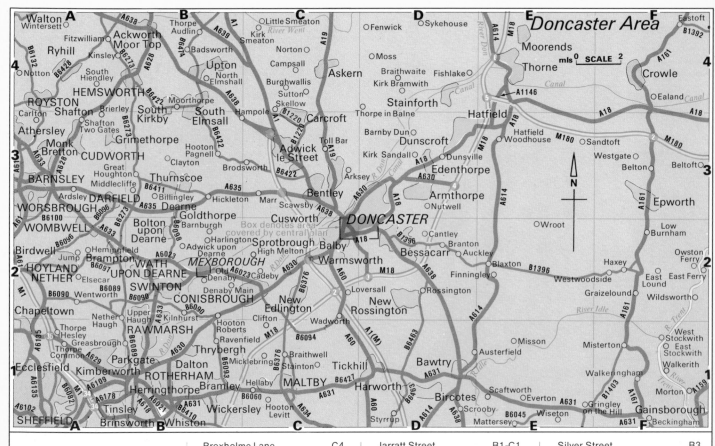

Key to Town Plan and Area Plan

Town Plan
- A A Recommended roads
- Other roads
- Restricted roads
- Buildings of interest   Hall
- Car Parks   P
- AA Service Centre   AA
- Parks and open spaces
- One way streets

Area Plan
- A roads
- B roads
- Locations   Ashton O
- Urban area

Street Index — with grid reference

Central Doncaster

Alderson Drive	D2-E2-E3
Apley Road	C2
Ardeen Road	E4-F4
Avondale Road	F3
Bawtry Road	F1-F2
Belle Vue Avenue	E1-F1-F2
Bennetthorpe	D2-E2
Broxholme Lane	C4
Buckingham Road	E4
Carr House Road	C1-D1-E1-E2
Chequer Avenue	C1-D1-E1
Chequer Road	C1-C2-C3
Christchurch Road	B4-C4-C3
Church View	A4-B4
Church Way	B4-C4
Cleveland Street	A1-A2-B2-B3
Clumber Road	E1
College Road	B2-C2
Copley Road	B4-C4
Craithie Road	E4-F4-F3
Cunningham Road	C1-C2
Danum Road	D1-E1-E2
Dockin Hill Road	B4-C4
Dublin Road	F4
Duke Street	A3-B3-B2
East Laithe Gate	B3-C3
Elmfield Road	C1-C2
Firbeck Road	D2-E2
Franklin Crescent	E2-E3
Glamis Road	F3
Glyn Avenue	C4
Goldsborough Road	E3-F3
Granby Crescent	E2
Greendyke Road	A1-B1
Grey Friar's Road	A4-B4
Hallgate	B3-C3
Hamilton Road	D1
Hampton Road	E3-E4
Harewood Road	F3
High Street	B3
Highfield Road	C4-D4
Holyrood Road	E4-E3-F3
Imperial Crescent	E4
Jarratt Street	B1-C1
King's Road	C4
Lakeen Road	F4
Lawn Avenue	C3-D3
Lawn Road	C3-D3
Leger Way	F2-F3
Leicester Avenue	F3
Limetree Avenue	D1-E1
Low Fisher Gate	B4
Neterhall Road	B4-C4
North Bridge Road	A4
Manor Drive	E2-E3
Marlborough Road	E4
Milton Walk	B1-B2
Osborne Road	E4
Oxford Street	B1
Palmer Street	C1
Park Road	C3-C4
Queens Road	C4-D4
Rainton Road	C1
Regent Square	C3
Roberts Road	A1
Roman Road	D1-D2
Rufford Road	E1
St Anne's Road	F1-F2
St Cecilia's Road	E1-F1
St Helen's Road	E1-F1
St Hilda's Road	E1-F1
St James Street	A1-A2-B2
St Mary's Road	D4
St Sepulchre Gate West	A1-A2
St Ursula's Road	F1
Sandy Lane	E1
Sandbeck Road	E1-E2
Sandringham Road	E3-F3-F4
Shaftesbury Avenue	F3
Silver Street	B3
South Parade	C3-C2-D2
South Street	C1
Stockil Road	D1
Theobald Avenue	D1
Thoresby Avenue	E1
Thorne Road	C3-C4-D4
Trafford Way	A3-A2-B2-B1-C1
Town Moor Avenue	D4-E4-E3-F3-F2
Tudor Road	F4
Waterdale	B2-B3-C3
Welbeck Road	D2-E2
Whitburn Road	C2
Windsor Road	D4-E4
Wood Street	B3
Zetland Road	E4-F4-F3

Mexborough

Adwick Road	C2-C3-C4-B4
Albert Road	B3-B4
Alexandra Road	B3-C3
Argyle Road	B3
Auckland Road	C3
Bank Street	B2-B1-C1
Carlyle Road	B2-B3
Cemetery Road	A4-B4
Church Street	C1
College Road	B2-C2
Cromwell Road	B2
Dolcliff Road	A2-A3-A2-B2
Garden Street	A2-B2
Genoa Street	C2-C3

Doncaster

Diana Rigg, Kevin Keegan and Freddie Trueman are just a few of the popular figures of fame who come from Doncaster, a busy commercial and industrial town which is set in a predominantly coalmining area and happens to be the birthplace of a good many celebrities. The town is also notable for its racecourse, which has been the site of the St Leger since the late 18th century, and it is well provided with professional football from Doncaster Rovers, who play in the Canon League.

Amongst the town's interesting older buildings, the 19th-century Church of St George was designed by Sir Gilbert Scott, and one of the few surviving Victorian Mansion Houses can also be seen here. The local Museum and Art Gallery offers displays of geology, natural history and the past of the Doncaster area. A museum of social history is housed in the attractive setting of Cusworth Hall, a fine 18th-century Palladian mansion which stands on the outskirts of the town.

Mexborough was a small village until the changes of the early 19th century fostered its expansion into an industrial town. The modern developments of streets and housing in more recent years have left Mexborough very little in the way of older buildings, but the Parish Church of St John the Baptist has retained vestiges of its Norman origins.

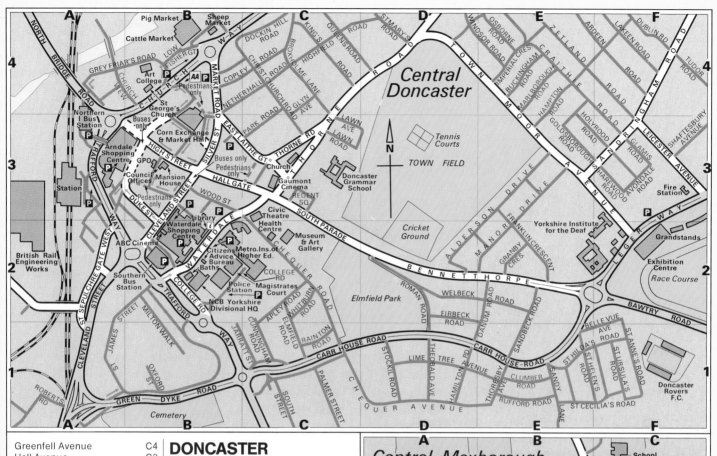

Central Doncaster

DONCASTER

public buildings and places of interest

AA Road Service Centre	**B4**
Central Library and Tourist Information Centre, Waterdale Shopping Centre	**B2**
Corn Exchange and Market Hall	**B3-B4**
Doncaster Grammar School	**C3**
Mansion House. An impressive building of 1748 containing several finely decorated public rooms. Adjacent are the Metropolitan Borough Council Offices	**B3**
Museum and Art Gallery	**C2**
St George's Church Designed by Sir Gilbert Scott and completed in 1858, it stands on the site of a Norman church destroyed by fire in 1853. The pinnacled tower rises to 170 feet.	**B4**
Technical College	**B2-C2**

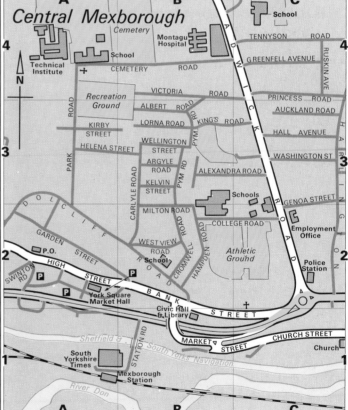

Central Mexborough

DONCASTER

Britain's oldest racecourse has long been a mecca for punters — amongst its better known visitors is Charles Dickens, who in 1875 watched the 110th St Leger from the ornate and still-used 18th-century grandstand.

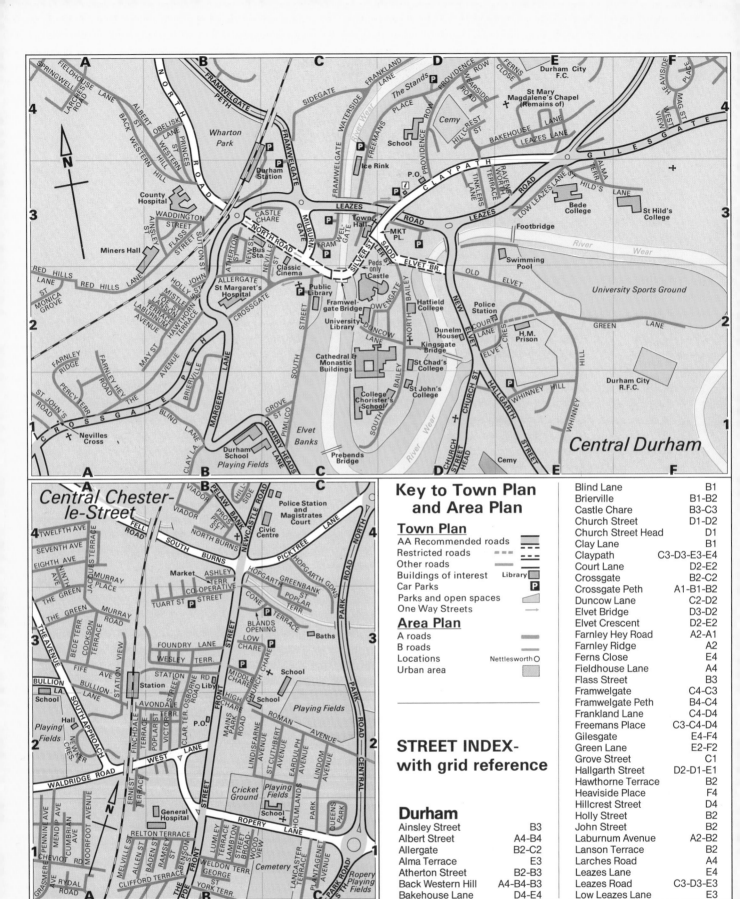

Central Durham

Central Chester-le-Street

Durham

The castle and the cathedral stand side by side high above the city like sentinels, dramatically symbolising the military and religious power Durham wielded in the past. Its origins date from about 995 when the remains of St Cuthbert arrived from Lindisfarne and his shrine was a popular centre of pilgrimage. Soon after that early fortifications were built, later replaced by a stone castle which became the residence of the Prince-Bishops of Durham – powerful feudal rulers appointed by the King. Today the city's university, the oldest in England after Oxford and Cambridge, occupies the castle and most of the buildings around peaceful, secluded Palace Green. The splendid Norman cathedral, sited on the other side of the Green, is considered to be one of the finest in Europe. Its combination of strength and size, tempered with grace and beauty, is awe-inspiring.

Under the shadow of these giants the old city streets, known as vennels, ramble down the bluff past the 17th-century Bishop Cosin's House and the old grammar school, to the thickly-wooded banks of the Wear. Here three historic bridges link the city's heart with the pleasant Georgian suburbs on the other side of the river.

Although Durham is not an industrial city, it has become the venue for the North-East miners' annual Gala Day in July.

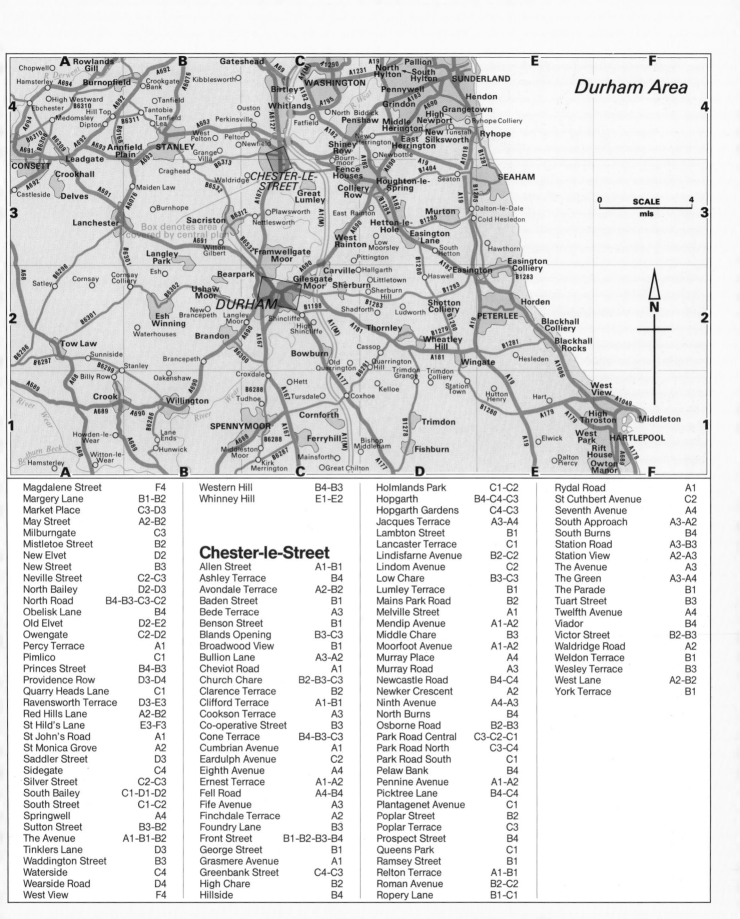

Durham Area

SCALE
0 ——— 4
mls

N

Box denotes area covered by central plan

Magdalene Street	F4	Western Hill	B4-B3	Holmlands Park	C1-C2	Rydal Road	A1
Margery Lane	B1-B2	Whinney Hill	E1-E2	Hopgarth	B4-C4-C3	St Cuthbert Avenue	C2
Market Place	C3-D3			Hopgarth Gardens	C4-C3	Seventh Avenue	A4
May Street	A2-B2			Jacques Terrace	A3-A4	South Approach	A3-A2
Milburngate	C3	**Chester-le-Street**		Lambton Street	B1	South Burns	B4
Mistletoe Street	B2			Lancaster Terrace	C1	Station Road	A3-B3
New Elvet	D2	Allen Street	A1-B1	Lindisfarne Avenue	B2-C2	Station View	A2-A3
New Street	B3	Ashley Terrace	B4	Lindom Avenue	C2	The Avenue	A3
Neville Street	C2-C3	Avondale Terrace	A2-B2	Low Chare	B3-C3	The Green	A3-A4
North Bailey	D2-D3	Baden Street	B1	Lumley Terrace	B1	The Parade	B1
North Road	B4-B3-C3-C2	Bede Terrace	A3	Mains Park Road	B2	Tuart Street	B3
Obelisk Lane	B4	Benson Street	B1	Melville Street	A1	Twelfth Avenue	A4
Old Elvet	D2-E2	Blands Opening	B3-C3	Mendip Avenue	A1-A2	Viador	B4
Owengate	C2-D2	Broadwood View	B1	Middle Chare	B3	Victor Street	B2-B3
Percy Terrace	A1	Bullion Lane	A3-A2	Moorfoot Avenue	A1-A2	Waldridge Road	A2
Pimlico	C1	Cheviot Road	A1	Murray Place	A4	Weldon Terrace	B1
Princes Street	B4-B3	Church Chare	B2-B3-C3	Murray Road	A3	Wesley Terrace	B3
Providence Row	D3-D4	Clarence Terrace	B2	Newcastle Road	B4-C4	West Lane	A2-B2
Quarry Heads Lane	C1	Clifford Terrace	A1-B1	Newker Crescent	A2	York Terrace	B1
Ravensworth Terrace	D3-E3	Cookson Terrace	A3	Ninth Avenue	A4-A3		
Red Hills Lane	A2-B2	Co-operative Street	B3	North Burns	B4		
St Hild's Lane	E3-F3	Cone Terrace	B4-B3-C3	Osborne Road	B2-B3		
St John's Road	A1	Cumbrian Avenue	A1	Park Road Central	C3-C2-C1		
St Monica Grove	A2	Eardulph Avenue	C2	Park Road North	C3-C4		
Saddler Street	D3	Eighth Avenue	A4	Park Road South	C1		
Sidegate	C4	Ernest Terrace	A1-A2	Pelaw Bank	B4		
Silver Street	C2-C3	Fell Road	A4-B4	Pennine Avenue	A1-A2		
South Bailey	C1-D1-D2	Fife Avenue	A3	Picktree Lane	B4-C4		
South Street	C1-C2	Finchdale Terrace	A2	Plantagenet Avenue	C1		
Springwell	A4	Foundry Lane	B3	Poplar Street	B2		
Sutton Street	B3-B2	Front Street	B1-B2-B3-B4	Poplar Terrace	C3		
The Avenue	A1-B1-B2	George Street	B1	Prospect Street	B4		
Tinklers Lane	D3	Grasmere Avenue	A1	Queens Park	C1		
Waddington Street	B3	Greenbank Street	C4-C3	Ramsey Street	B1		
Waterside	C4	High Chare	B2	Relton Terrace	A1-B1		
Wearside Road	D4	Hillside	B4	Roman Avenue	B2-C2		
West View	F4			Ropery Lane	B1-C1		

DURHAM
High above the wooded banks of the River Wear, Durham's castle and cathedral crown the steep hill on which the city is built. They share the site with several of the university's attractive old buildings.

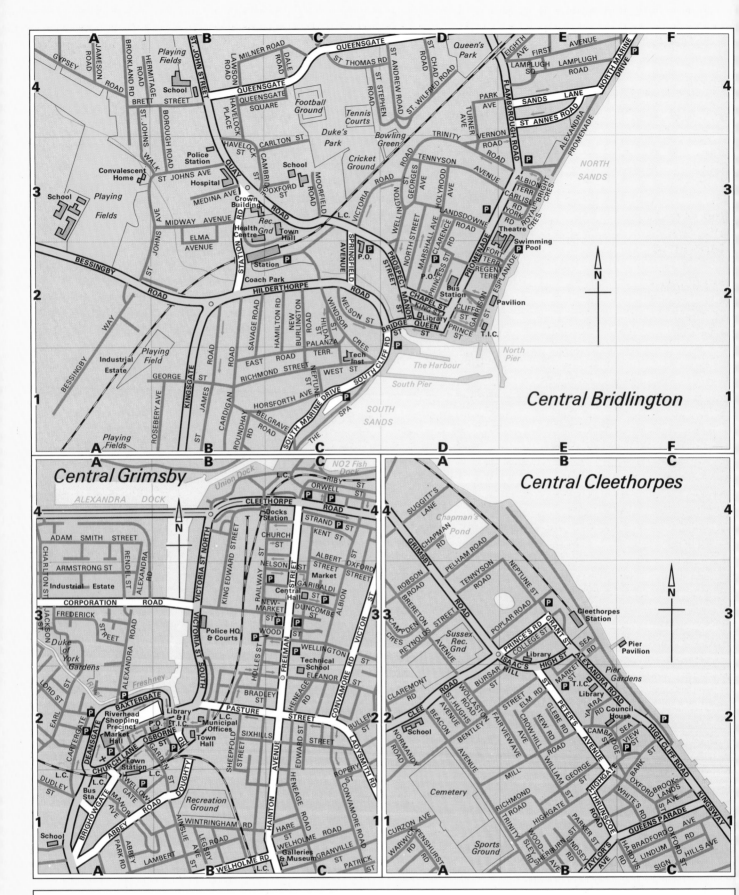

Central Bridlington

Central Grimsby

Central Cleethorpes

East coast towns

Scarborough is a classic seaside resort. It has good beaches and all the amusements required of a popular holiday destination, and it also shares in the grandeur of the impressive 12th-century castle ruins which stand on a headland between its two principal beaches.

Bridlington has thrived and flourished as a resort, with fine beaches sheltered by towering Flamborough Head. The older part of the town has several Georgian buildings, and the Bayle Gate (part of former priory) is now a museum. Nearby Sewerby Hall is a Georgian country house set in extensive parkland, and includes a small zoo.

Grimsby was little more than a village not so very long ago, but in the 19th century it rapidly expanded into a major River Humber port. The medieval Parish Church of St James still has some 14th-century features, and also worth seeing are the Welholme Galleries' museum and art gallery.

Cleethorpes has dealt effectively with the vagaries of tide and weather by installing an artificial beach and wave machine in its seafront Leisure Centre pool. Succulent oysters were the pride of the town in its fishing village days, but now visitors prefer to come for the sandy beaches and the entertainments which have made it such a popular resort. Sidney Park is noted for its aviaries and an arch made from a whale's jawbone.

28

Central Scarborough

North Bay

South Bay

29

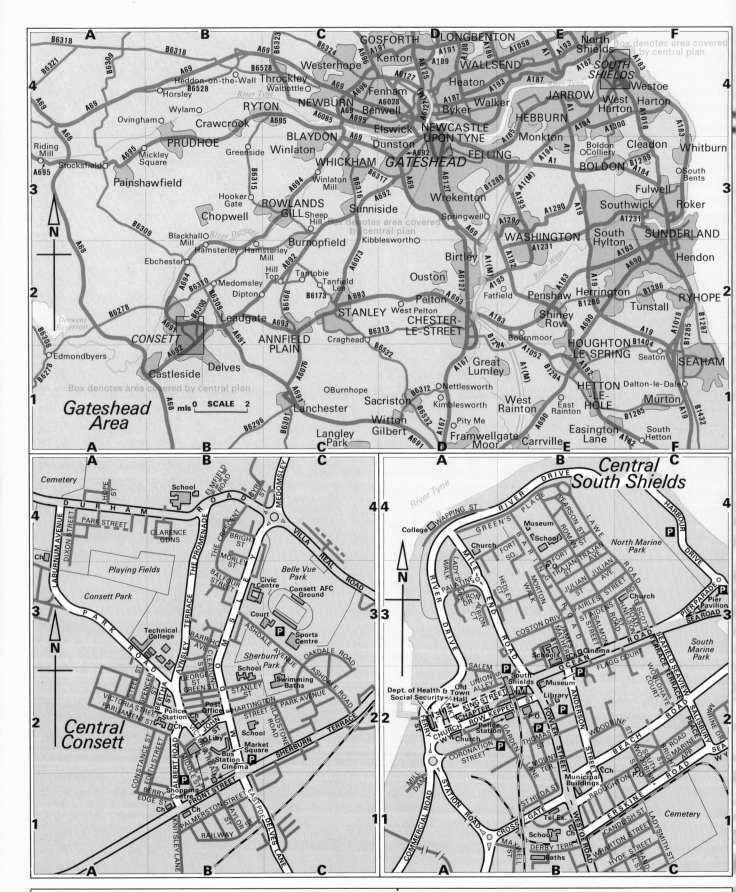

Gateshead

Seven bridges make the link across the Tyne to Newcastle from Gateshead, which is largely a modern town: a disastrous fire in the 19th century destroyed most of its older buildings. One notable escape from the fire was St Mary's Church, which has been heavily restored but still has some of its 12th-century features, and serves as a reminder that this is in fact an ancient Tyneside settlement. The town has suffered in this century too, with the decline of its dock area, but light engineering has come to take the place of its older industries, and the town has world renown today as a venue for national and international events at its celebrated athletics stadium.

South Shields has safe, sandy beaches and a good selection of entertainments and amusements for visitors, and another of its attractions is the South Tyneside Leisure and Gymnastics Centre, where the extensive swimming complex includes a wave machine. Overlooking the market square is the fine 18th-century Old Town Hall — irreverently known by locals as the Pepperpot. The Metal Arts Precinct features the work of local artists, and the Arbeia Roman Fort and Museum can be visited in Baring Street.

Consett was once a steel producing town, and has a pleasant Derwentside setting with a number of attractive parks.

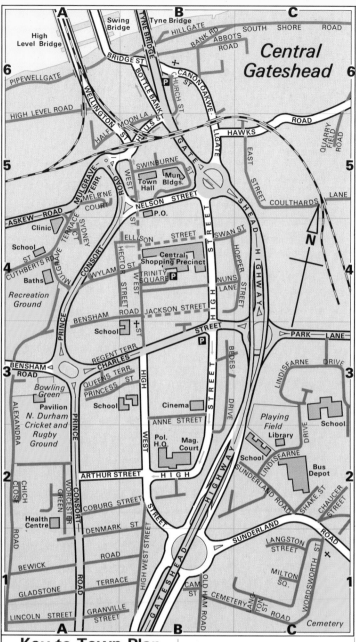

Central Gateshead

Key to Town Plan and Area Plan

Town Plan
AA Recommended roads
Other roads
Restricted roads
Buildings of interest   Cinema
One Way Streets
Parks and open spaces
Car Parks   P
Churches   +
Metro Stations   M

Area Plan
A roads
B roads
Locations   Ripley O
Urban area

Street Index with Grid Reference

Gateshead

Abbots Road	B6-C6
Alexandra Road	A1-A2-A3
Anne Street	B3
Arthur Street	A2-B2
Askew Road	A4-A5
Bank Road	B6
Bedes Drive	B2-B3
Bensham Road	A3-A4-B4
Bewick Road	A1-B1
Bottle Bank	B5-B6
Bridge Street	A6-B6
Camilla Street	B1
Canon Street	B6
Cemetery Road	B1-C1
Charles Street	A3-B3-C3
Chaucer Street	C2
Chichester Close	A2
Church Street	B5-B6
Coburg Street	A2-B2
Coulthards Lane	C5
Denmark Street	A1-B1-B2
East Street	C5
Ellison Street	A4-B4
Gateshead Highway	B1-B2-C2-C3-C4-C5-B5-B6
Gladstone Terrace	A1-B1
Granville Street	A1-B1
Half Moon Lane	A5-B5
Hawks Road	B5-C5-C6
Hector Street	A4-B4
High Level Road	A5-A6
High Street	B2-B3-B4-B5
High West Street	B1-B2-B3
Hillgate	B6
Hills Street	B5
Hopper Street	B4-C4-B4
Jackson Street	B4
Langton Street	C1
Lincoln Street	A1
Lindisfarne Drive	C2-C3
Melbourne Court	A5
Milton Square	C1
Mulgrave Terrace	A4-A5
Nelson Street	B5
Nuns Lane	B4-C4
Oakwell Gate	B5-B6
Old Ham Road	B1
Park Lane	C3
Pipewell Gate	A6
Prince Consort Road	A1-A2-A3-A4-A5-B5
Princess Street	A3-B3
Quarryfield Road	C5-C6
Queens Terrace	A3-B3
Regent Terrace	A3-B3
St Cuthberts Road	A4
Shakespeare Street	C2
South Shore Road	B6-C6
Sunderland Road	B1-C1-C2-C1
Swan Street	B4-C4
Swinburne Street	B5
Trinity Square	B4
Tyne Bridge	B6
Wellington Street	A6-A5-B5
West Street	B3-B4-B5
Worcester Green	A1-A2
Wordsworth Street	C1
Wylam Street	A4-B4

Consett

Albert Road	B1-B2
Ashdale Avenue	B3-C3
Ashdale Road	C2
Aynsley Terrace	B2-B3
Balfour Street	B3
Barr House Avenue	B3
Berry Edge Street	A1-B1
Bertha Street	B2
Bright Street	B4
Clarence Gardens	B4
Cleadon Street	B2-B3
Constance Road	A1-A2-B2
Cyril Street	B4-C4
Delves Lane	B1-C1
Dixon Street	A3-A4
Durham Road	A4-B4
East Parade	B1
Edith Street	A1-B1-B2
Elmfield Road	B4
Front Street	B1
George Street	B2
Gladstone Road	C2
Green Street	B2
Hartington Street	B2-C2
Hope Street	A4
John Street	B2
Knitsley Lane	B1
Laburnum Avenue	A3-A4
Medomsley	B2-B3-B4-C4
Middle Street	B1-B2
Morley Street	B4
Oakdale Road	C2-C3
Palmerston Street	B1
Park Avenue	C2
Park Road	A3-B3-B2-A2
Park Street	A4
Parliament Street	A2-B2
Railway Street	B1
Sherburn Terrace	B2-C2
Spencer Street	A2-B2
Stanley Street	B2
Steel Street	A2-A3
The Crescent	B4
The Promenade	B3-B4
Taylor Street	B1
Victoria Road	B1-B2
Victoria Street	A2-B2
Villa Real Road	C3-C4

South Shields

Albion Court	A3
Anderson Street	B1-B2
Baring Road	B3-B4
Beach Road	B1-B2-C2
Bright Street	C2
Broughton Road	B1-C1-C2
Candlish Street	B1-C1
Chapter Row	A2
Church Way	A2
Commercial Road	A1-A2
Coronation Street	A2
Coston Drive	B3
Crossgate	A1-B1
Derby Terrace	B1
Erskine Road	B1-C1-C2
Fairles Street	B3-C3
Ferry Street	A2
Flagg Court	B2-B3-C3
Fort Square	B3-B4
Fowler Street	B1-B2
Garden Lane	B1-B2
Greens Place	A4-B4
Handel Street	C1
Harbour Drive	C3-C4
Hedley Court	A3-B3
Henry Nelson Street	C3
Heron Drive	A3
Hyde Street	B1-C1
James Mather Street	B3
Julian Avenue	B3-C3
Julian Street	B3
Keppel Street	A2-B2
King Street	A2-B2
Lady's Walk	A3-A4
Ladysmith Street	C1
Lawe Road	B4-C4-C3
Market Place	A2
Marine Approach	C2
Marine Drive	C2
Maxwell Street	A1-B1
Mile End Road	A4-A3-B3-B2
Milldam	A1
Morton Walk	B3
Mount Terrace	B2
Ocean Road	B2-B3-C3
Palatine Street	A3
Pearsons Street	B4
Pier Parade	C3
River Drive	A2-A3-A4-B4-C4
Roman Road	B4-B3-C3
St Aidens Road	B3-C3
St Hilda Street	B1
Salem Street	A2
Salisbury Place	C2
Salmon Street	B3
Scott Road	C3
Sea Road	C3
Sea Way	C2
Seafield Terrace	C2-C3
Seaview Terrace	C2
South Woodbine Street	C1-C2
Station Road	A1-A2
Thomas Street	B2
Trajan Avenue	B4
Trajan Street	B3-B4
Union Alley	A2-B2
Wapping Street	A4
Westoe Road	B1
Wharton Street	B1-C1
Woodbine Street	B2-C2
Wouldhaye Court	C2

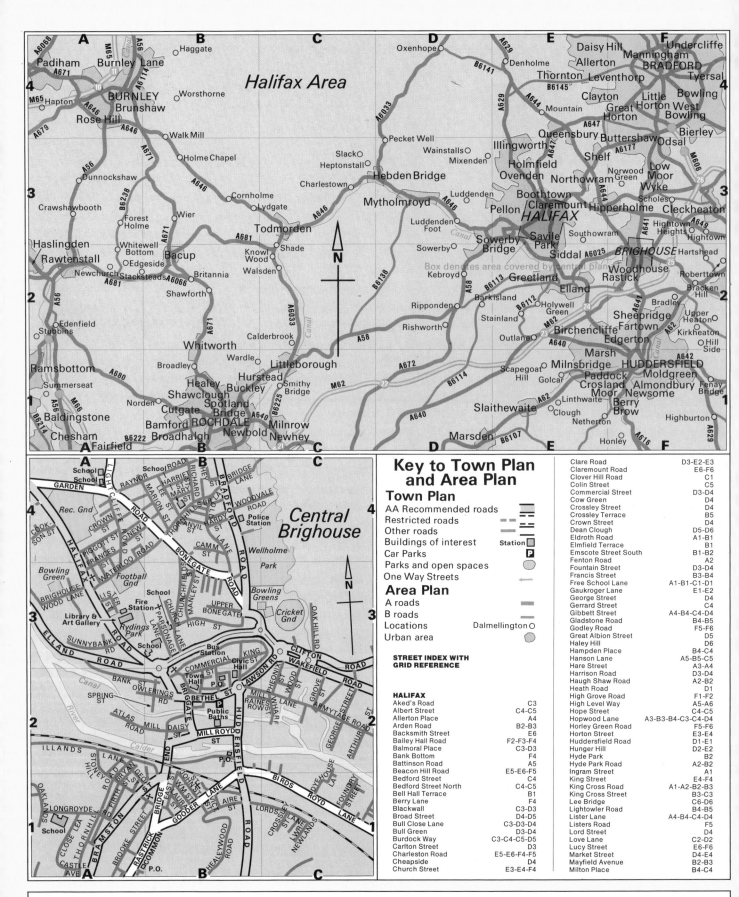

Key to Town Plan and Area Plan

Town Plan

AA Recommended roads	
Restricted roads	
Other roads	
Buildings of interest	Station ▢
Car Parks	Ⓟ
Parks and open spaces	
One Way Streets	←

Area Plan

A roads	
B roads	
Locations	Dalmellington ○
Urban area	

STREET INDEX WITH GRID REFERENCE

HALIFAX

Aked's Road	C3
Albert Street	C4-C5
Allerton Place	A4
Arden Road	B2-B3
Backsmith Street	E6
Bailey Hall Road	F2-F3-F4
Balmoral Place	C3-D3
Bank Bottom	F4
Battinson Road	A5
Beacon Hill Road	E5-E6-F5
Bedford Street	C4
Bedford Street North	C4-C5
Bell Hall Terrace	B1
Berry Lane	F4
Blackwall	C3-D3
Broad Street	D4-D5
Bull Close Lane	C3-D3-D4
Bull Green	D3-D4
Burdock Way	C3-C4-C5-D5
Carlton Street	D3
Charleston Road	E5-E6-F4-F5
Cheapside	D4
Church Street	E3-E4-F4
Clare Road	D3-E2-E3
Claremount Road	E6-F6
Clover Hill Road	C1
Colin Street	C5
Commercial Street	D3-D4
Cow Green	D4
Crossley Street	D4
Crossley Terrace	B5
Crown Street	D4
Dean Clough	D5-D6
Eldroth Road	A1-B1
Elmfield Terrace	B1
Emscote Street South	B1-B2
Fenton Road	A2
Fountain Street	D3-D4
Francis Street	B3-B4
Free School Lane	A1-B1-C1-D1
Gaukroger Lane	E1-E2
George Street	C4
Gerrard Street	C4
Gibbett Street	A4-B4-C4-D4
Gladstone Road	B4-B5
Godley Road	F5-F6
Great Albion Street	D5
Haley Hill	D6
Hampden Place	B4-C4
Hanson Lane	A5-B5-C5
Hare Street	A3-A4
Harrison Road	D3-D4
Haugh Shaw Road	A2-B2
Heath Road	D1
High Grove Road	F1-F2
High Level Way	A5-A6
Hope Street	C4-C5
Hopwood Lane	A3-B3-B4-C3-C4-D4
Horley Green Road	F5-F6
Horton Street	E3-E4
Huddersfield Road	D1-E1
Hunger Hill	D2-E2
Hyde Park	B2
Hyde Park Road	A2-B2
Ingram Street	A1
King Street	E4-F4
King Cross Road	A1-A2-B2-B3
King Cross Street	B3-C3
Lee Bridge	C6-D6
Lightowler Road	B4-B5
Lister Lane	A4-B4-C4-D4
Listers Road	F5
Lord Street	D4
Love Lane	C2-D2
Lucy Street	E6-F6
Market Street	D4-E4
Mayfield Avenue	B2-B3
Milton Place	B4-C4

Halifax

Rising up from the eastern edge of the Pennine Hills, this old industrial town occupies a magnificent setting and offers an unexpected wealth of fine buildings. Jewel in the crown is Piece Hall, a unique 18th-century cloth hall built around a quadrangle, which serves as a fitting testimony to the town's long history of textile manufacture. The Perpendicular style Parish Church is 15th-century; the Town Hall was designed by the same architect as the Houses of Parliament, and is thought by some to be one of the finest in the country. Most eccentric of the town's monuments must be Wainhouse Tower, designed as a chimney, but never used as such. It is now an ornamental tower and viewpoint. Halifax also has no less than three model villages: purpose-built to house textile workers these would have been ahead of their time when first constructed. Not content with the history to be seen in its buildings, the town also offers the insights into the past of Bankfield Museum and Shibbden Hall.

Brighouse is the reputed burial place of Robin Hood, who might have fared far worse than this friendly and welcoming town nestling in the valley of the River Calder. An industrial centre with a charming setting, it has several pleasant open spaces, and country walks can be enjoyed only a short distance from the town centre.

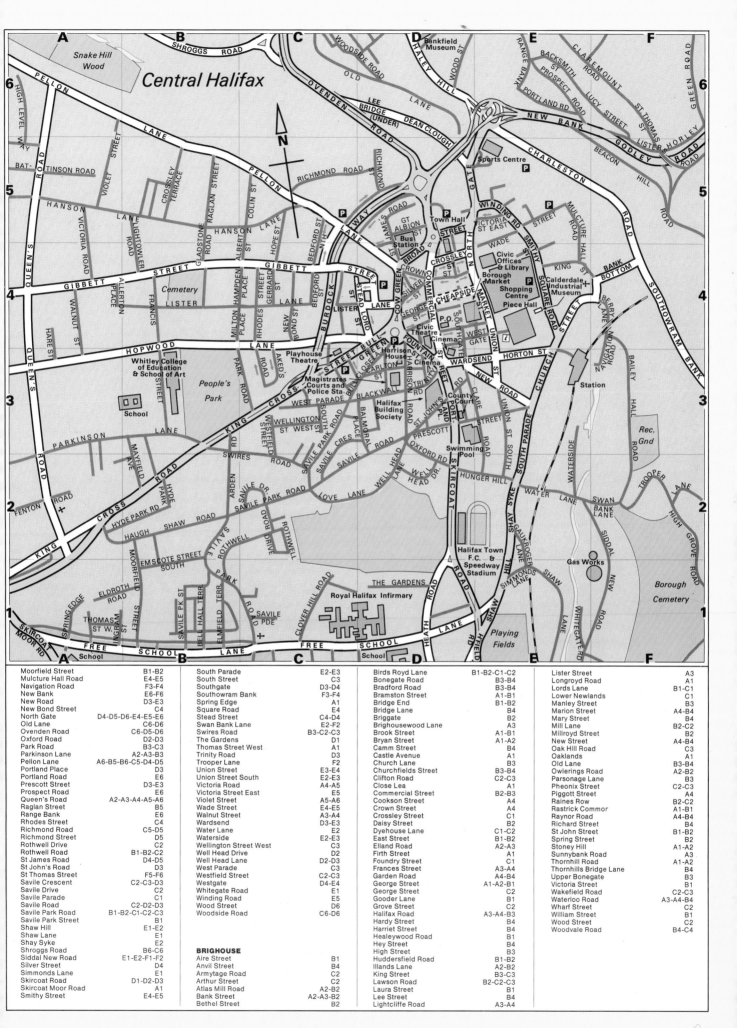

Central Halifax

Street	Grid	Street	Grid	Street	Grid	Street	Grid
Moorfield Street	B1-B2	South Parade	E2-E3	Birds Royd Lane	B1-B2-C1-C2	Lister Street	A3
Mulcture Hall Road	E4-E5	South Street	C3	Bonegate Road	B3-B4	Longroyd Road	A1
Navigation Road	F3-F4	Southgate	D3-D4	Bradford Road	B3-B4	Lords Lane	B1-C1
New Bank	E6-F6	Southowram Bank	F3-F4	Bramston Street	A1-B1	Lower Newlands	C1
New Road	D3-E3	Spring Edge	A1	Bridge End	B1-B2	Manley Street	B3
New Bond Street	C4	Square Road	E4	Bridge Lane	B4	Marion Street	A4-B4
North Gate	D4-D5-D6-E4-E5-E6	Stead Street	C4-D4	Briggate	B2	Mary Street	B4
Old Lane	C6-D6	Swan Bank Lane	E2-F2	Brighousewood Lane	A3	Mill Lane	B2-C2
Ovenden Road	C6-D5-D6	Swires Road	B3-C2-C3	Brook Street	A1-B1	Millroyd Street	B2
Oxford Road	D2-D3	The Gardens	D1	Bryan Street	A1-A2	New Street	A4-B4
Park Road	B3-C3	Thomas Street West	A1	Camm Street	B4	Oak Hill Road	C3
Parkinson Lane	A2-A3-B3	Trinity Road	D3	Castle Avenue	A1	Oaklands	A1
Pellon Lane	A6-B5-B6-C5-D4-D5	Trooper Lane	F2	Church Lane	B3	Old Lane	B3-B4
Portland Place	D3	Union Street	E3-E4	Churchfields Street	B3-B4	Owlerings Road	A2-B2
Portland Road	E6	Union Street South	E2-E3	Clifton Road	C2-C3	Parsonage Lane	B3
Prescott Street	D3-E3	Victoria Road	A4-A5	Close Lea	A1	Pheonix Street	C2-C3
Prospect Road	E6	Victoria Street East	E5	Commercial Street	B2-B3	Piggott Street	A4
Queen's Road	A2-A3-A4-A5-A6	Violet Street	A5-A6	Cookson Street	A4	Raines Row	B2-C2
Raglan Street	B5	Wade Street	E4-E5	Crown Street	A4	Rastrick Commor	A1-B1
Range Bank	E6	Walnut Street	A3-A4	Crossley Street	C1	Raynor Road	A4-B4
Rhodes Street	C4	Wardsend	D3-E3	Daisy Street	B2	Richard Street	B3
Richmond Road	C5-D5	Water Lane	E2	Dyehouse Lane	C1-C2	St John Street	B1-B2
Richmond Street	D5	Waterside	E2-E3	East Street	B1-B2	Spring Street	B2
Rothwell Drive	C2	Wellington Street West	C3	Elland Road	A2-A3	Stoney Hill	A1-A2
Rothwell Road	B1-B2-C2	Well Head Drive	D2	Firth Street	A1	Sunnybank Road	A3
St James Road	D4-D5	Well Head Lane	D2-D3	Foundry Street	C1	Thornhill Road	A1-A2
St John's Road	D3	West Parade	C3	Frances Street	A3-A4	Thornhills Bridge Lane	B4
St Thomas Street	F5-F6	Westfield Street	C2-C3	Garden Road	A4-B4	Upper Bonegate	B3
Savile Crescent	C2-C3-D3	Westgate	D4-E4	George Street	A1-A2-B1	Victoria Street	B1
Savile Drive	C2	Whitegate Road	E1	George Street	C2	Wakefield Road	C2-C3
Savile Parade	C1	Winding Road	E5	Gooder Lane	B1	Waterloo Road	A3-A4-B4
Savile Road	C2-D2-D3	Wood Street	D6	Grove Street	A3	Wharf Street	C2
Savile Park Road	B1-B2-C1-C2-C3	Woodside Road	C6-D6	Halifax Road	A3-A4-B3	William Street	B1
Savile Park Street	B1			Hardy Street	B4	Wood Street	C2
Shaw Hill	E1-E2			Harriet Street	B4	Woodvale Road	B4-C4
Shaw Lane	E1	**BRIGHOUSE**		Healeywood Road	B1		
Shay Syke	E2	Aire Street	B1	Hey Street	B4		
Shroggs Road	B6-C6	Anvil Street	B4	High Street	B3		
Siddal New Road	E1-E2-F1-F2	Armytage Road	C2	Huddersfield Road	B1-B2		
Silver Street	D4	Arthur Street	C2	Illands Lane	A2-B2		
Simmonds Lane	E1	Atlas Mill Road	A2-B2	King Street	B3-C3		
Skircoat Road	D1-D2-D3	Bank Street	A2-A3-B2	Lawson Road	B2-C2-C3		
Skircoat Moor Road	A1	Bethel Street	B2	Laura Street	B1		
Smithy Street	E4-E5			Lee Street	B4		
				Lightcliffe Road	A3-A4		

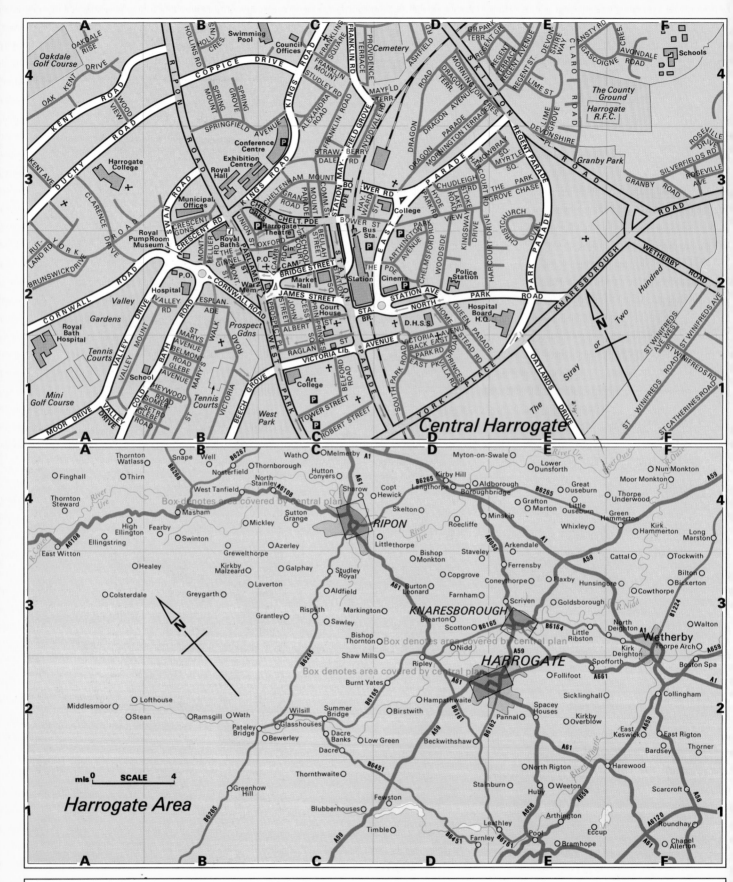

Harrogate

Dignified Victorian stone buildings and lovely gardens reflect Harrogate's 19th-century popularity as a spa town and its Royal Baths, opened in 1897, became one of the largest hydrotherapy establishments in the world. More recently the town has become a busy conference centre, the main venues being the Royal Hall and the elegant old Assembly Rooms. A glass-covered walkway in Valley Gardens leads to the Sun Pavilion and part of the lovely Harlow Car Gardens is used for experimental horticulture.

Ripon, known as the Gateway to the Dales, stands at the junction of three rivers; the Ure, the Skell and the Laver. Its small cathedral, a delightful 12th-century building occupying the site of an Anglo-Saxon church, has a small museum of church treasures in the original crypt. One corner of the town's rectangular market square is marked by the medieval Wakeman's house, now a local museum and tourist information centre.

Knaresborough Here buildings scramble higgledy-piggledy up a rocky outcrop from the banks of the River Nidd to the town's ruined 14th-century castle. The keep, two baileys and two gatehouses have survived, and there is a museum in the grounds. The town is able to claim two records; it has the oldest linen-mill and the oldest chemist's shop in England.

34

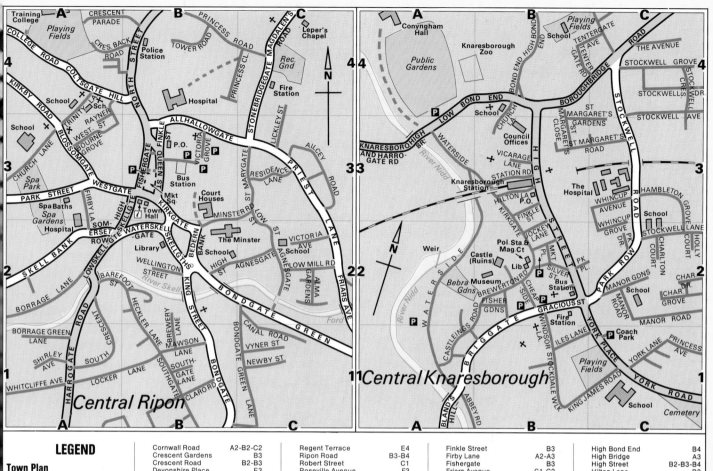

Central Ripon

Central Knaresborough

LEGEND

Town Plan

AA recommended route
Restricted roads
Other roads
Buildings of interest — Station
Car parks — P
Parks and open spaces
One way streets

Area Plan

A roads
B roads
Locations — Nidd ○
Urban area

Street Index with Grid Reference

Harrogate

Albert Street	C2
Alexandra Road	C4
Ansty Road	E4-F4
Arthington Avenue	D2
Ashfield Road	D4
Avondale Road	F4
Back East Park Road	D1
Beech Grove	B1-C1
Belford Road	C1
Belmont Road	B1
Beulah Street	C2
Bower Road	C3-D3
Bower Street	C3-D3
Brunswick Drive	A2
Cambridge Road	C2
Cambridge Street	C2
Chelmsford Road	D2-D3
Cheltenham Crescent	B3-C3
Cheltenham Mount	C3
Cheltenham Parade	C3
Christchurch Oval	E2-E3
Chudleigh Road	D3
Clarence Drive	A2-A3
Claro Road	E3-E4
Cold Bath Road	A1-B1-B2
Commercial Street	C3
Coppice Drive	B4-C4
Cornwall Road	A2-B2-C2
Crescent Gardens	B3
Crescent Road	B2-B3
Devonshire Place	E3
Devonshire Way	E4
Dragon Avenue	D3-D4
Dragon Parade	D3-D4
Dragon Road	D3-D4
Dragon Terrace	D4
Duchy Road	A3-A4-B4
East Parade	D2-D3-E3-E4
East Park Road	D1-D2
Esplanade	B2
Franklin Mount	C4
Franklin Road	C3-C4
Franklins Square	C4
Gascoigne Crescent	E4-F4
Glebe Avenue	B1
Glebe Road	A1-B1
Granby Road	F3
Granville Road	C3
Grove Park Terrace	D4-E4
Harcourt Drive	D2-D3
Harcourt Road	D3
Hayward Street	C3-D3
Heywood Road	B1
Hollins Crescent	B4
Hollins Road	B4
Homestead Road	D1-D2
Hyde Park Road	D3
James Street	C2
John Street	C2
Kent Avenue	A3
Kent Road	A3-A4-B4
King's Road	B3-C3-C4
Kingsway Drive	D2-D3
Knaresborough Road	E1-E2-F2-F3
Lime Grove	E3-E4
Lime Street	E4
Mayfield Grove	C3-C4
Mayfield Terrace	C4-D4
Montpellier Road	B2
Montpellier Street	B2
Moor Drive	A1
Mornington Crescent	D4-E4
Mornington Terrace	D3-D4
Mount Parade	C3
Mowbray Square	D3-E3
Myrtle Square	E3
North Park Road	D2-E2
Nyddvale Road	C3-C4-D4
Oakdale Rise	A4
Oak Kent Drive	A4
Oatlands Drive	E1
Oxford Street	B2-C2-C3
Park Chase	E3
Park Parade	E1-E2-E3
Park View	D3
Parliament Street	B3-B2-C2
Princes Square	C1-C2
Princes Street	C2
Princes Villa Road	D1
Prospect Place	C1-C2
Providence Terrace	C4
Queen Parade	D2-D1-E1
Raglan Street	C2
Regent Avenue	E4
Regent Grove	D4-E4
Regent Parade	E3-E4
Regent Street	E4

Regent Terrace	E4
Ripon Road	B3-B4
Robert Street	C1
Roseville Avenue	F3
Roseville Drive	F3
Rutland Road	A2
St Catherine's Road	F1
St Marys Avenue	B1
St Mary's Walk	B1-B2
St Winifreds Avenue	F1-F2
St Winifreds Avenue West	F1-F2
St Winifreds Road	F1
School Court	C2
Silverfields Road	F3
Skipton Road	D4-E4-E3-F3
Somerset Road	A1-B1
South Park Road	D1
Springfield Avenue	B4-B3-C3-C4
Spring Grove	B4
Spring Mount	B4
Station Avenue	D2
Station Bridge	C2
Station Parade	C3-C2-C1-D1
Station Square	C2
Stoke Lake Road	D3
Strawberry Dale Road	C3
Studley Road	C4
Swan Road	B2-B3
The Ginnel	B2
The Grove	D3-E3
The Parade	C2-D2
Tower Street	C1
Union Street	B2-B3
Valley Drive	A1-A2-B2
Valley Mount	A1-B1-B2
Valley Road	B2
Victoria Avenue	C1-D1-D2
Victoria Road	B1-B2
West Park	C1-C2
Wetherby Road	F2
Woodside	D2-D3
Wood View	A4
York Place	D1-E1
York Road	A3-A2-A3-B3

Ripon

Agnesgate	B2-C2
Ailcey Road	C3
Allhallowgate	B3-C3
Alma Gardens	C2
Barefoot Street	A2-B2
Bedern Bank	B2
Blossomgate	A3
Bondgate	B1
Bondgate Green	B2-C2-C1
Bondgate Green Lane	C1-C2
Borrage Green Lane	A1
Borrage Lane	A2
Brewery Road	B1-B2
Canal Road	C1-C2
Church Lane	A3
Claro Road	B1
College Road	A4
Coltsgate Hill	A4-B4
Crescent Back Road	A4-B4
Crescent Parade	A4-B4

Finkle Street	B3
Firby Lane	A2-A3
Fishergate	B3
Friars Avenue	C1-C2
Harrogate Road	A1-A2
Heckler Lane	B1-B2
High Skellgate	A3-A2-B2-B3
High Street	B2
King Street	B1-B2
Kirkby Road	A3-A4
Kirkgate	B2-B3
Lickley Street	C3-C4
Locker Lane	A1-B1
Low Mill Lane	C2
Lowskellgate	A2
Low Street	C2-C3
Magdalen's Road	C4
Mawson Lane	B1
Minster Road	B2-B3-C3
Newby Street	C1
North Lane	B3-B4
Park Street	A3
Priest Lane	C2-C3
Princess Close	B4-C4
Princes Road	B4-C4
Queen Street	B3
Rayner Street	A3-A4
Residence Lane	C3
St Agnesgate	C2
St Marygate	C3
Shirley Avenue	A1
Skell Bank	A2
Skellgarths	B2
Somerset Row	A2
South Crescent	A1-A2
Southgate	B1
Southgate Lane	B1
Stonebridgegate	C3-C4
Tower Road	B4
Trinity Lane	A3-A4
Victoria Avenue	C2
Victoria Grove	B3
Vyner Street	C1
Waterskellgate	A2-B2
Wellington Street	B2
Westbourne Grove	A3
Westgate	A3-B3
Whitcliffe Avenue	A1

Knaresborough

Abbey Road	A1-B1
Bland's Hill	A1
Bond End	B4
Boroughbridge Road	B4-C4
Brewerton Road	B2
Briggate	A1-B1-B2
Castleings Road	A1-B1-B2
Charlton Court	C2
Charlton Drive	C2
Charlton Grove	C2
Cheapside	B2
Church Lane	B3-B4
Finkle Street	B3
Fisher Gardens	B2
Gracious Street	B2
Hambleton Grove	C2-C3

High Bond End	B4
High Bridge	A3
High Street	B2-B3-B4
Hilton Lane	B3
Holly Court	C2
Iles Lane	B1-C1
Jockey Lane	B2-B3
King James Road	B1-C1
Kirkgate	B2-B3
Knaresborough and Harrogate Road	A3
Low Bond End	A3-A4-B4
Manor Gardens	C2
Manor Road	C2
Market Place	B2
Park Place	B2-C2
Park Row	C2
Princess Avenue	C1
St Margaret's Close	B3-B4
St Margaret's Gardens	B3-C3
St Margaret's Road	B3-C3
Silver Street	B2
Station Road	B3
Stockdale Walk	B1
Stockwell Avenue	C4
Stockwell Crescent	C4
Stockwell Drive	C4
Stockwell Grove	C4
Stockwell Lane	C2
Stockwell Road	C2-C3-C4
Tentergate Avenue	B4-C4
Tentergate Road	B4-C4
The Avenue	C4
Vicarage Lane	B3
Waterside	A1-A2-B2-B3-A3
Whincup Avenue	C2
Whincup Grove	C2-C3
Windsor Lane	B1-B2
York Lane	C1
York Place	B2-C2-C2
York Road	C1

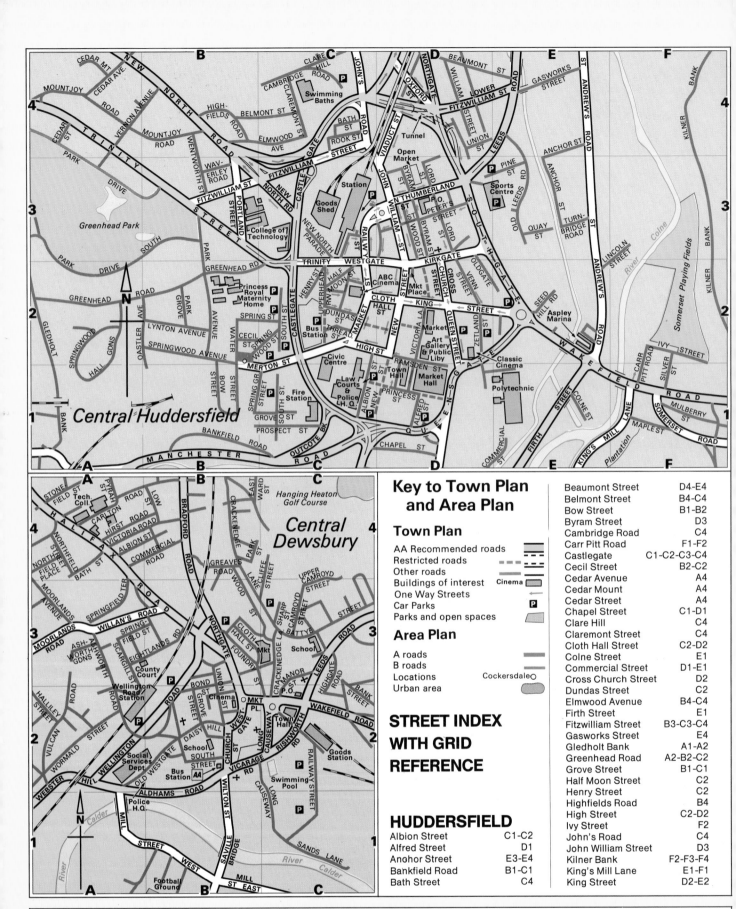

Key to Town Plan and Area Plan

Town Plan

AA Recommended roads	▬▬
Restricted roads	----
Other roads	▬
Buildings of interest	Cinema ▭
One Way Streets	←
Car Parks	P
Parks and open spaces	▰

Area Plan

A roads	▬
B roads	▬
Locations	Cockersdale○
Urban area	▰

STREET INDEX WITH GRID REFERENCE

HUDDERSFIELD

Albion Street	C1-C2
Alfred Street	D1
Anchor Street	E3-E4
Bankfield Road	B1-C1
Bath Street	C4
Beaumont Street	D4-E4
Belmont Street	B4-C4
Bow Street	B1-B2
Byram Street	D3
Cambridge Road	C4
Carr Pitt Road	F1-F2
Castlegate	C1-C2-C3-C4
Cecil Street	B2-C2
Cedar Avenue	A4
Cedar Mount	A4
Cedar Street	A4
Chapel Street	C1-D1
Clare Hill	C4
Claremont Street	C4
Cloth Hall Street	C2-D2
Colne Street	E1
Commercial Street	D1-E1
Cross Church Street	D2
Dundas Street	C2
Elmwood Avenue	B4-C4
Firth Street	E1
Fitzwilliam Street	B3-C3-C4
Gasworks Street	E4
Gledholt Bank	A1-A2
Greenhead Road	A2-B2-C2
Grove Street	B1-C1
Half Moon Street	C2
Henry Street	C2
Highfields Road	B4
High Street	C2-D2
Ivy Street	F2
John's Road	C4
John William Street	D3
Kilner Bank	F2-F3-F4
King's Mill Lane	E1-F1
King Street	D2-E2

Huddersfield

With a long history of textile making and a more recent involvement in chemicals and engineering, Huddersfield has for many years been a busy industrial and commercial centre. But another aspect of the town is its fine old buildings: the best area for these is around St George's Square, where the railway station's mid-19th-century colonnaded facade is thought by some to be one of the finest in the country.

Yet another side to Huddersfield is its role as a venue for local choirs and bands, who regularly come here for performances at the Town Hall. A good collection of English watercolours can be seen in the art gallery in Princess Alexandra Walk, and the Tolson Memorial Museum in Ravensknowle Park deals with geology, natural history and the area's own rich past. Near the village of Almondsbury to the south stands Castle Hill, an ancient hill fort topped with a 19th-century tower.

Dewsbury is one of the main towns of the West Yorkshire Heavy Woollen District, and is well known for its manufacture of blankets and carpets. Lying on the River Calder, this is a popular market and shopping centre, and has its own museum and art gallery. Places of interest include the parish church, which has retained some 12th-century features.

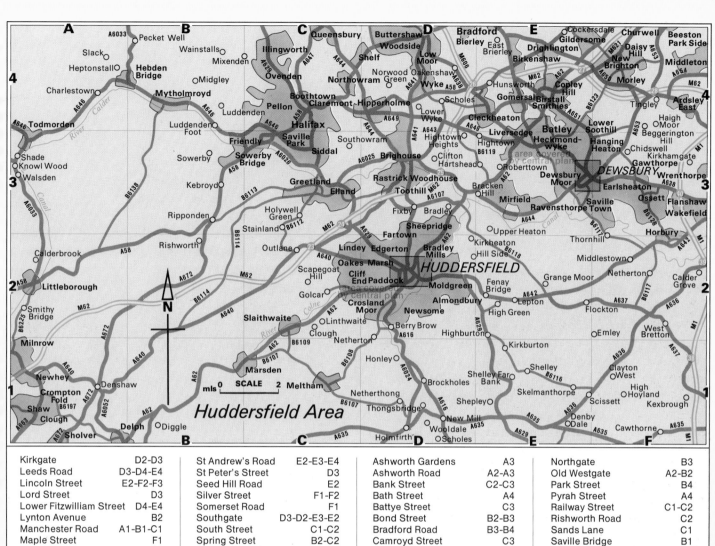

Huddersfield Area

SCALE — mls 0 ... 2 — N

Kirkgate	D2-D3	St Andrew's Road	E2-E3-E4
Leeds Road	D3-D4-E4	St Peter's Street	D3
Lincoln Street	E2-F2-F3	Seed Hill Road	E2
Lord Street	D3	Silver Street	F1-F2
Lower Fitzwilliam Street	D4-E4	Somerset Road	F1
Lynton Avenue	B2	Southgate	D3-D2-E3-E2
Manchester Road	A1-B1-C1	South Street	C1-C2
Maple Street	F1	Spring Street	B2-C2
Market Street	C2	Spring Grove Street	B1-C1
Merton Street	B2-B1-C1-C2	Springwood Avenue	B2
Mountjoy Road	A4-B4	Springwood Hall Gardens	
Mulberry Street	F1		A1-A2
New Street	C1-D1-D2	Springwood Street	B2-C2
New North Parade	C3	Threadneedle Street	C2
New North Road	A4-B4-B3-C3	Trinity Street	A4-A3-B3-C3-C2
Northgate	D4	Turnbridge Road	E3
Northumberland Street	D3	Union Street	D4
Oastler Avenue	B1-B2-A2	Upperhead Row	C2
Oldgate	E2-D2-D3	Vernon Avenue	A4-B4
Old Leeds Road	E3-E4	Venn Street	D2
Outcote Bank	C1	Viaduct Street	D3-D4
Oxford Street	D4	Victoria Lane	D2
Park Avenue	B2-B3	Wakefield Road	E2-E1-F1
Park Drive	A4-A3-B3	Water Street	B1-B2
Park Drive South	A3-A2-A3-B3	Waverley Road	B3
Park Grove	B2	Wentworth Street	B3-B4
Pine Street	D3-E3	Trinity Westgate	C3-C2-D2-D3
Portland Street	B3	William Street	D4
Princess Street	D1	Wood Street	D3
Prospect Street	B1-C1	Zetland Street	D2
Quay Street	E3		
Queensgate	D1-D2-E2	**DEWSBURY**	
Queen Street	D1-D2	Albion Street	A4-B4
Railway Street	C3	Aldhams Road	A2-A1-B1-B2
Ramsden Street	D1-D2		
Rook Street	C4		

Ashworth Gardens	A3	Northgate	B3
Ashworth Road	A2-A3	Old Westgate	A2-B2
Bank Street	C2-C3	Park Street	B4
Bath Street	A4	Pyrah Street	A4
Battye Street	C3	Railway Street	C1-C2
Bond Street	B2-B3	Rishworth Road	C2
Bradford Road	B3-B4	Sands Lane	C1
Camroyd Street	C3	Saville Bridge	B1
Carlton Road	A4	Scargill Street	A2-A3
Church Street	B2	Sharp Street	C3
Cliffe Street	B3-C3-C4	South Street	B2
Cloth Hall Street	B3	Springfield Street	A3-B3
Commercial Road	A4-B4	Springfield Terrace	A3
Crackenedge Lane	B3-B4-C2-C3	Stonefield Street	A4
Daisy Hill	B2	Union Street	B2-B3
East Ward Street	B4	Upper Camroyd Street	C3-C4
Eightlands Road	A3-B3	Vicarage Road	B2-C2
Foundry Street	B3-C3-C2	Victoria Road	A4-B4
Greaves Road	B4	Vulcan Road	A2-A3
Grove Street	B2	Wakefield Road	C2
Halifax Road	A4-A3-B3	Webster Hill	A1-A2
Halliley Street	A2	Wellington Road	A2-B2-B3
Highgate Road	C2-C3	Westgate	B2
Hirst Road	A4-B4	Willan's Road	A3-B3
Leeds Road	C2-C3	Wilton Street	B1-B2
Long Causeway	B2-C2-C1	Wood Street	B4-B3-C3
Low Street	A4	Wormald Street	A2
Manor Street	C2-C3		
Market Place	B2-C2		
Mill Street East	B1-C1		
Mill Street West	A1-B1		
Moorlands Avenue	A3-A4		
Moorlands Road	A3		
Northfield Place	A4		
Northfield Street	A4		

HUDDERSFIELD
Designed by J. P. Pritchett and built in the 1840s, the splendid railway station is one of the earlier ones, but is quite outstanding with its Corinthian columns and pediment flanked by fine colonnades.

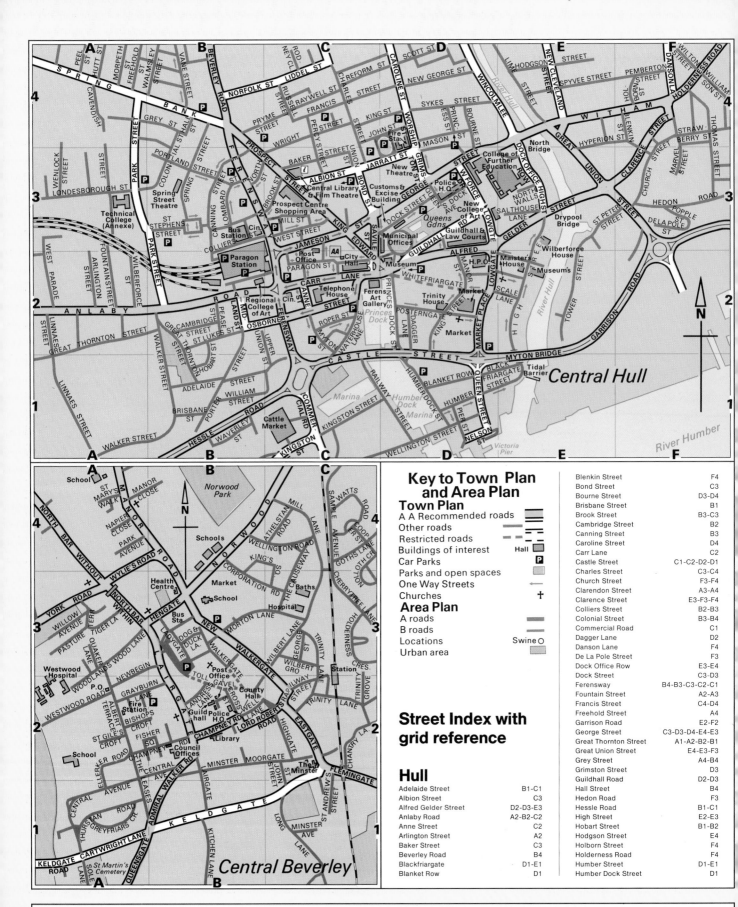

Central Hull

Central Beverley

Key to Town Plan and Area Plan

Town Plan
A A Recommended roads	
Other roads	
Restricted roads	
Buildings of interest	Hall
Car Parks	P
Parks and open spaces	
One Way Streets	
Churches	+

Area Plan
A roads	
B roads	
Locations	Swine O
Urban area	

Street Index with grid reference

Hull

Adelaide Street	B1-C1
Albion Street	C3
Alfred Gelder Street	D2-D3-E3
Anlaby Road	A2-B2-C2
Anne Street	C2
Arlington Street	A2
Baker Street	C3
Beverley Road	B4
Blackfriargate	D1-E1
Blanket Row	D1

Blenkin Street	F4
Bond Street	C3
Bourne Street	D3-D4
Brisbane Street	B1
Brook Street	B3-C3
Cambridge Street	B2
Canning Street	B3
Caroline Street	D4
Carr Lane	C2
Castle Street	C1-C2-D2-D1
Charles Street	C3-C4
Church Street	F3-F4
Clarendon Street	A3-A4
Clarence Street	E3-F3-F4
Colliers Street	B2-B3
Colonial Street	B3-B4
Commercial Road	C1
Dagger Lane	D2
Danson Lane	F4
De La Pole Street	F3
Dock Office Row	E3-E4
Dock Street	C3-D3
Ferensway	B4-B3-C3-C2-C1
Fountain Street	A2-A3
Francis Street	C4-D4
Freehold Street	A4
Garrison Road	E2-F2
George Street	C3-D3-D4-E4-E3
Great Thornton Street	A1-A2-B2-B1
Great Union Street	E4-E3-F3
Grey Street	A4-B4
Grimston Street	D3
Guildhall Road	D2-D3
Hall Street	B4
Hedon Road	F3
Hessle Road	B1-C1
High Street	E2-E3
Hobart Street	B1-B2
Hodgson Street	E4
Holborn Street	F4
Holderness Road	F4
Humber Street	D1-E1
Humber Dock Street	D1

Hull

Officially Kingston-upon-Hull, this ancient port was specially laid out with new docks in 1293, on the decree of Edward I, and echoes of the town's past can be seen in the Town Docks Museum. The docks and the fishing industry are synonymous with Hull – it has Britain's busiest deep-sea fishing port – although flour-milling, vegetable oil extraction and petrochemical production are also important. The centre of Hull consists of broad streets and spacious squares and parks, such as Queen's Gardens, laid out on the site of what used to be Queen's Dock. The older part of the town which lies south-east of here between the docks and the River Hull is full of character, with a number of Georgian buildings and places of interest.

Beverley is one of England's most distinguished towns. Between its two principal buildings – the famous Minster and St Mary's Church – are medieval streets and pleasing market squares graced by redbrick Georgian houses built by the landed gentry of the East Riding during the town's heyday as a fashionable resort. The Minster's twin towers soar above the rooftops of the town as a constant reminder that here is one of the most beautiful pieces of Gothic architecture in Europe. The wealth of beauty and detail throughout is immense, but carving in both stone and wood is one of its most outstanding features.

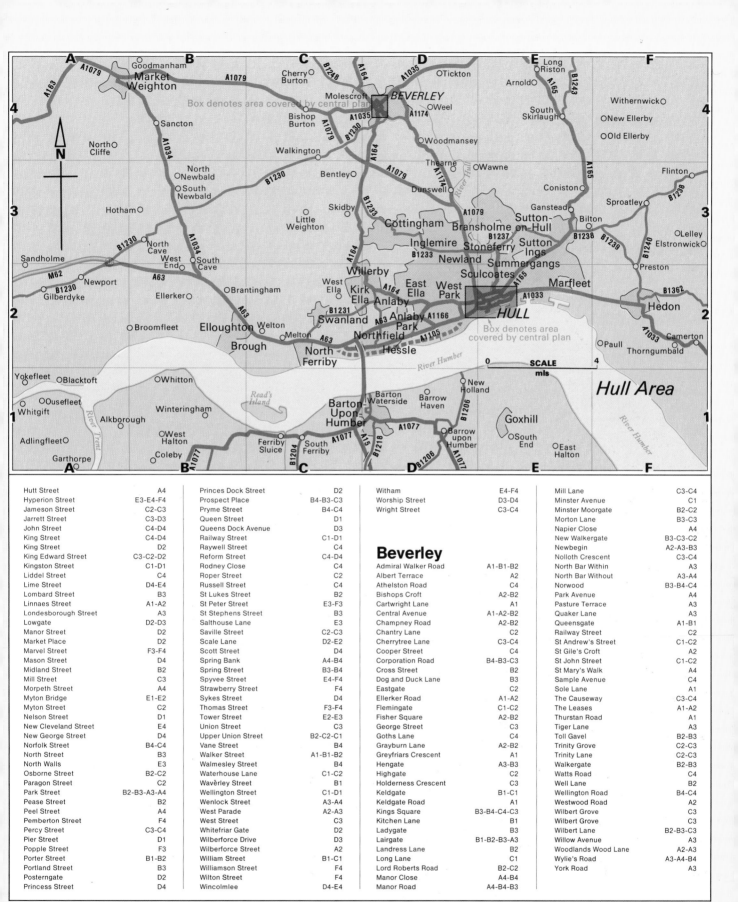

Hull Area

Box denotes area covered by central plan

SCALE
0 _____ 4
mls

Hutt Street	A4	Princes Dock Street	D2
Hyperion Street	E3-E4-F4	Prospect Place	B4-B3-C3
Jameson Street	C2-C3	Pryme Street	B4-C4
Jarrett Street	C3-D3	Queen Street	D1
John Street	C4-D4	Queens Dock Avenue	D3
King Street	C4-D4	Railway Street	C1-D1
King Street	D2	Raywell Street	C4
King Edward Street	C3-C2-D2	Reform Street	C4-D4
Kingston Street	C1-D1	Rodney Close	C4
Liddel Street	C4	Roper Street	C2
Lime Street	D4-E4	Russell Street	C4
Lombard Street	B3	St Lukes Street	B3
Linnaes Street	A1-A2	St Peter Street	E3-F3
Londesborough Street	A3	St Stephens Street	B3
Lowgate	D2-D3	Salthouse Lane	E3
Manor Street	D2	Saville Street	C2-C3
Market Place	D2	Scale Lane	D2-E2
Marvel Street	F3-F4	Scott Street	D4
Mason Street	D4	Spring Bank	A4-B4
Midland Street	B2	Spring Street	B3-B4
Mill Street	C3	Spyvee Street	E4-F4
Morpeth Street	A4	Strawberry Street	F4
Myton Bridge	E1-E2	Sykes Street	D4
Myton Street	C2	Thomas Street	F3-F4
Nelson Street	D1	Tower Street	E2-E3
New Cleveland Street	E4	Union Street	C3
New George Street	D4	Upper Union Street	B2-C2-C1
Norfolk Street	B4-C4	Vane Street	B4
North Street	B3	Walker Street	A1-B1-B2
North Walls	E3	Walmesley Street	B4
Osborne Street	B2-C2	Waterhouse Lane	C1-C2
Paragon Street	C2	Waverley Street	B1
Park Street	B2-B3-A3-A4	Wellington Street	C1-D1
Pease Street	B2	Wenlock Street	A3-A4
Peel Street	A4	West Parade	A2-A3
Pemberton Street	F4	West Street	C3
Percy Street	C3-C4	Whitefriar Gate	D2
Pier Street	D1	Wilberforce Drive	D3
Popple Street	F3	Wilberforce Street	A2
Porter Street	B1-B2	William Street	B1-C1
Portland Street	B3	Williamson Street	B4
Posterngate	D2	Wilton Street	F4
Princess Street	D4	Wincolmlee	D4-E4

Witham	E4-F4
Worship Street	D3-D4
Wright Street	C3-C4

Beverley

Admiral Walker Road	A1-B1-B2
Albert Terrace	A2
Athelston Road	C4
Bishops Croft	A2-B2
Cartwright Lane	A1
Central Avenue	A1-A2-B2
Champney Road	A2-B2
Chantry Lane	C2
Cherrytree Lane	C3-C4
Cooper Street	C4
Corporation Road	B4-B3-C3
Cross Street	B2
Dog and Duck Lane	B3
Eastgate	C2
Ellerker Road	A1-A2
Flemingate	C1-C2
Fisher Square	A2-B2
George Street	C3
Goths Lane	C4
Grayburn Lane	A2-B2
Greyfriars Crescent	A1
Hengate	A3-B3
Highgate	C2
Holderness Crescent	C3
Keldgate	B1-C1
Keldgate Road	A1
Kings Square	B3-B4-C4-C3
Kitchen Lane	B1
Ladygate	B3
Lairgate	B1-B2-B3-A3
Landress Lane	B2
Long Lane	C1
Lord Roberts Road	B2-C2
Manor Close	A4-B4
Manor Road	A4-B4-B3

Mill Lane	C3-C4
Minster Avenue	C1
Minster Moorgate	B2-C2
Morton Lane	B3-C3
Napier Close	A4
New Walkergate	B3-C3-C2
Newbegin	A2-A3-B3
Nolloth Crescent	C3-C4
North Bar Within	A3
North Bar Without	A3-A4
Norwood	B3-B4-C4
Park Avenue	A4
Pasture Terrace	A3
Quaker Lane	A3
Queensgate	A1-B1
Railway Street	C2
St Andrew's Street	C1-C2
St Gile's Croft	A2
St John Street	C1-C2
St Mary's Walk	A4
Sample Avenue	C4
Sole Lane	A1
The Causeway	C3-C4
The Leases	A1-A2
Thurstan Road	A1
Tiger Lane	A3
Toll Gavel	B2-B3
Trinity Grove	C2-C3
Trinity Lane	C2-C3
Walkergate	B2-B3
Watts Road	C4
Well Lane	B2
Wellington Road	B4-C4
Westwood Road	A2
Wilbert Grove	C3
Wilbert Grove	C3
Wilbert Lane	B2-B3-C3
Willow Avenue	A3
Woodlands Wood Lane	A2-A3
Wylie's Road	A3-A4-B4
York Road	A3

HULL
Schemes to cross the Humber estuary were first discussed over 100 years ago, but it was not until 1981 that the mammoth project was sucessfully completed. At 4626ft, the Humber Bridge has the longest main span in the world.

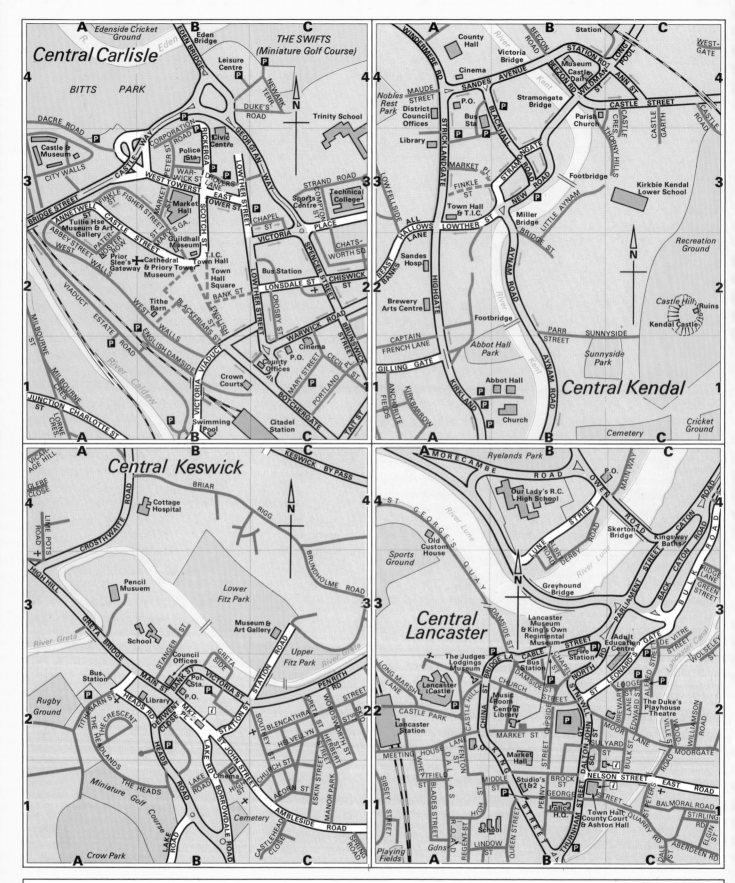

Lake District

Keswick With the River Greta running through it and Skiddaw looming above, this is a charming, quiet market town set amid beautiful scenery at the southern end of Derwentwater. The Fitz Park Museum and Art Gallery houses a collection of manuscripts by the numerous authors and poets who took their inspiration from the Lakeland.

Windermere has remained unspoiled despite the enormous popularity it has won as a holiday resort. Centred around its extensive lake, it stands in a setting which has been exalted by poets and artists for years. Windermere's architecture is mainly Victorian, as a result of the railway coming in the mid-19th century and bringing prosperity to the town. But conservationists campaigned to stop the railway going any further, and so the natural peace of the area was preserved.

Lancaster Dominating the city from its hilltop site, Lancaster Castle was once the headquarters of the Duchy and is still in use today — as a prison. Its late Georgian courtrooms and the beautiful Shire Hall are open to visitors. Close by stands the Priory, an architectural gem, and also of interest is the early 17th-century Judge's Lodgings house, which provided accommodation for assize judges for 150 years. The building now houses a display of dolls, with beautiful

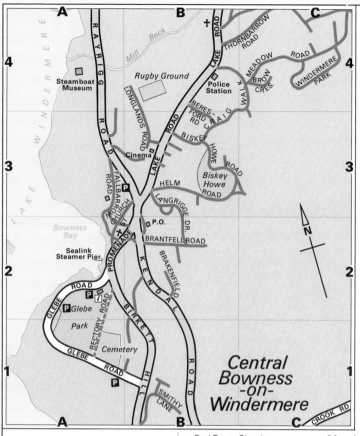

Central Bowness -on- Windermere

LEGEND

AA Recommended roads	
Restricted roads	
Other roads	
Buildings of interest	Library ▢
Car Parks	🅿
Parks and open spaces	
One Way Streets	←
Churches	†

Street Index with Grid Reference

Carlisle

Abbey Street	A2-A3
Annetwell Street	A3
Bank Street	B2-C2
Blackfriars Street	B1-B2
Botchergate	C1
Bridge Street	A3
Brunswick Street	C1-C2
Castle Street	A3-A2-B2
Castle Way	A3-B3-B4
Cecil Street	C1
Chapel Street	C3
Charlotte Street	A1
Chatsworth Square	C2
Chiswick Street	C2
City Walls	A3
Compton Street	C3
Corporation Road	B3-B4
Crosby Street	C1-C2
Dacre Road	A3-A4
Drovers Lane	B3
Duke's Road	B4-C4
East Tower Street	B3
Eden Bridge	B4
English Damside	B1-B2
English Street	B2
Finkle Street	A3
Fisher Street	A3-B3
Georgian Way	B4-B3-C3
Junction Street	A1
Lonsdale Street	C2
Lorne Crescent	A1
Lowther Street	B3-B2-C2
Market Street	B3
Mary Street	C1
Milbourne Crescent	A1
Millbourne Street	A1-A2
Newark Terrace	C4
Paternoster Row	A2-A3
Peter Street	B3
Portland Place	C1
Rickergate	B3
St Mary's Gate	B2-B3
Scotch Street	B2-B3
Spencer Street	C2
Strand Road	C3
Tait Street	C1
Viaduct Estate Road	A2-A1-B1
Victoria Place	C2-C3
Victoria Viaduct	B1
Warwick Road	C1-C2
Warwick Street	B3
West Tower Street	B3
West Walls	A2-B2-B1

Kendall

All Hallows Lane	A2-A3
Anchorite Fields	A1
Ann Street	C4
Aynam Road	B1-B2-B3
Beast Banks	A2
Beezon Road	B4
Blackhall Road	A4-B4-B3
Bridge Street	B3
Captain French Lane	A1
Castle Crescent	C3-C4
Castle Garth	C3-C4
Castle Road	C3-C4
Castle Street	B4-C4
Finkle Street	A3
Gilling Gate	A1
Highgate	A1-A2
Kirkbarrow	A1
Kirkland	A1
Little Aynam	B2-B3
Longpool	C4
Low Fellside	A3
Lowther Street	A3-B3
Market Place	A3
Maude Street	A4
New Road	B3
Parr Street	B1-B2
Sandes Avenue	A4-B4
Station Road	B4
Stramongate	B3
Stricklandgate	A3-A4
Sunnyside	B1-C1
Thorny Hills	B3-C3
Westgate	C4
Wildman Street	B4
Windermere Road	A4

Keswick

Acorn Street	C1
Ambleside Road	C1
Bank Street	B2
Blencathra Street	C2
Borrowdale Road	B1
Briar Rigg	A4-B4-C4
Brundholme Road	C3-C4
Castlehead Close	C1
Church Street	C1
Crosthwaite Road	A3-A4
Derwent Close	B2
Eskin Street	C1-C2
Glebe Close	A4
Greta Bridge	A2-A3
Greta Side	B2
Greta Street	C2
Heads Road	A2-B2-B1
Helvellyn Street	C2
High Hill	A3
Keswick By Pass	C4
Lake Road	B1-B2
Lime Pots Road	A3-A4
Main Street	B2
Manor Park	C1
Market Place	B2
Penrith Road	C2
St Herbert Street	C1-C2
St John Street	B2-B1-C1
Southey Street	C1-C2
Spring Road	C1
Stanger Street	B2-B3
Station Road	C2-C3
Station Street	B2
The Crescent	A2
The Headlands	A1-A2
The Heads	A1-B1
Tithebarn Street	A2
Vicarage Hill	A4
Victoria Street	B2
Wordsworth Street	C1

Lancaster

Aberdeen Road	C1
Albert Road	B3-B4
Alfred Street	C2-C3
Balmoral Road	C1
Black Caton Road	C3-C4
Blades Street	A1
Brewary Lane	C2
Bridge Lane	A2-B2-B3
Brock Street	B1
Bulk Road	C3-C4
Bulk Street	C1-C2
Cable Street	B2-B3
Castle Hill	A2
Castle Park	A2
Caton Road	C4
Chapel Street	B2
Cheapside	B2
China Street	A2
Church Street	B2
Dale Street	C1
Dallas Road	A1-A2
Dalton Square	B1-B2
Damside Street	A3-B3-B2
Derby Road	B3-B4
De Vitre Street	C3
East Road	C1
Edward Street	C2
Elgin Street	C1
Fenton Street	A1-A2
George Street	B1-C1
Great John Street	B2
Green Street	C3
High Street	A1
King Street	A2-B2-B1
Lindow Street	A1-B1
Lodge Street	C2
Long Marsh Lane	A2
Lune Street	B3-B4
Main Way	C4
Market Street	B2
Meeting House Lane	A2
Middle Street	A1-B1
Moorgate	C2
Moor Lane	B2-C2
Morecambe Road	A4-B4
Nelson Street	B1-C1
North Road	B2-B3
Owen Road	B4-C4
Parliament Street	C3-C4
Penny Street	B1-B2
Quarry Road	C1
Queen Street	B1
Regent Street	A1
Ridge Lane	C3
St George's Quay	A3-A4
St Leonard's Gate	B2-C2-C3
St Peter's Road	C1-C2
Sibsey Street	A1
Stirling Road	C1
Stonewell	B2
Sulyard Street	B2-C2
Thurnham Street	B1
Wheatfield Street	A1-A2
Williamson Road	C2
Wolseley Street	C2-C3
Woodville Street	C2

Bowness-on-Windermere

Beresford Road	B3-B4
Birkett Hill	A2-B2-B1
Biskey Howe Road	B3-C3
Brakenfield	B2
Brantfell Road	B2
Brow Crescent	C4
Church Street	A2-A3-B3
Craig Way	B4-C4-B4-B3
Crook Road	C1
Fallbarrow Road	A2-A3
Glebe Road	A2-A1-B1
Helm Road	B3
Kendall Road	B1-B2
Lake Road	B3-B4
Langridge Drive	B2-B3
Longlands Road	B3-B4
Meadow Road	C4
Promenade	A2-B2
Rayrigg Road	A4-A3-B3
Rectory Road	A1-A2
Smithy Lane	B1
Thornbarrow Road	B4-C4
Windermere Park	C4

furniture from Gillows and other cabinet makers.

Kendal's motto is "Wool Is My Bread" — a constant reminder that wool was the town's staple trade for over 600 years and brought it the prosperity which it still enjoys today. Flemish weavers started the industry when they settled here in the 14th century, and the town is now a centre for the production of such different products as turbines, carpets, shoes, socks and hornware — although its best known product must be

the sustaining Kendal Mint Cake. An interesting local feature are the numerous named and numbered yards which lie tucked away through Kendal's archways and down alleyways, and were once a focus of small industry.

Carlisle Bonnie Prince Charlie proclaimed his father King of England from the steps of Carlisle Cross before marching south to be taken prisoner by the Duke of Cumberland, and Carlisle Castle was the centre of turbulent scenes between English and

Scots from Norman times to the Jacobite rebellion. This is the 'Border City', capital of the Border area between England and Scotland. But as well as a past of conflict it can also claim to have some beautiful buildings. Finest of all perhaps is the cathedral; other places of interest are the Guildhall, which is 15th-century, Tullie House (a fine Jacobean building with Victorian extensions), and the city's museum and art gallery, which has a good collection of artefacts from its past.

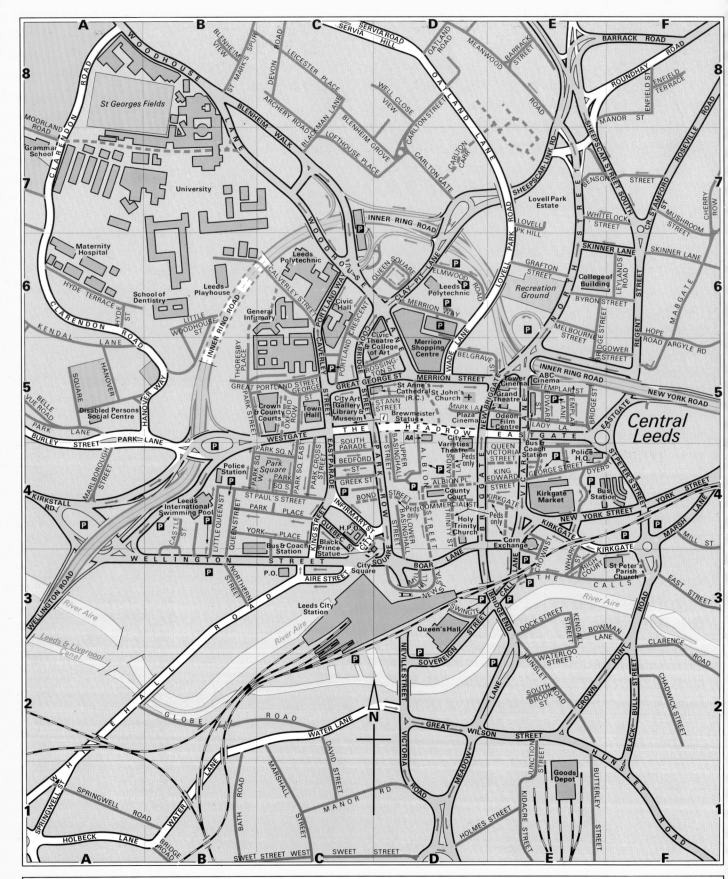

Leeds

In the centre of Leeds is its town hall – a monumental piece of architecture with a 225ft clock-tower. It was opened by Queen Victoria in 1858, and has been a kind of mascot for the city ever since. It exudes civic pride; such buildings could only have been created in the heyday of Victorian prosperity and confidence. Leeds' staple industry has always been the wool trade, but it only became a boom town towards the end of the 18th century, when textile mills were introduced. Today, the wool trade and ready-made clothing (Mr Hepworth and Mr Burton began their work here) are still important, though industries like paper, leather, furniture and electrical equipment are prominent.

Across Calverley Street from the town hall is the City Art Gallery, Library and Museum. Its collections include sculpture by Henry Moore, who was a student at Leeds School of Art. Nearby is the Headrow, Leeds' foremost shopping thoroughfare. On it is the City Varieties Theatre, venue for many years of the famous television programme 'The Good Old Days'. Off the Headrow are several shopping arcades, of which Leeds has many handsome examples. Leeds has a good number of interesting churches; perhaps the finest is St John's, unusual in that it dates from 1634, a time when few churches were built.

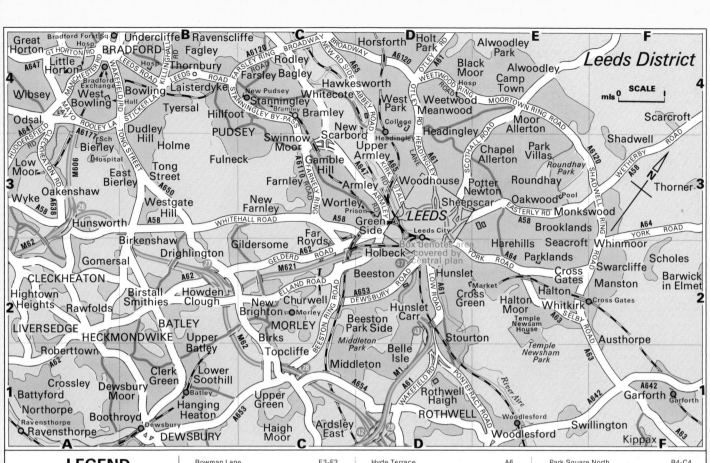

LEGEND

Town Plan

AA Recommended roads	
Other roads	
Restricted roads	
Buildings of interset	Museum
AA Service Centre	AA
Parks and open spaces	
Car Parks	P
Churches	†
One way streets	←

District Plan

A roads	
B roads	
Stations	Kirkgate ●
Urban area	
Buildings of interest	Hospital

Street Index with Grid Reference

Leeds

Aire Street	C3
Albion Place	D4
Albion Street	D3-D4-D5
Archery Road	C7-C8
Argyle Road	F5
Barrack Road	E8-F8
Barrack Street	E8
Bath Road	B1-B2
Bedford Street	C4
Belgrave Street	D5-E5
Belle Vue Road	A5
Benson Street	E7-F7
Black Bull Street	F1-F2-F3
Blackman Lane	C7-C8
Blenheim Grove	C8-C7-D7
Blenheim View	B8
Blenheim Walk	B8-C8-C7
Boar Lane	D3-D4
Bond Street	C4-D4

Bowman Lane	E3-F3
Bridge End	D3-E3
Bridge Road	B1
Bridge Street	E5-E6
Briggate	D3-D4-D5
Burley Street	A4-A5
Butterley Street	E1-E2
Byron Street	E6-F6
Call Lane	E3
Calverley Street	C5-C6
Carlton Carr	D7
Carlton Gate	D7
Carlton Street	D7-D8
Castle Street	B3-B4
Chadwick Street	F2
Chapleltown Road	E8
Cherry Row	F7
City Square	C3-C4-D4-D3
Clarence Road	F2-F3
Clarendon Road	A8-A7-A6-A5-B5
Clay Pit Lane	D6
Commercial Street	D4
Cookridge Street	C5-C6-D6
Cross Stamford Street	F6-F7
Crown Street	E3-E4
Crown Point Road	E2-F2-F3
David Street	C1-C2
Devon Road	C8
Dock Street	E3
Dyer Street	E4-F4
East Parade	C4-C5
East Street	F3
Eastgate	E5-F5
Edward Street	E5
Elmwood Road	D6
Enfield Street	F8
Enfield Terrace	F8
George Street	C5
George Street	E4
Globe Road	A2-B2-C2
Gower Street	E5-F5
Grafton Street	E6
Great George Street	C5-D5
Great Portland Street	B5-C5
Great Wilson Street	D2-E2
Greek Street	C4-D4
Hanover Square	A5
Hanover Way	A5-B5
High Court	E3
Holbeck Lane	A1-B1
Holmes Street	D1-E1
Hope Road	F5-F6
Hunslett Road	E3-E2-E1-F1-F2
Hyde Street	A6

Hyde Terrace	A6
Infirmary Street	C4-D4
Inner Ring Road	B5-B6-C6-C7-D7-D6-E6-E5-F5
Junction Street	E1-E2
Kendal Lane	A5-A6
Kendal Street	E3
Kidacre Street	E1
King Street	C3-C4
King Edward Street	D4-E4
Kirkgate	E4-E3-F3-F4
Kirkstall Road	A4
Lady Lane	E5
Lands Lane	D4-D5
Leicester Place	C8
Leylands Road	F6
Lisbon Street	B3-B4
Little Queen Street	B3-B4
Little Woodhouse Street	B6
Lofthouse Place	C7-D7
Lovell Park Hill	E7
Lovell Park Road	D6-E6-E7
Lower Basinghall Street	D3-D4
Mabgate	F6
Manor Road	C1-D1
Manor Street	E8-F8
Mark Lane	D5
Marlborough Street	A4
Marsh Lane	F4
Marshall Street	D1-D2-E2-E3
Meadow Lane	D1-D2-E2-E3
Meanwood Road	D8-E8
Melbourne Street	E6
Merrion Street	D5-E5
Merrion Way	D6
Mill Hill	D3
Mill Street	F4
Moorland Road	A7-A8
Mushroom Street	F6-F7
Neville Street	D2-D3
New Briggate	D5-E5
New Station Street	D3
New York Road	F5
New York Street	E4-F4
North Street	E5-E6-E7
Northern Street	B3
Oatland Lane	D8-D7-E7
Oatland Road	D8
Oxford Row	C5
Park Cross Street	C4-C5
Park Lane	A5-B5-B4
Park Place	B4-C4
Park Row	C4-C5-D5-D4
Park Square East	C4

Park Square North	B4-C4
Park Square South	C4
Park Square West	B4
Park Street	B5-C5
Portland Crescent	C5-C6
Portland Way	C6
Quebec Street	C3-C4
Queen Street	B3-B4
Queen Square	C6-D6
Queen Victoria Street	D4-E4
Regent Street	F5-F6
Roseville Road	F7-F8
Rossington Street	C5-D5
Roundhay Road	E8-F8
St Ann Street	C5-D5
St Mark's Spur	B8-C8
St Paul's Street	B4-C4
St Peter's Street	E4-F4
Servia Hill	C8-D8
Servia Road	C8-D8
Sheepscar Link Road	E7-E8
Sheepscar Street North	E8
Sheepscar Street South	E8-E7-F7
Skinner Lane	E6-F6
South Brook Street	E2
South Parade	C4
Sovereign Street	D2-D3-E3
Springfield Mount	A1-B1
Springwell Street	A1
Sweet Street	C1-D1
Sweet Street West	B1-C1
Swinegate	D3
The Calls	E3-F3
The Headrow	C5-D5
Templar Lane	E5
Templar Street	E5
Thoresby Place	B5-B6
Trinity Street	D4
Upper Basinghall Street	D4-D5
Vicar Lane	E4-E5
Victoria Road	D1-D2
Wade Lane	D5-D6
Water Lane	B1-B2-C2-D2
Waterloo Street	E2-E3
Well Close View	D8
Wellington Road	A3
Wellington Street	A3-B3-C3
Westgate	B4-B5-C5-C4
Wharf Street	E3-E4
Whitehall Road	A1-A2-B2-B3-C3
Whitelock Street	E7-F7
Woodhouse Lane	A8-B8-B7-C7-C6-D6-D5
York Place	B4-C4
York Street	F4

LEEDS
Offices now occupy the handsome twin-towered Civic Hall
which stands in Calverley Street in front of the new
buildings of Leeds Polytechnic. This area of the city – the
commercial centre – has been extensively redeveloped

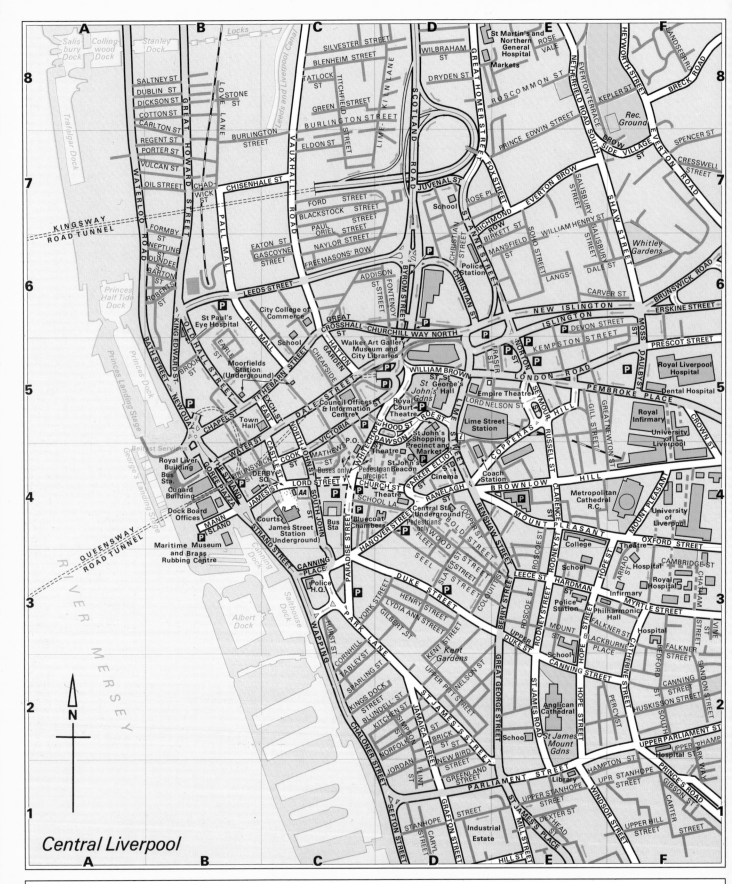

Central Liverpool

Liverpool

Although its dock area has been much reduced, Liverpool was at one time second only to London in pre-eminence as a port. Formerly the centrepiece of the docks area were three monumental buildings – the Dock Board Offices, built in 1907 with a huge copper-covered dome; the Cunard Building, dating from 1912 and decorated with an abundance of ornamental carving; and best-known of all, the world-famous Royal Liver Building, with the two 'liver birds' crowning its twin cupolas.

Some of the city's best industrial buildings have fallen into disuse in recent years, and have been preserved as monuments of the industrial age. One has become a maritime museum housing full-sized craft and a workshop where maritime crafts are demonstrated. Other museums and galleries include the Walker Art Gallery, with excellent collections of European painting and sculpture; Liverpool City Libraries, one of the oldest and largest public libraries in Britain, with a vast collection of books and manuscripts; and Bluecoat Chambers, a Queen Anne building now used as a gallery and concert hall. Liverpool has two outstanding cathedrals: the Roman Catholic, completed in 1967 in an uncompromising controversial style; and the Protestant, constructed in the great tradition of Gothic architecture, but begun in 1904 and only recently completed.

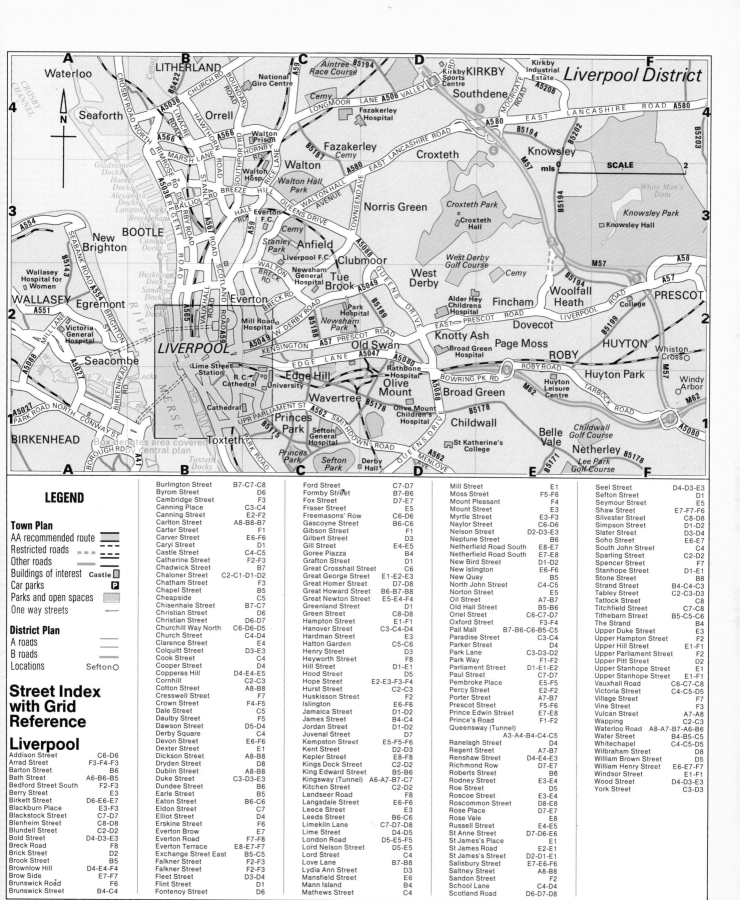

Liverpool District

Map labels: Waterloo, LITHERLAND, Seaforth, Orrell, National Giro Centre, Aintree Race Course, KIRKBY, Kirkby Sports Centre, Kirkby Industrial Estate, Southdene, Knowsley, Croxteth, Fazakerley, Fazakerley Hospital, Walton Prison, Walton Hosp., Walton Hall Park, Norris Green, Croxteth Park, Croxteth Hall, Knowsley Park, Knowsley Hall, White Man's Dam, BOOTLE, New Brighton, Stanley Park, Anfield, Liverpool F.C., Everton F.C., Clubmoor, Tue Brook, Newsham General Hospital, West Derby, West Derby Golf Course, Cemy, Woolfall Heath, Fincham, PRESCOT, WALLASEY, Egremont, Victoria General Hospital, Wallasey Hospital for Women, Everton, Mill Road Hospital, Newsham Park, Knotty Ash, Broad Green Hospital, Page Moss, Dovecot, ROBY, HUYTON, Whiston Cross, Seacombe, LIVERPOOL, Lime Street Station, R.C. Cathedral, University, Edge Hill, Olive Mount, Wavertree, Rathbone Hospital, Broad Green, Old Swan, Huyton Leisure Centre, Huyton Park, Roby Road, Windy Arbor, BIRKENHEAD, Cathedral, Princes Park, Sefton General Hospital, Toxteth, Olive Mount Children's Hospital, Childwall, St Katherine's College, Belle Vale, Childwall Golf Course, Netherley, Lee Park Golf Course, Derby Hall, Sefton Park, Princes Park, Toxteth Docks, Alder Hey Childrens Hospital, College

SCALE 0 mls 2

Box denotes area covered by central plan

LEGEND

Town Plan
- AA recommended route
- Restricted roads
- Other roads
- Buildings of interest — Castle
- Car parks — P
- Parks and open spaces
- One way streets

District Plan
- A roads
- B roads
- Locations — Sefton○

Street Index with Grid Reference

Liverpool

Street	Grid
Addison Street	C6-D6
Arrad Street	F3-F4-F3
Barton Street	B6
Bath Street	A6-B6-B5
Bedford Street South	F2-F3
Berry Street	E3
Birkett Street	D6-E6-E7
Blackburn Place	E3-F3
Blackstock Street	C7-D7
Blenheim Street	C8-D8
Blundell Street	C2-D2
Bold Street	D4-D3-E3
Breck Road	F8
Brick Street	D2
Brook Street	B5
Brownlow Hill	D4-E4-F4
Brow Side	E7-F7
Brunswick Road	F6
Brunswick Street	B4-C4
Burlington Street	B7-C7-C8
Byrom Street	D6
Cambridge Street	F3
Canning Place	C3-C4
Canning Street	E2-F2
Carlton Street	A8-B8-B7
Carter Street	F1
Carver Street	E6-F6
Caryl Street	D1
Castle Street	C4-C5
Catherine Street	F2-F3
Chadwick Street	B7
Chaloner Street	C2-C1-D1-D2
Chatham Street	F3
Chapel Street	B5
Cheapside	C5
Chisenhale Street	B7-C7
Christian Street	D6
Christian Street	D6-D7
Churchill Way North	C6-D6-D5
Church Street	C4-D4
Clarence Street	E4
Colquitt Street	D3-E3
Cook Street	C4
Cooper Street	D4
Copperas Hill	D4-E4-E5
Cornhill	C2-C3
Cotton Street	A8-B8
Cresswell Street	F7
Crown Street	F4-F5
Dale Street	C5
Daulby Street	F5
Dawson Street	D5-D4
Derby Square	C4
Devon Street	E6-F6
Dexter Street	E1
Dickson Street	A8-B8
Dryden Street	D8
Dublin Street	A8-B8
Duke Street	C3-D3-E3
Dundee Street	B6
Earle Street	B5
Eaton Street	B6-C6
Eldon Street	C7
Elliot Street	D4
Erskine Street	F6
Everton Brow	E7
Everton Road	F7-F8
Everton Terrace	E8-E7-F7
Exchange Street East	B5-C5
Falkner Street	F2-F3
Falkner Street	F2-F3
Fleet Street	D3-D4
Flint Street	D1
Fontenoy Street	D6
Ford Street	C7-D7
Formby Street	B7-B6
Fox Street	D7-E7
Fraser Street	E5
Freemasons' Row	C6-D6
Gascoyne Street	B6-C6
Gibson Street	F1
Gilbert Street	D3
Gill Street	E4-E5
Goree Piazza	B4
Grafton Street	D1
Great Crosshall Street	C6
Great George Street	E1-E2-E3
Great Homer Street	D7-D8
Great Howard Street	B6-B7-B8
Great Newton Street	E5-E4-F4
Greenland Street	D1
Green Street	C8-D8
Hampton Street	E1-F1
Hanover Street	C3-C4-D4
Hardman Street	E3
Hatton Garden	C5-C6
Henry Street	D3
Heyworth Street	F8
Hill Street	D1-E1
Hood Street	D5
Hope Street	E2-E3-F3-F4
Hurst Street	C2-C3
Huskisson Street	F2
Islington	E6-F6
Jamaica Street	D1-D2
James Street	B4-C4
Jordan Street	D1-D2
Juvenal Street	D7
Kempston Street	E5-F5-F6
Kent Street	D2-D3
Kepler Street	E8-F8
Kings Dock Street	C2-D2
King Edward Street	B5-B6
Kingsway (Tunnel)	A6-A7-B7-C7
Kitchen Street	C2-D2
Landseer Road	F8
Langsdale Street	E6-F6
Leece Street	E3
Leeds Street	B6-C6
Limekiln Lane	C7-D7-D8
Lime Street	D4-D5
London Road	D5-E5-F5
Lord Nelson Street	D5-E5
Lord Street	C4
Love Lane	B7-B8
Lydia Ann Street	D3
Mansfield Street	E6
Mann Island	B4
Mathews Street	C4
Mill Street	E1
Moss Street	F5-F6
Mount Pleasant	F4
Mount Street	E3
Myrtle Street	E3-F3
Naylor Street	C6-D6
Nelson Street	D2-D3-E3
Neptune Street	B6
Netherfield Road South	E8-E7
Netherfield Road South	E7-E8
New Bird Street	D1-D2
New Islington	E6-F6
New Quay	B5
North John Street	C4-C5
Norton Street	E5
Oil Street	A7-B7
Old Hall Street	B5-B6
Oriel Street	C6-C7-D7
Oxford Street	F3-F4
Pall Mall	B7-B6-C6-B5-C5
Paradise Street	C3-C4
Parker Street	D4
Park Lane	C3-D3-D2
Park Way	F1-F2
Parliament Street	D1-E1-E2
Paul Street	C7-D7
Pembroke Place	E5-F5
Percy Street	E2-F2
Porter Street	A7-B7
Prescot Street	F5-F6
Prince Edwin Street	E7-E8
Prince's Road	F1-F2
Queensway (Tunnel)	A3-A4-B4-C4-C5
Ranelagh Street	D4
Regent Street	A7-B7
Renshaw Street	D4-E4-E3
Richmond Row	D7-E7
Roberts Street	B6
Rodney Street	E3-E4
Roe Street	D5
Roscoe Street	E3-E4
Roscommon Street	D8-E8
Rose Place	D7-E7
Rose Vale	E8
Russell Street	E4-E5
St Anne Street	D7-D6-E6
St James's Place	E1
St James Road	E2-E1
St James's Street	D2-D1-E1
Salisbury Street	E7-E6-F6
Saltney Street	A8-B8
Sandon Street	F2
School Lane	C4-D4
Scotland Road	D6-D7-D8
Seel Street	D4-D3-E3
Sefton Street	D1
Seymour Street	E5
Shaw Street	E7-F7-F6
Silvester Street	C8-D8
Simpson Street	D1-D2
Slater Street	D3-D4
Soho Street	E6-E7
South John Street	C4
Sparling Street	C2-D2
Spencer Street	F7
Stanhope Street	D1-E1
Stone Street	B8
Strand Street	B4-C4-C3
Tabley Street	C2-C3-D3
Tatlock Street	C8
Titchfield Street	C7-C8
Tithebarn Street	B5-C5-C6
The Strand	B4
Upper Duke Street	E3
Upper Hampton Street	F2
Upper Hill Street	E1-F1
Upper Parliament Street	F2
Upper Pitt Street	D2
Upper Stanhope Street	E1
Upper Stanhope Street	E1-F1
Vauxhall Road	C6-C7-C8
Victoria Street	C4-C5-D5
Village Street	F7
Vine Street	F3
Vulcan Street	A7-A8
Wapping	C2-C3
Waterloo Road	A8-A7-B7-A6-B6
Water Street	B4-B5-C5
Whitechapel	C4-C5-D5
Wilbraham Street	D8
William Brown Street	D5
William Henry Street	E6-E7-F7
Windsor Street	E1-F1
Wood Street	D4-D3-E3
York Street	C3-D3

LIVERPOOL
The Metropolitan Cathedral of Christ the King is one of Liverpool's most striking landmarks. Crowning the conical roof is a tower of stained glass which throws a pool of coloured light on to the altar below.

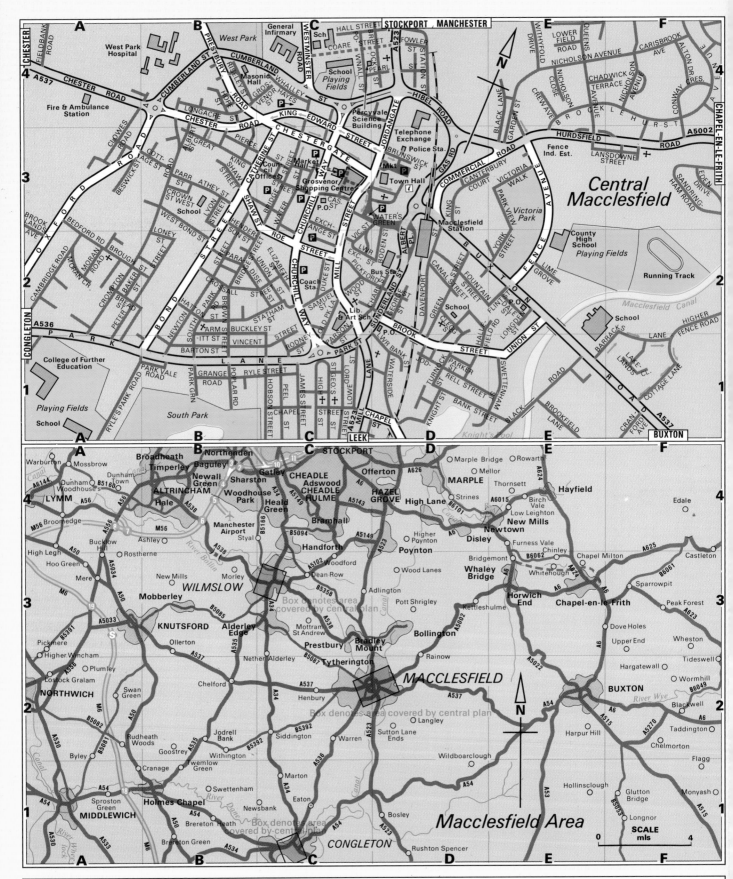

Macclesfield

One hundred and eight steps rise up to the Church of St Michael, which makes a striking and dramatic backdrop to the town that rises to meet it. The church can also be entered on the level from the market place, and its large monuments are amongst the best in Cheshire. The church is the finest reminder of the town's medieval origins, and other buildings of architectural interest include some early mills and Georgian houses. Once the centre of the English silk industry, Macclesfield today concentrates on the production of man-made fibres, and still remains a pleasant market town. Amongst its open spaces, West Park is one of the oldest public parks in the country, and has at its entrance the Macclesfield Museum and Art Gallery, where a fine Egyptian collection can be seen.

Congleton Stone Age man is thought to have built the chambered tomb known as Bridestones

which stands on the road to Leek, so Congleton can claim to date from Neolithic times. The town's medieval street plan is still intact, and it has some fine Tudor buildings — a legacy to its prosperity at this time. Now an important cattle market and textile town, its focal point is the fine Venetian-Gothic style Victorian Town Hall.

Wilmslow nestles in the valleys of the Bollin and Dean. With one of the area's most picturesque positions, this is a pleasant dormitory town.

46

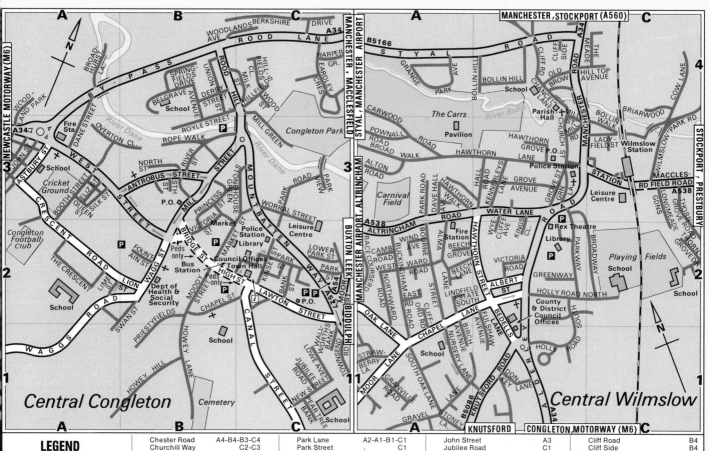

Central Congleton

Central Wilmslow

LEGEND

Town Plan

AA recommended route	
Restricted roads	
Other roads	
Buildings of interest	Hall
Car parks	P
Parks and open spaces	

Area Plan

A roads	
B roads	
Locations	Littleton
Urban area	

Street Index with Grid Reference

Macclesfield

Albert Place	D2-D3
Albert Street	B3-B4
Alton Drive	F4
Armitt Street	B2-B1
Athey Street	B3
Baker Street	A2
Bank Street	D1-E1
Barracks Lane	E1-F1-F2
Barton Street	B1
Bedford Road	A3-A2
Beswick Street	A3
Black Lane	E3-E4
Black Road	E1
Boden Street	D2-D3
Bond Street	A1-B2-B3
Bread Street	A2
Bridge Street	B2-C2-C3
Brock Street	D4
Brocklehurst Avenue	E3-E4-F4
Brook Street	D2-D1-E1
Brookfield Lane	E1
Brooklands Avenue	A3-A2
Brough Street	A2-B2
Brown Street	B2-B1
Brunswick Street	D3
Buckley Street	B2-B1-C1-C2
Buxton Road	D3-D2-E2-E1-F1
Cambridge Road	A2
Canal Street	D2
Canterbury Court	D3
Carisbrook Avenue	F4
Castle Street	C3
Catherine Street	B3-C3
Chadwick Terrace	E4-F4
Chapel Street	C1-D1
Charlotte Street	D2
Chestergate	C4-C3
Chester Road	A4-B4-B3-C4
Churchill Way	C2-C3
Clegg Street	D2
Clowes Road	A3-A4
Coare Street	C4-D4
Commercial Road	D3-D4
Conway Crescent	F4
Cottage Lane	F1
Cottage Street	A3-B3
Cranford Avenue	F1
Crew Avenue	E4
Crompton Road	A2-B2-B3
Crossall Street	B2-C2
Crown Street West	B3
Cumberland Street	B4-C4
Dale Street	E2
Davenport Street	D1-D2-D3
Duke Street	C2
Eden Drive	F3
Elizabeth Street	C2
Exchange Street	C3-C2
Fence Avenue	E2-E3
Fieldbank Road	A4
Flint Street	E2
Fountain Street	D2
Fowler Street	D4
Garden Street	E3-E4
Gas Road	D3
George Street	D2
Grange Road	B1
Great King Street	B3-C3
Green Street	D1-D2
Grosvenor Street	B4-C4
Hallefield Road	D1-D2
Hall Street	C4-D4
Hatton Street	B2
Henderson Street	B3-B2
Hibel Road	D4-D3
High Street	C1
Higher Fence Road	F1-F2
Hobson Street	C1
Hope Street	B4
Hurdsfield Road	E3-F3
James Street	C1
Jodrell Street	D1-E1
Jordangate	D3-D4
King Street	D3
King Edward Street	C4-C3-D3
Knight Street	D1
Lakelands Close	F1
Lansdowne Street	E3-F3
Lime Grove	E2
Loney Street	B2
Longacre Street	B4
Longden Street	E2
Lord Street	C1
Lowe Street	C1
Lower Bank Street	D2-D1
Lower Exchange Street	C2-D2
Lower Field Road	E4
Lyon Street	B3
Mill Lane	C1
Mill Street	C2-C3
Moran Crescent	A2
Moran Road	A2
Newton Street	B1-B2
Nicholson Avenue	E4-F4
Nicholson Close	E4
Old Park Lane	C1-C2
Oxford Road	A2-A3-B3-B4
Paradise Street	B2-C2
Park Green	B1

Park Lane	A2-A1-B1-C1
Park Street	C1
Park View	E3
Parker Street	D1-E1
Park Vale Road	A1-B1
Parr Street	B3
Parsonage Street	C1-C2
Pearl Street	C4-D4
Peel Street	C1
Peter Street	A1-A2-B2
Pickford Street	C2-D2
Pierce Street	B3-C3
Poplar Road	B1
Pownall Street	C4
Prestbury Road	B4-C4
Queens Avenue	E4-E3
Riseley Street	B4
Rodney Street	C1
Roe Street	B3-C2
Ryle Street	B1-C1
Ryle's Park Road	A1
St George's Street	C1
Samuel Street	C2
Sandringham Road	F3
Shaw Street	B3-C3
South Park Road	B1-B2
Statham Street	B2-C2
Station Street	D4
Sunderland Street	C1-C2-D2
Swettenham Street	E1
Turnock Street	D1
Union Street	B2-C2
Union Street	E1-E2
Victoria Street	C2-C3-D3
Victoria Walk	E3
Vincent Street	B1-C1-C2
Waterside	D1
Water Street	C2-C3
Water's Green	D3
West Bond Street	B3-B2
Westminster Road	C4
Whalley Hayes	C4
Withyfold Drive	E4
Wood Street	C2
York Street	E2

Congleton

Antrobus Street	B3
Astbury Street	A3
Bank Street	C2
Belgrave Avenue	B4-B3
Berkshire Drive	B4-C4
Booth Street	A2-A3
Bridge Street	B2
Broadhurst Lane	A4
By-Pass	A3-A4-B4
Canal Street	C2-C1
Chapel Street	B2-C2
Crescent Road	A3-A2
Dane Street	A3-A4
Derby Street	B4
Eardley Crescent	C4
Elizabeth Street	A3
Fountain Street	B2
Harper Grove	C4
High Street	B2-C2
Hillfields	C4
Hillfields Close	C4
Howey Lane	B2-B1
Howey Hill	A1-B1

John Street	A3
Jubilee Road	C1
Kinsey Street	C2
Lawton Street	C2
Lime Street	A2
Lion Street	A2-B2
Lowe Avenue	C1
Lower Park Street	C1
Market Street	B2-C2-C3
Milk Street	B4-C4
Mill Green	C4-C3
Mill Street	B3-C3
Moody Street	B2
Moor Street	C2
Mountbatten Way	C3-C2
New Street	C1
North Street	B3
Overton Close	A3-B3
Park Road	C3
Park Street	C2
Park View	C3
Pear Tree Bank	C1
Priestyfields	B1-B2
Princess Street	B2-B3
Queen Street	A3
River Street	B3
Rood Hill	B4-C4
Rood Lane	B4-C4
Rope Walk	B3
Royle Street	B3-B4-C4
Silk Street	A3
South Street	B3
Springfields Drive	B4
Stonehouse Green	C3
Swan Street	A1-A2-B2
The Crescent	A2
Townsend Road	C1
Union Street	B4
Victoria Street	B2-B3
Wagg Street	B2
Waggs Road	A1-A2-B2
Wallworths Bank	C1
West Street	A3-B3-B2
Wood Street	C4
Woodland Park	A3-A4
Woodlands Avenue	B4-C4
Worral Street	C3-C2

Wilmslow

Albert Street	B2
Alderley Road	B1-B2-B3-C3
Alma Lane	A2
Alton Road	A3
Altrincham Road	A2-A3-B3
Bedells Lane	B2-B1
Beech Grove	A2
Beech Lane	A2
Birch Avenue	A2-A1
Bollin Hill	B4
Bollin Walk	B4
Bourne Street	A2
Briarwood	C4
Broad Walk	A3
Broadway	B3-B2-C2
Buckingham Road	A2-A1
Cambridge Road	A2
Carwood Road	A4-A3
Chancel Lane	B4
Chapel Lane	A1-A2-B2
Church Street	B3

Cliff Road	B4
Cliff Side	B4
Clifford Road	A2-A1
Cow Lane	C4
Dave Hall Avenue	A3
Donkey Lane	B1
Eastwood Road	A2
Fulshaw Avenue	B2-B1
Granville Road	A1
Gravel Lane	A1
Green Lane	B3
Greenway	B2
Grove Avenue	B3
Grove Street	B3
Hall Road	B3
Hawthorn Grove	B3
Hawthorn Lane	A3-B3
Hawthorn Street	A2-B2-B3
Hawthorn Walk	B3
Hill Top Avenue	B4-C4
Holly Road North	B2-C2
Holly Road South	B1-B2
Kennerleys Lane	B3
Kings Close	B2-B3
Knutsford Road	A1-B1
Ladyfield Street	C3
Lindfield Estate South	A2
Longmeade Gardens	C3-C2
Macclesfield Road	C3
Manchester Road	B3-C3-C4-B4
Mill Road	B3
Mill Street	B4-B3
Moor Lane	A1
Northward Road	A2-A1
Nursery Lane	A1-B1
Oak Lane	A2-A1
Old Brow	B4
Park Avenue	A4
Park Road	A3
Parkway	B3-B2
Pownall Road	A3
Race Course Road	A2
South Oak Lane	A1
Station Road	C3
Stoney Lane	A1
Strawberry Lane	A1
Styal Road	A4-B4
The Meade	C4
Thorngrove Drive	C2
Thorngrove Road	C3-C2
Victoria Road	B3
Wates Road	A2
Westward Road	A2
Wilmslow Park Road	C3-C4
Windsor Avenue	A2
Wyecliffe Avenue	B2-B3

47

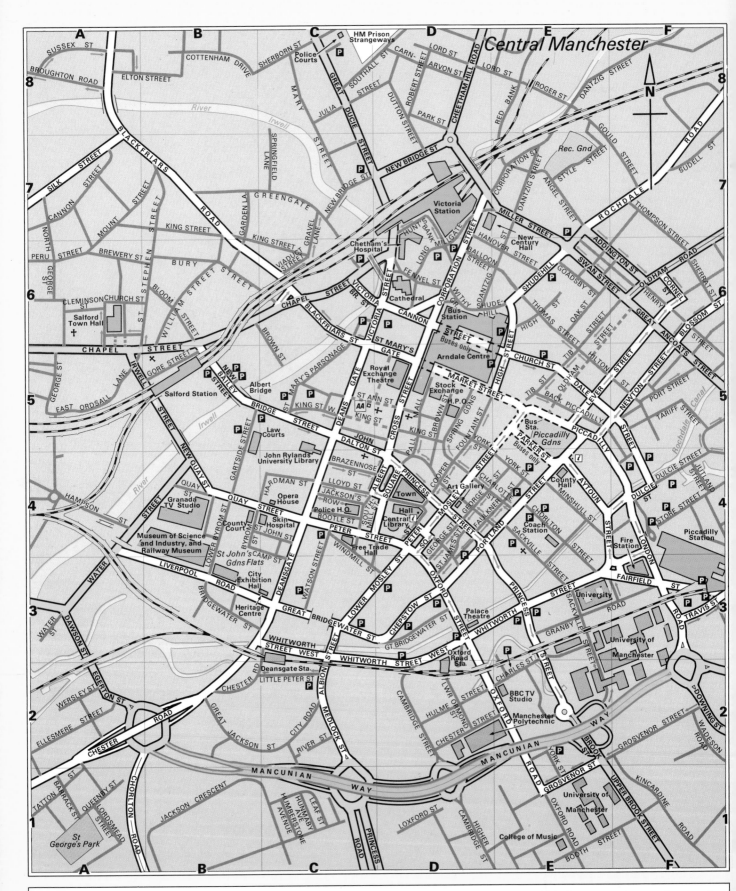

Manchester

The gigantic conurbation called Greater Manchester covers a staggering 60 square miles, reinforcing Manchester's claim to be Britain's second city. Commerce and industry are vital aspects of the city's character, but it is also an important cultural centre – the Halle Orchestra has its home at the Free Trade Hall (a venue for many concerts besides classical music), there are several theatres, a library (the John Rylands) which houses one of the most important collections of books in the world, and a number of museums and galleries, including the Whitworth Gallery with its lovely watercolours.

Like many great cities it suffered badly during the bombing raids of World War II, but some older buildings remain, including the town hall, a huge building designed in Gothic style by Alfred Waterhouse and opened in 1877. Manchester Cathedral dates mainly from the 15th century and is noted for its fine tower and outstanding carved woodwork. Nearby is Chetham's Hospital, also 15th-century and now housing a music school. Much new development has taken place, and more is planned. Shopping precincts cater for the vast population, and huge hotels have provided services up to international standards. On the edge of the city is the Belle Vue centre, a large entertainments complex including concert and exhibition facilities, and a speedway stadium.

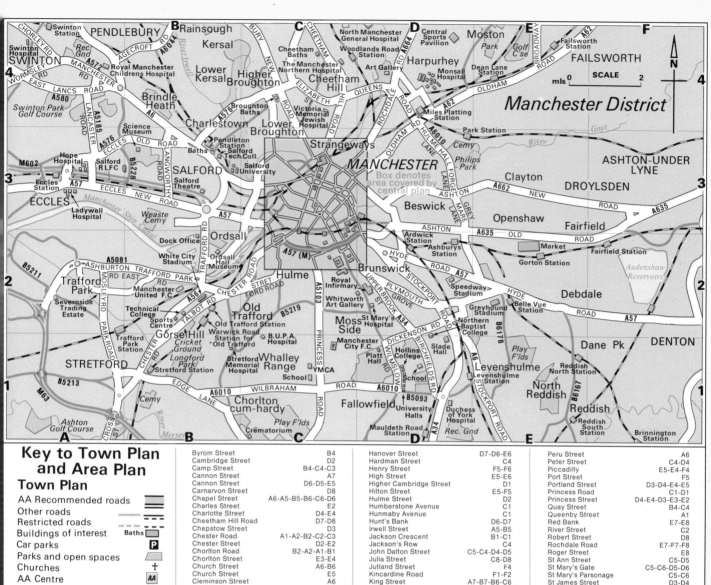

Manchester District map

MANCHESTER
The Barton Swing Bridge carries the Bridgewater Canal over the Manchester Ship Canal, which links Manchester with the sea nearly 40 miles away. Completed in 1894, the canal is navigable by vessels up to 15,000 tons.

49

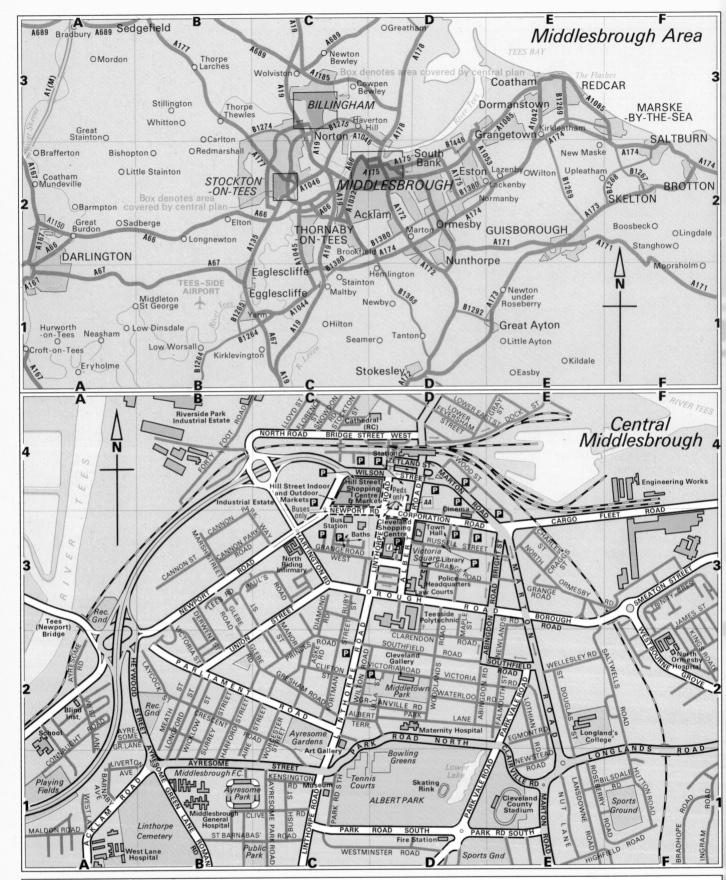

Middlesbrough

Heavy industry dominates Middlesbrough. It has been a centre of iron and steel manufacture since the 1840s although much of the steel-making has moved eastwards to a new works near Redcar. Its rise had begun ten years before, when the Stockton and Darlington Railway purchased land here and turned what had been a quiet riverside village into a busy coal exporting town. Middlesbrough's most notable structure is the Transporter Bridge, built across the Tees in 1911. It is one of only two bridges of its type left in Britain. The town centre is modern with spacious shopping areas and new public buildings. The Dorman Museum covers the region's history and there are two major art galleries.

Stockton has a place in transport history; it was here, on 27 September 1825, that the world's first steam passenger railway service began. The town, also situated on the River Tees, became an engineering and shipbuilding centre and is still an important industrial centre today. It has a town hall of 1763 standing in the middle of one of the widest main streets in England.

Billingham also stands on the Tees, and the river was one of the factors which encouraged various chemical industries to become established here. North Sea oil has given a boost to that industry, and the town centre has been completely rebuilt with every facility.

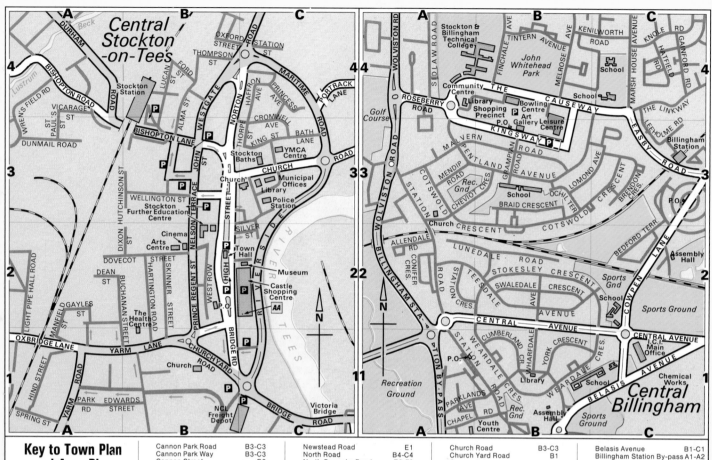

Key to Town Plan and Area Plan

Town Plan

AA Recommended roads	
Other roads	
Restricted roads	
Buildings of interest	
Car Parks	P
Parks and open spaces	
One way street	←

Area Plan

A roads	
B roads	
Locations	Aycliffe ○
Urban area	

Street Index with Grid Reference

Middlesbrough

Abingdon Road	D2-E2-E3
Acklam Road	A1-B1
Aire Street	B1-B2-C2
Albert Road	D3-D4
Albert Terrace	C2-D2
Aske Road	C2
Ayresome Green Lane	A2-B2-B1
Ayresome Park Road	C1
Ayresom Road	A2
Ayresome Street	B1-C1
Barnaby Avenue	A1
Bilsdale Road	E1-F1
Blake Road	D4-E4-E3
Borough Road	C3-D3-E3
Bradhope Road	F1
Bright Street	E3
Bridge Street West	C4-D4
Bush Street	C1
Cannon Park Road	B3-C3
Cannon Park Way	B3-C3
Cannon Street	B3
Cargo Fleet Road	E3-F3-F4
Charles Street	E3
Clairville Road	E1-E2
Clarendon Road	D2-D3
Clifton Street	C2
Clive Road	B1-C1
Connaught Road	A1-A2
Corporation Road	D4-D3-E3
Craggs Street	E3
Crescent Road	B2-C2-C1
Derwent Street	B2-B3
Diamond Road	C2-C3
Dock Street	E4
Egmont Road	E2
Falmouth Street	E2
Florence Street	E2
Forty Foot Road	B4-C4
Glebe Road	B3-B2-C2
Grange Road	D3-E3
Grange Road West	C3-D3
Granville Road	C2-D2
Gray Street	D4-E4-E3
Gresham Road	C2
Hartford Street	B1-B2
Hartinton Road	C3
Heywood Street	A2-B2
Highfield Road	E1-F1
Hutton Road	F1
Ingram Road	F1
James Street	F2-F3
Kensington Road	C1
Kings Road	F2-F3
Lansdowne Road	E1
Laycock Street	B2
Lees Road	B3
Linthorpe Road	C1-C2-C3-D3-D4
Liverton Avenue	A1-B1
Lloyd Street	C4
Longford Street	B1-B2
Longlands Road	E1-F1-F2
Lothian Road	E1-E2
Lower East Street	D4-E4
Lower Feversham Street	D4
Maldon Road	A1
Manor Street	C2-C3
Maple Street	D2-D3
Marsh Street	B3
Marton Road	D4-D3-E3-E2-E1
Meath Street	B2
Newlands Road	E2-E3
Newport Road	B2-B3-C3-C4-D4-D3
Newstead Road	E1
North Road	B4-C4
North Ormesby Road	E3-F3
Nut Lane	E1
Park Lane	D2-E2
Park Road North	C1-C2-D2-E2
Park Road South	C1-D1-E1
Park Vale Road	D1-E1-E2
Parliament Road	B2-C2
Portman Street	C2-C3
Princes Road	C2
Roman Road	B1
Roseberry Road	E1-F1
Ruby Street	C3
Russell Street	D3-E3
St Barnabas' Road	B1-C1
St Douglas Street	E1-E2
St Paul's Road	C3-B3-C3
Saltwells Road	E3-E2-F2
Smeaton Street	F3
Snowdon Road	C4
Southfield Road	C2-D2-E2
Stockton Street	C4
Surrey Street	B1-B2
Trinity Crescent	F2-F3
Ulla Street	D2
Union Street	B2-C2-C3
Victoria Road	C2-D2-E2
Victoria Street	B2-B3
Waterloo Road	D2-E2
Wellesley Road	E2
West Lane	A1-A2
Westbourne Grove	F2-F3
Westminster Road	C1-D1
Wicklow Street	B1-B2
Wilson Street	C4-D4
Wilton Road	C2-D2
Woodlands Road	D2-D3
Wood Street	D4
Worcester Street	C1-C2
Zetland Street	D4

Stockton-on-Tees

Alma Street	B3-B4
Bath Lane	C3
Bishopton Lane	A3-B3
Bishopton Road	A4-A3
Bridge Road	B2-B1-C1
Buchanan Street	A1-A2
Church Road	B3-C3
Church Yard Road	B1
Cromwell Avenue	C3
Dean Street	A2
Dixon Street	B2
Dovecot Street	A2-B2
Dunmail Road	A3
Durham Road	A4
Edwards Street	A1-B1
Ford Street	B4
Gayles Street	A2
Haffron Avenue	C3-C4
Hartington Road	B1-B2
High Street	B2-B3
Hind Street	A1
Hutchinson Street	B3
John Street	B3
King Street	C3
Light Pipe Hall Road	A1-A2
Lucan Street	B4
Manfield Street	A1-A2
Maritime Road	C3-C4
Mill Street	B3
Nelson Terrace	B2-B3
Norton Road	B3-B4-C4
Oxbridge Lane	A1
Oxford Street	B4-C4
Park Road	A1
Parliament Street	B1
Portrack Lane	C4
Prince Regent Street	B1-B2
Princes Avenue	C4
Riverside	C1-C2-C3
St Paul's Street	A3-A4
Silver Street	B2-C2
Skinner Street	B1-B2
Spring Street	A1
Station Street	C4
Thompson Street	B4
Thorpe Street	C3
Vicarage Street	A4
Wellington Street	B3
Westbourne Street	A1-B1
Westgate	B3-B4
West Row	B2
Wren's Field Road	A3-A4
Yarm Lane	A1-B1-B2
Yarm Road	A1

Billingham

Allendale Road	A2
Bedford Terrace	C2-C3
Belasis Avenue	B1-C1
Billingham Station By-pass	A1-A2
Braid Crescent	B3
Brendon Crescent	C3
Central Avenue	A2-B2-B1-C1-C2
Chapel Road	A1-B1
Cheviot Crescent	A3-B3
Conifer Crescent	A2
Cotswold Crescent	A3-A2-B2-B3-C3
Cowpen Lane	C1-C2-C3
Cumberland Crescent	B1
Easby Road	C3-C4
Finchale Avenue	B4
Gainford Road	C4
Grampian Road	B3
Hatfield Road	C4
Kenilworth Road	B4-C4
Kingsway	A4-A3-B3-B4
Knole Road	C4
Leeholme Road	C3-C4
Lomond Road	B3-C3
Lunedale Road	A2-B2
Malvern Road	A3-B3
Marsh House Avenue	C4
Melrose Avenue	B4
Mendip Road	A3
Ochil Terrace	B3
Parklands Avenue	A1-B1
Pentland Avenue	A3-B3-B4-C3-C4
Roseberry Road	A4
Sidlaw Road	A2
Station Crescent	A2
Station Road	A3-A2-A1-B1
Stokesley Crescent	B2-C2
Swaledale Crescent	B2
Teesdale Avenue	A2-B2-C2
Tintern Avenue	B4
The Causeway	A4-B4-C4
The Linkway	C4
Weardale Crescent	A2-A1-B2-B1-C1
Wharfdale Avenue	B1-B2
Wolviston Road	A2-A3-A4
York Crescent	B1-C1

MIDDLESBROUGH
In 1911 the Transporter Bridge was built to replace the river ferry between Port Clarence and Middlesbrough. It is still used today and a special viewing platform has been built to enable visitors to watch the bridge in operation.

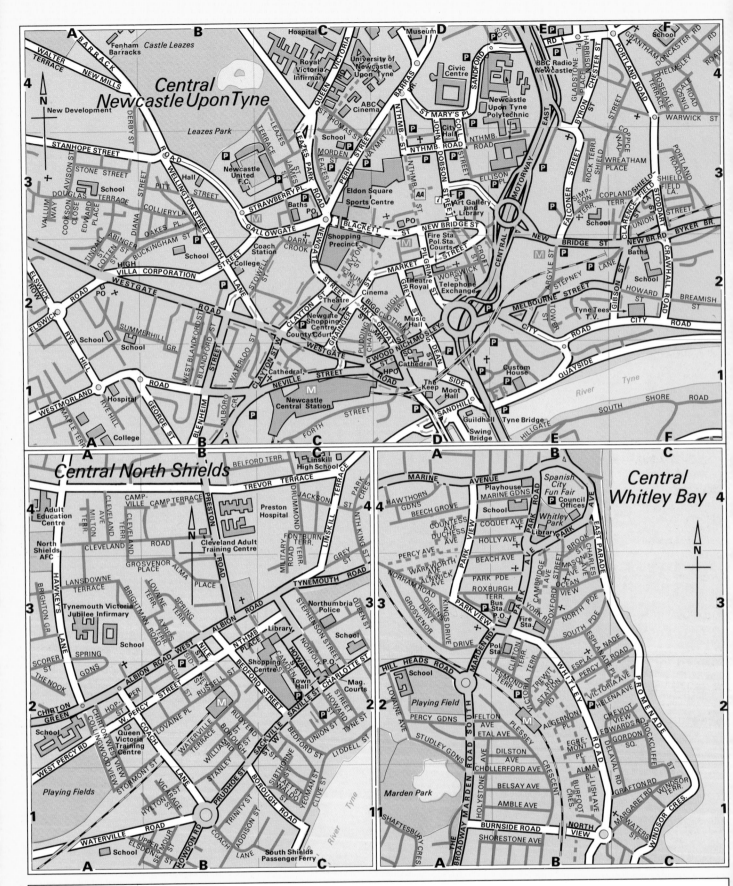

Newcastle

Six bridges span the Tyne at Newcastle; they all help to create a striking scene, but the most impressive is the High Level Bridge, built by Robert Stephenson in 1845-49 and consisting of two levels, one for the railway and one for the road. It is from the river that some of the best views of the city can be obtained. Grey Street is Newcastle's most handsome thoroughfare. It dates from the time, between 1835 and 1840, when much of this part of the city was replanned and rebuilt. Elegant façades curve up to Grey's Monument. Close to the Monument is the Eldon Centre, combining sports facilities and shopping centre to form an integrated complex which is one of the largest of its kind in Europe. Newcastle has many museums. The industrial background of the city is traced in the Museum of Science and Engineering, while the Laing Art Gallery and Museum covers painting, costumes and local domestic history. The Hancock Museum has an exceptional natural history collection and the John George Joicey Museum has period displays in a 17th-century almshouse. In Black Gate is one of Britain's most unusual museums – a collection of over 100 sets of bagpipes. Within the University precincts are three further museums. Of the city's open spaces, Town Moor is the largest. At nearly 1,000 acres it is big enough to feel genuinely wild.

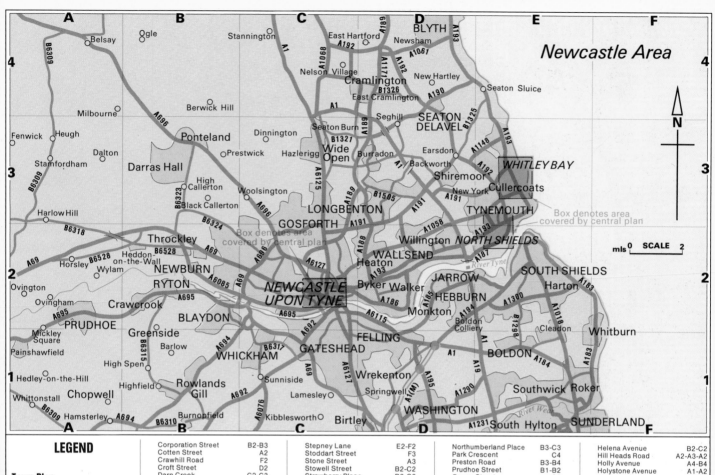

LEGEND

Town Plan

AA recommended route
Restricted roads
Other roads
Buildings of interest   Hall
Car parks   P
Parks and open spaces
Metro stations   M
One way streets

Area Plan

A roads
B roads
Locations   Craghead O
Urban area

Street Index with Grid Reference

Newcastle

Abinger Street	A2
Argyle Street	E2
Avison Street	A3
Barrack Road	A4-B4-B3
Barras Bridge	D4
Bath Lane	B2-C2
Bigg Market Street	C2-D2
Blackett Street	C3-D3-D2
Blandford Street	B1-B2
Blenheim Street	B1-B2
Breamish Street	F2
Buckingham Street	A2-B2-B3
Byker Bridge	F2-F3
Byron Street	E3-E4
Central Motorway	E1-D1-D2-E2-E3-E4
Chester Street	E4
City Road	E1-E2-F2
Clarence Street	F2-F3
Clayton Street	C2
Clayton Street West	B1-C1-C2
Clothmarket	D2
College Street	D3-D4
Colliery Lane	B3
Collingwood Street	C1-D1
Cookson Close	A3
Copland Terrace	E3-F3
Coppice Way	F3
Corporation Street	B2-B3
Cotten Street	A2
Crawhill Road	F2
Croft Street	D2
Darn Crook	C2-C3
Dean Street	D1-D2
Derby Street	A3-A4
Diana Street	A2-A3-B3
Dinsdale Road	F4
Doncaster Road	F4
Douglas Terrace	A3-B3
Edward Place	A3
Ellison Place	D3-E3
Elswick Road	A2
Elswick Row	A2
Falconer Street	E3
Forth Street	C1-D1
Gallowgate	B3-C3
George Street	A1-B1
Gibson Street	F2
Gladstone Place	E4
Grainger Street	C1-C2-D2
Grantham Road	F4
Grey Street	D2
Great Market	D1-D2
Harrison Place	F4
Haymarket	D3-D4
Helmsley Road	F4
High Bridge	D2
High Villa	A2
Hillgate	E1
Howard Street	F2
John Dobson Street	D3-D4
Leazes Lane	C3
Leazes Park Road	C3-C4
Leazes Terrace	C3-C4
Maple Terrace	A1
Market Street	D2
Marlborough Crescent	B1
Melbourne Street	E2-F2
Morden Street	C1
Moseley Street	D1-D2
Neville Street	C1
New Bridge Road	F2-F3
New Bridge Street	D3-E3-E2-F2
Newgate Street	C2-C3
New Mills	A4
Northumberland Street	D4-D3-E4
Nun Street	C2
Oakes Place	A2-B2-B3
Perry Street	C3-D3-D4
Pilgrim Street	D2
Pitt Street	B3
Portland Road	F3-F4
Pudding Chape	C1-C2
Quayside	D1-E1-F1-F2
Queen Victoria Road	C3
Rock Terrace	E3
Rosedale Terrace	F4
Rye Hill	A1-A2
St James Street	C3
St Mary's Place	D4
St Nicholas Square	D1-D2
St Thomas Street	C3-C4
Sandford Road	D4-E4
Sandhill	D1
Shield Street	E3-F3-F4
Sheildfield Lane	F3
Side	D1
Simpson Terrace	E3
South Shore Road	E1-F1
Stanhope Street	A3-B3
Stepney Lane	E2-F2
Stoddart Street	F3
Stone Street	F3
Stowell Street	B2-C2
Strawberry Place	B3-C3
Summerhill Grove	A2-B2-B1
Tindall Street	A2
Tower Street	E2
Union Street	F3
Vallum Way	A3
Victoria Square	E4
Walter Terrace	A4
Warwick Street	F4
Waterloo Street	B1-B2-C2
Wellington Street	B2
Westgate Road	A2-B2-C2-C1-D1
Westmorland Road	A1-B1
West Blandford Street	B1-B2
Worswick Street	D2
Wreatham Place	E3-F3

North Shields

Addison Street	B1
Albion Road	B3-C3
Albion Road West	A2-B2-B3
Alma Place	B3
Ayre's Terrace	B3
Bedford Street	B3-B2-B2
Belford Terrace	B4-C4
Borough Road	B2-B1-C1
Brightman Road	A3-B3
Brighton Grove	A3
Camden Street	C2-C3
Camp Terrace	B4
Campville	A4-B4
Cecil Street	B2
Charlotte Street	C2-C3
Chirton Green	A2
Chirton West View	A1-A2
Cleveland Avenue	A4
Cleveland Road	A4-B4
Cleveland Terrace	A3-A4
Clive Street	C1-C2
Coach Lane	A2-B2-B1
Collingwood View	A1-A2
Drummond Terrace	C3-C4
Fontbarn Terrace	C4
Grey Street	C3-C4
Grosvenor Place	A3-B3
Hawkey's Lane	A2-A3-A4
Hopper Street	A2
Howard Street	C2-C3
Howdon Road	B1
Hylton Street	A1-B1
Jackson Street	C4
Laet Street	C1
Lansdowne Terrace	A3
Liddell Street	C2
Linskill Terrace	C3-C4
Lovaine Place	B2
Lovaine Terrace	B3
Military Road	C3-C4
Milton Terrace	A4
Nile Street	B3
Norfolk Street	C2-C3
North King Street	C3-C4

North Shields (continued)

Northumberland Place	B3-C3
Park Crescent	C4
Preston Road	B3-B4
Prudhoe Street	B1-B2
Queen Street	C3
Rudyard Street	B2-C2-C1
Russell Street	B2
Sackville Street West	B2-C2
Saville Street	C2
Scorer Street	A2-A3
Seymour Street	B1
Sibthorne Street	C1-C2
Sidney Street	B2-B3
Spring Gardens	A2-A3
Spring Terrace	B3
Stanley Street	B1-B2
Stephenson Street	C2-C3
Stormont Street	A1-A2-B2
The Nook	A2
Trevor Terrace	B4-C4
Trinity Street	B1
Tyne Street	C2
Tynemouth Road	C3
Union Street	C2
Upper Elsdon Street	A1-B1
Vicarage Street	B1
Waldo Street	C1
Waterville Road	A1-B1
Waterville Terrace	B2
West Percy Road	A1-A2
West Percy Street	A2-B2-B1
William Street	B2-C2
Yeoman Street	C1-C2

Whitley Bay

Algernon Place	B2
Alma Place	B1
Alnwick Avenue	A3
Amble Avenue	A1-B1
Beach Avenue	A3-B3-B4
Beech Grove	A4
Belsay Avenue	A1-B1
Brook Street	B3-B4
Burfoot Crescent	B1
Burnside Road	A1-B1
Cambridge Avenue	B3-B4
Charles Avenue	B3-B4
Cheviot View	B2-C2
Chollerford Avenue	A1-B1
Clifton Terrace	B2-B3
Coquet Avenue	A4-B4
Countess Avenue	A4
Delaval Road	B2-C2-C1
Dilston Avenue	A2-B2
Duchess Avenue	A4
East Parade	B3-B4
Edwards Road	B2-C2
Egremont Place	B2
Esplanade	B2-B3-B3
Esplanade Place	B3-B2-C2
Etal Avenue	A2-B2
Felton Avenue	A2-B2
Gordon Square	C2
Grafton Road	C1
Grosvenor Drive	A3
Hawthorne Gardens	A4
Helena Avenue	B2-C2
Hill Heads Road	A2-A3-A2
Holly Avenue	A4-B4
Holystone Avenue	A1-A2
Jesmond Terrace	A2-B2
Kings Drive	A3
Lish Avenue	B1
Lovaine Avenue	A2
Marden Road	A2-A3-B3
Marden Road South	A1-A2
Margaret Road	C1
Marine Avenue	A4-B4
Marine Gardens	A4-B4
Mason Avenue	B3
Norham Road	A3
North Parade	B3
North View	B1
Ocean View	B3
Oxford Street	B3-B4
Park Avenue	B3-B4
Park Parade	A3-B3
Park Road	B4
Park View	A3-A4
Percy Avenue	A3-A4
Percy Gardens	A2
Percy Road	B2-C2-C3
Plessey Crescent	A2-B2-B1
Promenade	C1-C2-C3
Queens Drive	A3
Rockcliffe Street	C1-C2
Roxburgh Terrace	A3-B3
Shaftesbury Crescent	A1
Shorestone Avenue	A1-B1
South Parade	B3
Station Road	B2
Studley Gardens	A1-A2
The Broadway	A1
Trewit Road	B2
Victoria Avenue	B2-C2
Victoria Terrace	B2-B3
Warkworth Avenue	A3
Waters Street	C1
Whitley Road	B1-B2-B3
Windsor Crescent	C1
Windsor Terrace	C1
York Road	B3

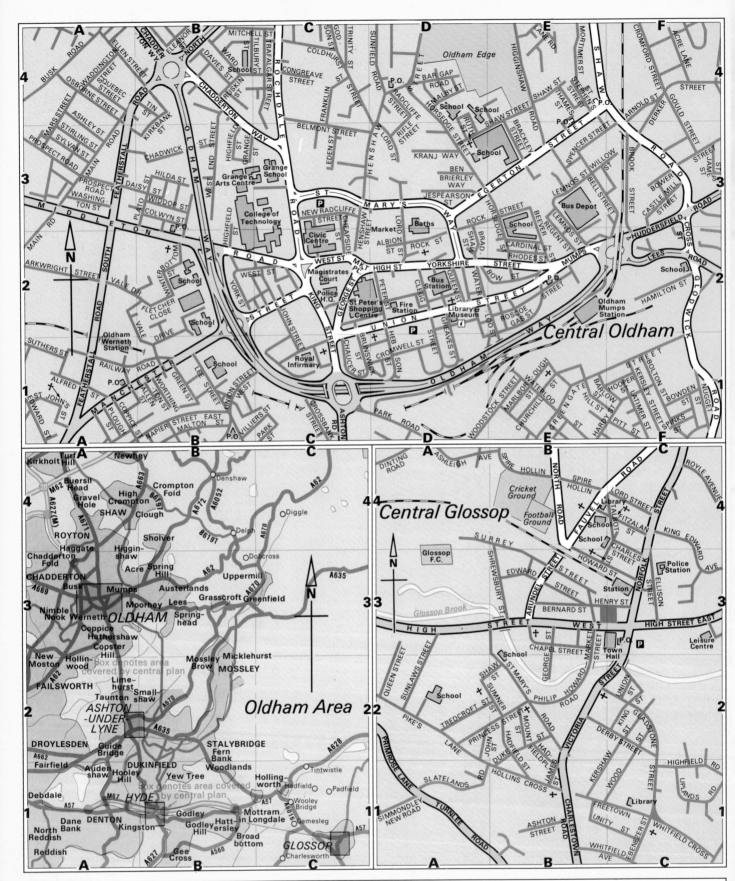

Oldham

Snooker championships are a feature of Oldham's Queen Elizabeth Hall, which is also in frequent use by the BBC for recording concerts. This ex-mill town has prospered with the coming of the M62, and as well as the Civic Centre, which is the site of the hall, it also has a fine modern Town Square Shopping Centre. In a pleasant combination of the old and new, it stands proudly alongside the old-established Tommyfield Market, said to be one of the country's largest permanent markets. The Local Interest Centre traces Oldham's past.

Ashton-under-Lyne Pride of Ashton-under-Lyne is the Parish Church of St Michael, noted for its fine 16th-century stained glass.

Glossop Cobbled streets, 17th-century stone houses and easy access to the Dark Peak moors are among the attractions of this High Peaks town. A popular touring centre, it also draws railway enthusiasts: nearby Dinting Railway Centre has a fine collection of steam locomotives offering rides most Sundays and Bank Holidays, while Manor Park is noted for its miniature steam railway. The park also draws the crowds for the annual local festival, which is held here each July.

Hyde lies in the Tame Valley and was once a centre for cotton manufacturing and for coal mining. Good shops and sports facilities can be found in the town.

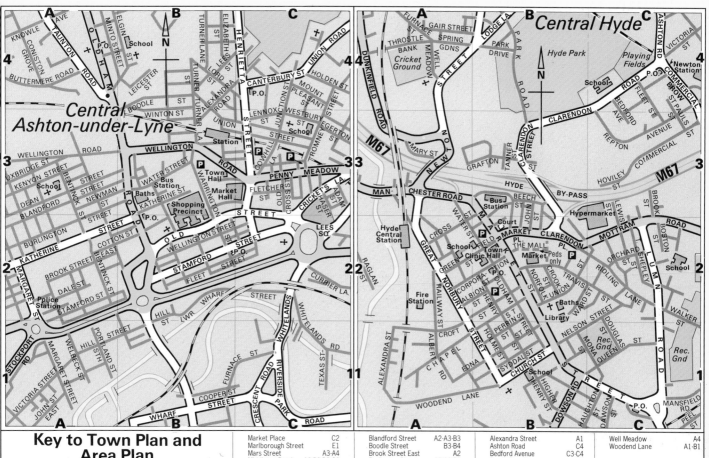

Key to Town Plan and Area Plan

Town Plan

- AA Recommended roads
- Restricted roads
- Other roads
- Buildings of interest — Theatre
- Car Parks — P
- Parks and open spaces

Area Plan

- A roads
- B roads
- Locations — Dobcross
- Urban area

STREET INDEX WITH GRID REFERENCE

OLDHAM

Acre Lane	F4
Albion Street	D2
Alfred Street	A1
Allen Street	B1
Arkwright Street	A2
Arnold Street	F4
Ashley Street	A3-A4
Ashton Road	C1
Bar Gap Road	D4
Barlow Street	E1-F1
Beever Street	E2-E3
Bell Street	E3-F3
Belmont Street	C4-C3-D3
Ben Brierley Way	D3
Bolton Street	B1
Bow Street	D2-E2
Bower Street	F3
Bowden Street	F1
Brackley Street	C4
Bradshaw Street	D2-D3
Brook Street	F2-F3
Brunswick Street	C1
Busk Road	A4
Cardinal Street	E2
Castle Mill Street	F3
Chadderton Way	B4-B3-C3
Chadwick Street	B3
Chaucer Street	C1
Cheapside Street	C2-C3
Churchill Street	C1
Clegg Street	D1-D2
Coldhurst Street	C4-D4-D3
Colwyn Street	B3
Congreave Street	C4
Coppice Street	A1-B1
Cromford Street	F4
Cromwell Street	C1-D1
Cross Street	F2-F3
Crossbank Street	C1
Daisy Street	A3-B3
Davies Street	B4
Derker Street	F3-F4
Eden Street	C3
Edward Street	A1
Egerton Street	D3-E3-E4
Eleanor Street	B4
Ellen Street	A4-B4
Featherstall Road North	A3-A4-B4
Featherstall Road South	A1-A2-A3
Fletcher Close	B2
Franklin Street	C4
Gas Street	E1-E2
George Street	C2
Glodwick Road	F1-F2
Godson Street	C4
Gould Street	F3-F4
Grange Street	B3-C3
Greaves Street	D1-D2
Green Street	B1
Greengate Street	E1-F1
Hamilton Street	F2
Hardy Street	E1-F1
Hebson Street	D1-D2
Henshaw Street	C2-C3-D3-D4
High Street	D2
Highfield Street	B2-B3
Higginshaw Road	E3-E4
Hilda Street	B3
Hill Street	E1-F1
Hooper Street	F1
Horsedge Street	D4-D3-E3-E2
Huddersfield Road	F2-F3
Jesperson Street	D3
John Street	C1-C2
Kersley Street	F1
King Street	C1-C2
Kirkbank Street	B3-B4
Kranj Way	D3
Lane Road	E4
Latimer Street	F1
Lee Street	B1
Lees Road	F2
Lemnos Street	E2-E3
Lord Street	D2-D3
Main Road	A2-A3-A4
Malby Street	D4
Malton Street	B1
Manchester Street	A1-B1-B2-C2
Market Place	C2
Marlborough Street	E1
Mars Street	A3-A4
Middleton Road	A3-B3-B2-C2
Mitchell Street	B4-C4
Mortimer Street	E4
Mumps	E2
Napier Street East	A1-B1
New Radcliffe Street	C3
Nugget Street	F1
Oldham Way	B4-B3-B2-B1-C1-D1-E1-E2-F2
Osborne Street	A4
Park Road	C1-D1
Park Street	C1
Peter Street	D2
Pitt Street	F1
Plato Street	B3
Plough Street	A1
Prospect Road	A3
Quebec Street	A4
Queen Street	D2
Radcliffe Street	D4
Railway Road	A1-B1
Regent Street	E2-E3
Rhodes Street	E2
Rifle Street	D3-D4
Rochdale Road	C2-C3-C4
Rock Street	D2-D3-E3
Roscoe Street	E2
Ruskin Street	B4
Ruth Street	D3-D4
St Jame's Street	F3
St John's Street	D1
St Mary's Way	C3-D3-D2
St Stephen's Street	E4
Shaw Road	E4-F4-F3
Shaw Street	D3-E3-E4
Spencer Street	E3-F3
Spinks Street	F1
Stirling Street	A3
Sunfield Road	D4
Suthers Street	A1
Sylvan Street	A3
Thames Street	E4
Tilbury Street	B4-C4
Tin Street	D1
Trafalgar Street	C4
Trinity Street	C4
Union Street	C1-C2-D2-E2
Union Street West	B1-C1
Vale Drive	A2-B2-B1
Villiers Street	B1-C1
Waddington Street	A4
Ward Street	B4-C4
Washington Street	A3
Waterloo Street	D2-E2-E1
West Street	B2-C2
West End Street	B3-B4
Widdop Street	B3
Willow Street	B3
Willow Street	E3-F3
Winterbottom Street	B2
Woodstock Street	D1-E1
Worthington Street	B1
York Street	B2
Yorkshire Street	D2-E2

ASHTON-UNDER-LYNE

Adam Street	C3
Alexandra Road	B3-B4-C4
Bentinck Street	A2-A3
Blandford Street	A2-A3-B3
Boodle Street	B3-B4
Brook Street East	A2
Burlington Street	A2-A3-B3
Buttermere Road	A4
Canterbury Street	C4
Coniston Grove	A4
Cooper Street	B1-C1
Cotton Street	A2-B2
Cowhill Lane	C3
Crescent Road	C1
Cricket's Lane	C3
Currier Lane	C2
Dale Street	A2
Dean Street	A2-A3-B3
Egerton Street	C3
Elgin Street	A4-B4
Elizabeth Street	B4
Fleet Street	B2-C2
Fletcher Street	C3
Furnace Street	B1-C1
Haser Street	C3
Henrietta Street	B4-C4-C3
Hill Street	A1-B1-B2
Holden Street	C4
John Street East	A1
Junction Street	C3-C4
Katherine Street	A2-B2-B3
Kenyon Street	A3
Knowle Avenue	A4
Lees Square	C2
Lees Street	B4
Leicester Street	B4
Lennox Street	C3
Lord Street	B4
Lower Wharf Street	B2-C2
Margaret Street	A1-A2
Minto Street	A4-B4
Mount Pleasant Street	C4
Newman Street	A3-B3
Old Street	B2-B3-C3-C2
Old Cross Street	C3
Oldham Road	A4-A3-B3-B2
Park Road	C1
Penny Meadow	C3
Portland Street South	A1
Riverside	C1
Romney Street	C3-C4
Stamford Street	A1-A2-B2-C2
Stockport Road	A1
Taunton Road	A4
Texas Street	C1
Turner Lane	B3-B4
Turner Street	B4
Union Road	C4
Union Street	B4-B3-C3
Uxbridge Street	A3
Victoria Street	A1
Warrington Street	B2-B3
Water Street	B3
Welbeck Street	A1
Wellington Road	A3-B3-C3
Wellington Street	B2-C2
Westbury Street	C3
Wharf Street	B1-C1
Whitelands	C1-C2
Whitelands Road	C1-C2
Winton Street	B3-B4

HYDE

Albert Road	A1
Albion Street	A2-B2
Alexandra Street	A1
Ashton Road	C4
Bedford Avenue	C3-C4
Beech Street	B3
Boston Street	C2
Brook Street	C3
Chapel Street	A1-B1-B2
Church Street	B1
Clarendon Place	B2
Clarendon Road	B3-B4-C4
Clarendon Street	B3
Commercial Brow	C3-C4
Commercial Street	C3
Corporation Street	A2-B2
Croft Street	A1-A2-B2
Crook Street	B2
Cross Street	A2-B2-B3
Dawson Street	C1
Douglas Street	C1-C2
Dowson Road	B1
Dunkinfield Road	A3-A4
Edna Street	A1-B1
Fleet Street	C3-C4
Furnace Street	A4
Gair Street	A4
Grafton Street	A3-B3
Great Norbury Street	A3-A2-A1-B1
Greenfield Street	A2-B2
Haughton Street	B1-C1
Henry Street	B1-B2
Higher Henry Street	B1
Holme Street	B1
Hoviley Street	C2
Hyde By-pass	A3-B3-C3
John Street	B2-B3
Lewis Street	C2-C3
Lodge Lane	B4
Lumn Road	C1-C2
Manchester Road	A3
Mansfield Road	C1
Market Place	B2
Market Street	B3-B2-B1-C1
Mary Street	A3
Mona Street	B1-C1
Mottram Road	C2
Nelson Street	B1-C1-C2
Newton Street	A3-A4
Norfolk Street	B2-B3
Oldham Street	B1-B2
Orchard Street	C2
Park Drive	B4
Park Road	B3-B4
Peel Street	C1
Perrin Street	B1-B2
Queen Street	C1
Raglan Street	A2
Railway Street	A1-A2
Ridling Lane	B2-C2
Repton Avenue	C3-C4
St Pauls Street	C3-C4
Spring Gardens	A4
Syddal Street	B1
Tanner Street	B3
The Mall	B2
Throstle Bank	A4
Tom Shepley Street	B2-C2
Travis Street	B2-C2
Union Street	B2-C2
Victoria Street	C4
Walker Street	C1-C2
Ward Street	B2-C2
Water Street	A3-A2-B2
Well Meadow	A4
Woodend Lane	A1-B1

GLOSSOP

Arundel Street	B3
Ashleigh Avenue	A4-B4
Ashton Street	B3
Bernard Street	B3
Chapel Street	B3
Charles Street	C3-C4
Charlestown Road	B1
Derby Street	B2-C2
Dinting Road	A4
Duke Street	B1-B2
Ebenezer Street	C1
Edward Street	B3
Ellison Street	C3
Fauvel Road	B4-C4
Fitzalan Street	C4
Freetown	B1-C1
George Street	B2-B3
Gladstone Street	B2-C2-C1
Hadfield Place	B1-B2
Hadfield Road	B1-B2
Henry Street	B3-C3
High Street East	C3
High Street West	A3-B3-C3
Highfield Road	C1
Hollins Cross	A1-B1
Howard Street	B4-B3-C3
James Street	B1
John Street	A2
Kershaw Street	B1-C1-C2
King Street	C2
King Edward Avenue	C3-C4
Lord Street	C4
Market Street	B2-B3
Mount Street	B2
Norfolk Street	C3-C4
North Road	B4
Philip Howard Road	B2
Pike's Lane	A1-A2
Primrose Lane	A1-A2
Princess Street	A2-B2
Queen Street	A2-A3
Royle Avenue	C4
St Mary's Road	B2-B3
Shaw Street	A2-B2
Simmondley New Road	A1
Slatelands Road	A1
Shrewsbury Street	B3-B4
Spire Hollin	B2
Sumner Street	A2-B2
Sunlaws Street	A2-A3
Surrey Street	A4-B4-B3
Talbot Street	B3-C3-C4
Tredcroft Street	A2-B2
Turnlee Road	A1-B1
Union Street	B1-C1
Unity Street	C1
Victoria Street	B2-C2-C3
Whitfield Avenue	B1-C1
Whitfield Cross	C1
Wood Street	B1-C1-C2

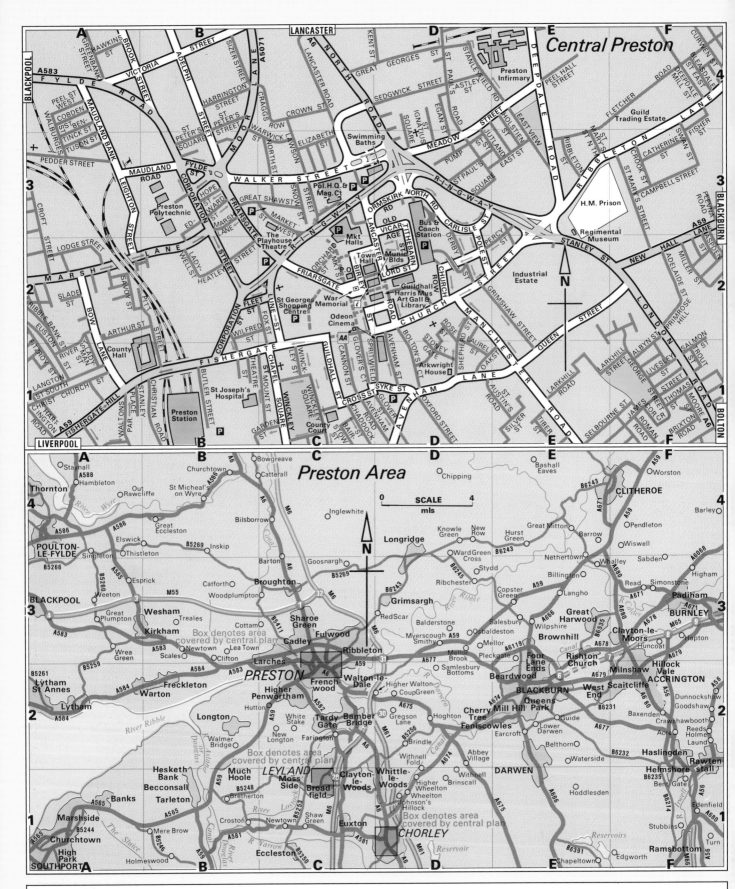

Preston

The decline of the cotton trade after World War I hit Preston badly: this was one of the most important centres in the 19th century.
But today the town is once again an important industrial centre, and one which is well-served by the motorway network.

By way of contrast, Preston also offers a generous number of parks and open spaces, and the River Ribble offers pleasant riverside walks. It has an impressive Market Square, where the neo-classical Harris Museum and Art Gallery houses an extensive collection of decorative and fine art, and displays on social history and archaeology can also be seen here.

Leyland was transformed by the setting up in 1892 of Leyland Motors, which later became Leyland Vehicles. Less well known is the town's restored 16th-century grammar school, now the home of the Museum and Exhibition Centre. Another attractive feature is Worden Park, which offers 160 acres of natural beauty and is also the venue of the Leyland Festival.

Chorley Fast expanding Chorley was once a major cotton centre and it's still a flourishing industrial town, although now its interests are more widely based. Close to the centre the wooded park and 16th-century house of Astley Hall are situated.

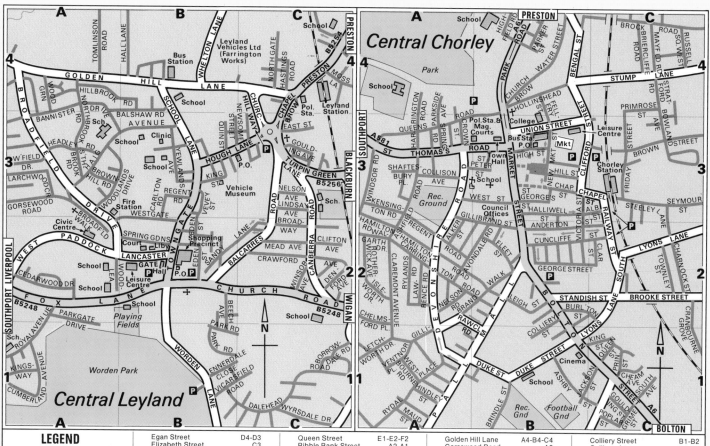

Central Chorley

Central Leyland

LEGEND

Town Plan

AA Recommended roads	▄▄▄
Other roads	▄▄
Restricted roads	▄ ▄ ▄
Buildings of interest	▢ Station
Churches	+
Car parks	P
Parks and open spaces	▢
One way streets	→

Area Plan

A roads	▄▄▄
B roads	▄▄
Locations	Warehorne ○
Urban area	▢

STREET INDEX

Preston

Adelaide Street	F2
Adelphi Street	B4-B3
Albyn Street	F1-F2
Arthur Street	A2-B2
Aspden Street	F3-F2
Astley Street	D4
Avenham Lane	D1-E1
Avenham Road	C1-D1
Avenham Street	D2-D1
Bairstow Street	C1
Bentinck Street	A3-A4
Birley Street	C2-D2
Bleasdale Street East	F4
Bolton's Court	D2-D1
Bow Lane	A2-A1
Brixton Road	F1
Brook Street	A4-B4
Butler Street	B1
Campbell Street	F3
Cannon Street	C2-C1
Carlisle Street	D3
Catherine Street	F3
Chaddock Street	C1
Chapel Street	C1
Christ Church Street	A1
Christian Road	B1
Church Row	D2
Church Street	D2-E2
Cobden Street	A4
Coronation Crescent	F1
Corporation Street	B3-B2-B1
Cragg's Row	C4
Croft Street	A3-A2
Crook Street	F3
Cross Street	C1-D1
Crown Street	C4
Curwen Street	F4
Deepdale Mill Street	F4
Deepdale Road	E4-E3
Derby Street	D3-D2
East Street	D3-E3
East View	E4-E3
Edward Street	B2-B3

Egan Street	D4-D3
Elizabeth Street	C3
Euston Street	A2-A1
Fishergate	B1-C1-C2
Fishergate Hill	A1
Fisher Street	F3-F4
Fitzroy Street	A2-A1
Fleet Street	B2-C2
Fletcher Road	E3-E4-F4
Fox Street	C2-C1
Friarsgate	B3-B2-C2-C3
Fylde Road	A4-B4
Fylde Street	B3
Garden Street	B1-C1
George Street	F1
Glover's Court	C2-C1
Glover Street	D1
Great Georges Street	C4-D4
Great Shaw Street	B3-C3
Greenbank Street	A4
Grimshaw Street	D2-E2-E1
Guildhall Street	C2-C1
Harrington Street	B4
Hartington Road	A1
Hawkins Street	A4
Heatley Street	B2
Holstien Street	E4-E3
Hope Street	B3
James Street	F1
Jutland Street	D3-E3
Kent Street	D4
Ladyman Street	A2-A1
Ladywell Street	B2
Lancaster Road	C4-C3-C2-D2-D3
Langton Street South	A1
Larkhill Road	D1
Larkhill Street	E1-F1
Laurel Street	D2-D1
Lawson Street	C4-C3
Leighton Street	A3-A2
Livesley Street	F1
Lodge Street	A2
London Road	F2-F1
Lord Street	D2
Lune Street	B2-C2
Manchester Road	D2-E2-E1
Market Street	C2
Market Street West	C3
Marsh Lane	A2-B2-B3
Maudland Bank	A4-A3
Maudland Road	A3-B3
Meadow Street	D3-D4-E4
Miller Street	F2
Moor Lane	B3-B4-C4
Moore Street	F1
Mount Street	C1
New Hall Lane	F2-F3
North Road	C4-D4-D3
North Street	C3
Oak Street	D1-E1
Old Vicarage	D3
Orchard Street	C2
Ormskirk Road	D3-D3
Oxford Street	D1
Peel Hall Street	E4
Peel Street West	A4
Pedder Street	A3
Percy Street	D2-E2-E3
Pitt Street	A2-B2-B1
Plevna Road	F3
Pole Street	D3-D2
Primrose Hill	F2
Pump Street	D3

Queen Street	E1-E2-F2
Ribble Bank Street	A2-A1
Ribbleton Lane	E3-F3-F4
Ribbleton Street	E3
Ringway	B2-C2-C3-D3-E3
River Street	A1-A2
Roman Road	F1
Rose Street	D2
St Austin's Road	D1-E1
St Ignatius Square	D4-D3
St Mary's Street	F3-F2
St Mary's Street North	E3
St Paul's Road	D4-D3
St Paul's Square	D3-E3
St Peter's Square	B3
St Peter's Street	B4
Salmon Street	F1-F2
Savoy Street	A2
Sedgwick Street	C4-D4
Selbourne Street	E1-E1
Shepherd Street	D1-D2
Silver Street	E1
Sizer Street	B4
Slade Street	A2
Snow Street	C3
Spritwield	C2-D2-C1-D1
Stanleyfield Road	D4-E4
Stanley Place	A1
Stanley Street	E2-F2
Stoney Gate	D2-D1
Syke Street	C1-D1
Swan Street	F4-F3
Theatre Street	B1
Thomas Street	F1
Tiber Street	E1
Tithebarn Street	D3-D2
Trout Street	E1
Tuson Street	A3-A4
Victoria Street	A4-B4
Walburges	A4-A3
Walker Street	B3-C3
Waltons Parade	A1
Warwick Street	B4-B3-C3
Wilfred Street	B2-C2
Winckley Square	C1
Winckley Street	C1

Leyland

Balcarres Road	B2-C2-C3
Balshaw Road	A4-B4
Bannister Drive	A3-A4
Beech Avenue	B1-B2
Borrowdale Road	C1
Broadfield Drive	B2-A2-A3-A4
Broadfield Walk	A2-A3
Broadway	C2
Brownhill Road	A3
Canberra Road	C2-C3
Carlton Road	B3
Cedarwood Drive	A2
Chapel Brow	C3-C4
Churchill Way	C3-C4
Church Road	B2-C2
Clifton Avenue	C2
Crawford Avenue	C2
Cumberland Avenue	A1
Dalehead Road	B1-C1
Denford Avenue	C2
East Street	C3
Eden Street	B2-B3
Ennerdale Close	B1-C1
Fox Lane	A2-B2

Chorley

Golden Hill Lane	A4-B4-C4
Gorsewood Road	A3
Goulding Avenue	C3
Haig Avenue	A3-B3
Hall Lane	B4
Hastings Road	C4
Headley Road	A3
Hillbrook Road	A4-B4
Hough Lane	B3-C3
King Street	B3
Kingsway	A1
Lancaster Gate	B2
Larchwood Crescent	A3
Lindsey Avenue	C3
Mead Avenue	C2
Moss Lane	C4
Nelson Avenue	C3
Newsome Street	B3
Northbrook Road	A3-A4
Northgate	C4
Parkgate Drive	A1-A2
Park Road	B1
Preston Road	C4
Quin Street	B3
Regent Road	B3
Royal Avenue	A1-A2
Sandy Lane	B2-C2
School Lane	B3-B4
Southbrook Road	A3
Spring Gardens	B2
Tomlinson Road	A4
Towngate	B1-B2-B3
Turpin Green Lane	C3
Vevey Street	B3
Vicarsfield Road	B1-C1
Westfield Drive	A3
Westgate	B2-B3
West Paddock	A2
Whelton Lane	B4
Winsor Avenue	C2
Wood Green	A4
Woodlands Drive	A3-B3
Woodlea	C2
Worden Lane	B1
Wyrsdale Drive	C1
Yewlands Avenue	B3

Albert Street	B3-C3
Alker Street	A2
Anderton Street	B2-C2
Ashby Street	B1-C1
Ashfield Road	A2-A3
Avondale Road	A2-B2
Bengal Street	B4
Bolton Road	B2-B1-C1
Bowland Avenue	C3-C4
Briercliffe Road	C4
Brindle Street	B1
Brooke Street	C2
Brock Road	B4-C4
Brown Street	C3
Burlington Street	B2-C2
Carrington Road	A2-B2
Chapel Street	B3-C3
Charnock Street	C1
Cheam Avenue	C1
Chelmsford Place	A2
Church Brow	B4
Claremont Avenue	A1-A2
Clarence Street	C2
Clifford Street	B4-B3-C3

Colliery Street	B1-B2
Collison Avenue	A3
Cranbourne Grove	C1-C2
Crown Street	A3
Cuncliffe Street	B2-C2
Devonshire Road	A1-A2-A3
Duke Street	B1
Fellery Street	B3-B4
Fleet Street	B2
Friday Street	C3-C4
George Street	B2-C2
Gillibrand Street	A3-A2-B2
Gillibrand Walk	A1-A2-B2
Goulding Street	C1
Grime Street	C1
Halliwell Street	B3
Hamilton Road	A3-A2-B2
Harington Road	A3-A4
Highfield Road	B4
High Street	B3
Hill Street	B3
Hindley Street	A1
Hollinshead	B4
Isleworth Drive	A2
Jackson Street	B1-C1
Kensington Road	A3
King Street	B1-C1
Lawrence Road	A2
Leigh Street	B2
Letchworth Drive	A1
Lyons Lane	C2
Lyons Lane South	B1-C1-C2
Market Street	B2-B3
Maud Street	A1
Mayfield Road	A2
Nelson Road	A2
New Market Street	B3
Pall Mall	A1-B1-B2
Parker Street	B4
Park Road	B4
Parkside Avenue	A3-A4
Poplar Street	C1
Primrose Street	C4
Princess Street	C1
Queens Road	A3-B3-B4
Queen Street	C2
Railway Street	C2-C3
Rawcliffe Road	A1-A2-B2-B1
Regent Road	A2-A3
Rotherwick Avenue	A2
Russell Square West	C4
Rydal Place	A1
Rylands Road	A2
St George's Street	B3
St Peter Street	A3-B3
St Thomas's Road	A3-B3
Seymour Street	C3
Shaftesbury Place	A3
South Avenue	C1
Spring Road	A3
Standish Street	B2-C2
Steeley Lane	C2-C3
Stratford Road	A3
Stump Lane	B4-C4
Townley Street	C2
Union Street	B3
Ventnor Place	A1
Victoria Street	B2-B3
Walgarth Drive	A2
Water Street	B4
Westbourne Road	A1
West Street	A3-B3
Windsor Road	A3

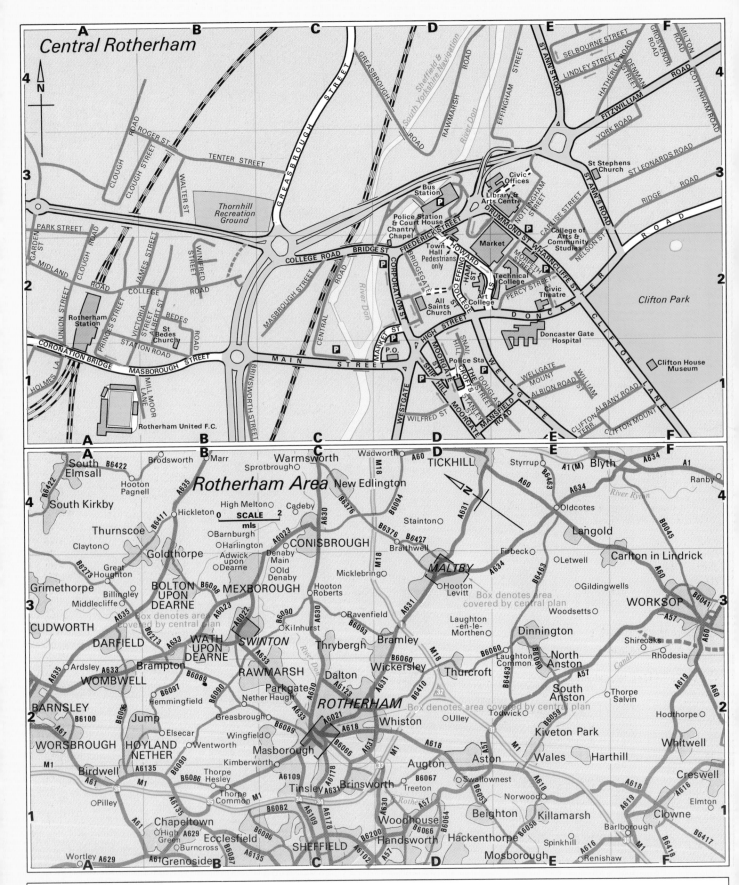

Central Rotherham

Rotherham

Evidence of Rotherham's industry goes back at least as far as the Romans, whose ironworking artefacts have been found here. They were followed by a group of 12th-century monks who established a mining site, and in the 18th century came the beginnings of Rotherham as a major industrial centre with iron smelting on a large scale. Today this is a pleasant town with broad, largely 19th- and 20th-century streets, and offering a pleasant blend of architectural styles. Outstanding in both senses is the large, Norman Perpendicular Church of All Saints with its majestic spire and interior, and another cause for pride is the medieval chapel on Rotherham Bridge. Typical of its time, this is now one of only three perfect examples surviving in the country.

Swinton Rich coal seams beneath the town are chiefly responsible for modern Swinton, but its name is more widely associated with Rockingham pottery which is much sought-after today. Just one kiln from the original pottery remains, and can be seen off the A633 Swinton to High Haugh road.

Maltby's coalfields only began to be worked about half a century ago, and more recent developments give it the feel of a bright modern town. But a pre-coal, pre-industrial Maltby still exists, and can be reached by steps and steep slopes from the main centre.

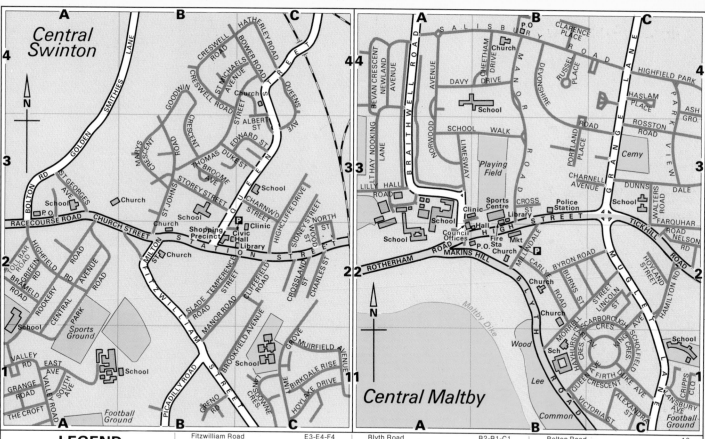

LEGEND

Town Plan

AA Recommended roads	
Other roads	
Restricted roads	
Buildings of interest	Station
Car Parks	**P**
Parks and open spaces	
One Way Streets	→

Area Plan

A roads	
B roads	
Locations	Nutwell ○
Urban area	

Street Index with Grid Reference

Central Rotherham

Albany Road	E1-F1
Albert Street	B1-B2
Albion Road	E1
Bedes Road	B1-B2
Bridge Street	C2-D2
Bridgegate	D2
Brinsworth Street	B1
Carlisle Street	E2-E3
Central Road	C1-C2
Clifton Lane	E2-F2-F1
Clifton Mount	E1-F1
Clifton Terrace	E1
Clough Road	A2, A3-A4-B4
Clough Street	A3-B3
College Road	A2-B2-C2
College Street	D2
Coronation Bridge	A1-A2
Corporation Street	D1-D2
Cottenham Road	F3-F4
Denham Street	F4
Doncaster Road	D2-E2-F2-F3
Douglas Street	D1-E1
Drummond Street	D3-E3-E2
Effingham Street	D2, E3-E4
Fitzwilliam Road	E3-E4-F4
Frederick Street	D2-D3
Garden Street	A2-A3
Greasbrough Road	C4-D4-D3
Greasbrough Street	C3-C4
Grosvenor Road	F4
Hatherley Road	E4-F4
High Street	D1-D2
Holmes Lane	A1
Howard Street	D2-E2-D2
James Street	B2-B3
Lindley Street	E4-F4
Main Street	B1-C1-D1
Mansfield Road	D1-E1
Market Street	D1-D2
Masborough Street	A1-B1
Midland Road	A2
Mill Moor Lane	A1-B1
Milton Road	F4
Moorgate	D1
Moorgate Street	D1-D2
Morpeth Street	E2
Nelson Street	E2-E3
Nottingham Street	E3
Park Street	A3
Percy Street	E2
Princes Street	A1-A2
Rawmarsh Road	D3-D4
Ridge Road	F3
Roger Street	A4-A3-B3
St Ann's Road	E4-E3-F3-F2
St Leonards Road	E3-F3
Selbourne Street	E4-F4
Ship Hill	D1
Snail Hill	D1-D2
Stanley Street	D1
Station Road	A2-A1-B1
Tenter Street	B3-C3
The Crofts	D1
Union Street	A1-A2
Victoria Street	A2-B2
Walter Street	B3
Wellgate	D2-D1-E1
Wellgate Mount	E1
Westgate	D1
Wharncliffe Street	E2
Wilfred Street	D1
William Street	E1
Winifred Street	B2
York Road	E3-F3-F4

Central Maltby

Alexandra Street	C1
Ash Grove	C4
Bevan Crescent	A4
Blyth Road	B2-B1-C1
Braithwell Road	A3-A4
Burns Street	B2
Byron Road	B2-C2
Carlye Road	B2
Charnwell Avenue	B3-C3
Cheetham Drive	B4
Clarence Place	B4-C4
Cripps Close	C1
Cross Street	B3
Davy Drive	A4-B4
Devonshire Road	B4-B3-C3
Duke Avenue	C1
Dunns Dale	C3
Earl Avenue	B2-B1-C1
Farquhar Road	C2-C3
Firth Crescent	B1-C1
Grange Lane	C3-C4
Hamilton Road	C2
Haslam Place	C4
Hayhurst Crescent	B1
High Street	A2-B2-B3-C3
Highfield Park	C4
Hoyland Street	C2
King Avenue	C1-C2
Lansbury Avenue	C1
Limesway	A3
Lilly Hall Road	A3
Lincoln Street	C2
Little Hay Wooking Lane	A3-A4
Makins Hill	A2-B2
Manor Road	B3-B4
Millindale	B2-B3
Morrell Street	B1-B2-C2
Muglet Lane	C1-C2-C3
Nelson Road	C2
Newland Avenue	A4
Norwood Avenue	A3-A4
Park View	C3-C4
Portland Place	B3
Queen Avenue	B1-C1
Rosston Road	C3
Rotherham Road	A2
Russel Place	B4
Salisbury Road	A4-B4-C4
Scarborough Crescent	B1-B2-C2
Scholfield Crescent	C1
School Walk	A3-B3
Tickhill Road	C2-C3
Victoria Street	B1-C1
Walters Road	C3

Central Swinton

Albert Street	C3-C4
Birkdale Rise	C1
Bolton Road	A3
Bower Road	B4-C4
Bramfield Road	A2
Brookfield Avenue	B1-C1-C2
Broome Avenue	B3
Central Avenue	A1-A2
Charles Street	C2
Charnwood Street	C3
Church Street	A3-A2-B2
Cliffefield Road	C2
Creswell Road	B4
Crossland Street	C2
Duke Street	B3-C3
East Avenue	A1
Edward Street	B3-C3
Fitzwilliam Street	B2-B1-C1
Golden Smithies Lane	A3-A4-B4
Goodwin Crescent	B3-B4
Grange Road	A1
Greno Road	B1
Griffin Road	A2
Hatherley Road	B4-C4
Highcliffe Drive	C2-C3
Highfield Road	A2
Hoylake Drive	C1
Landsdowne Crescent	C1
Lime Grove	C1-C2
Manor Road	B1-B2-C2
Marys Crescent	B3
Milton Street	B2
Muirfield Avenue	C1
North Street	C2-C3
Park Road	A1-A2
Picadilly Road	B1
Queen Street	B2-B3-C3-C4
Queens Avenue	C3-C4
Racecourse Road	A2-A3
Rookery Road	A1-A2
St Georges Avenue	A3
St Johns Road	B2-B3
St Michaels Avenue	B4-C4
Sidney Street	C2-C3
Slade Road	B2
South Avenue	A1
Station Road	B2-C2
Storey Street	B3
Temporence Street	B2-C2
The Croft	A1
Thomas Street	B3-B4-C4
Toll Bar Road	A2
Valley Road	A1
Wood Street	C2

ROTHERHAM
Begun in 1483 and used after the Reformation as an almshouse, town prison, plague isolation hospital and tobacconist's shop, the Chapel of Our Lady on Chantry Bridge was restored and rededicated in 1924.

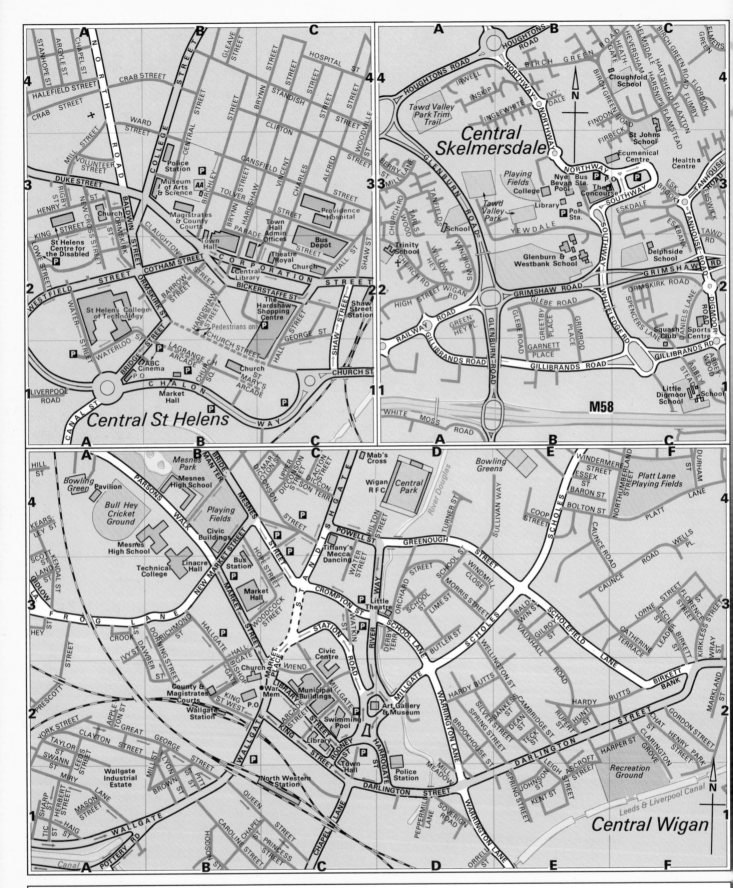

St Helens

Pilkington Glass have been manufacturing glassware here for over 150 years, and today there is a fascinating museum attached to the company's Prescot Road works. A town of fine sporting facilities, St Helens also offers the attractions of its noted Rugby League team and of horse racing at Haydock Park Racecourse, which lies to the north-east of the town.

Wigan is known to millions through George Orwell's book *The Road to Wigan Pier*, but has seen radical changes in recent years. Not least of these has been the development of the area around the Leeds and Liverpool Canal, where the original pier, or wharf, is being turned into a Leisure and Recreation Centre. Several old warehouses have been renovated and a working mill engine is on display, while providing visitors with food and drink is a new pub — the Orwell.

Skelmersdale's once-important coal mining has declined in recent years, but the establishment in the 1960s of a New Town offering all the appropriate facilities has helped to attract new industries. A history dating back to the Romans can be traced here.

Leigh stands on the Leeds and Liverpool Canal. Familiar to Rugby enthusiasts for its Rugby League team, it's also popular with anglers and sailors for 1,000-acre Pennington Flash Country Park.

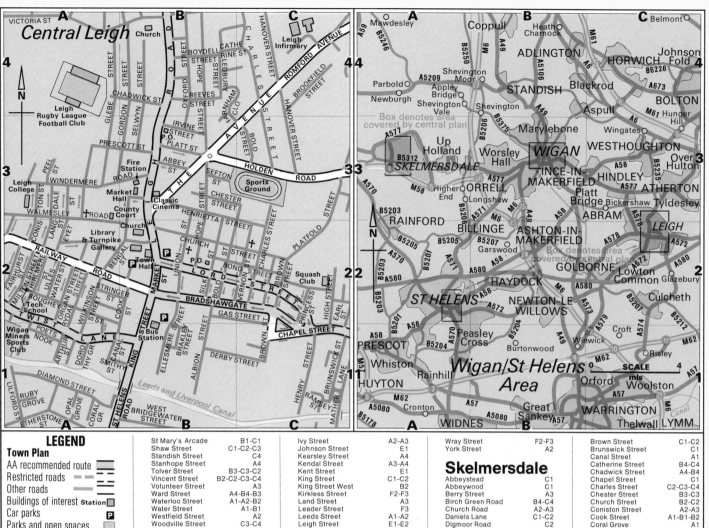

Central Leigh

Wigan/St Helens Area

Street index with Grid Reference

St Helens

Alfred Street	C3-C4
Argyle Street	A4
Baldwin Street	A2-A3
Barrow Street	B2
Bickerstaffe Street	B2-C2
Birchley Street	B2-B3-B4
Bridge Street	A1-B1-B2
Brynn Street	B3-B4-C4
Canal Street	A1
Cansfield Street	B3-C3
Central Street	B3-B4
Chalon Way	A1-B1-C1
Chapel Street	A4
Charles Street	C2-C3-C4
Church Square	B1
Church Street	B2-B1-C1
Claughton Street	A3-B3-B2
Clifton Street	B4-C4-C3
College Street	A3-B3-B4
Corporation Street	B2-C2
Cotham Street	B2
Crab Street	A4-B4
Duke Street	A3-B3
George Street	C1-C2
Gleave Street	B4
Halefield Street	A4
Hall Street	C1-C2-C3
Hardshaw Street	B2-B3-C3-C4
Henry Street	A3
Hospital Street	C4
King Street	A2-A3
Lagrange Arcade	A4
Liverpool Road	A1
Mill Street	A3-A4
New Cross Street	A2-A3
North Road	A3-A4
Ormskirk Street	A3-A2-B2
Parade Street	B3-B2-C2
Rigby Street	A3

St Mary's Arcade	B1-C1
Shaw Street	C1-C2-C3
Standish Street	C4
Stanhope Street	A4
Tolver Street	B3-C3-C2
Vincent Street	B2-C2-C3-C4
Volunteer Street	A3
Ward Street	A4-B4-B3
Waterloo Street	A1-A2-B2
Water Street	A1-B1
Westfield Street	A2
Woodville Street	C3-C4

Wigan

Acton Street	C4
Appleton Street	A2
Arcade Street	C2
Ascroft Street	E1-E2
Baldwin Street	E3
Bankes Street	D2-E2
Baron Street	E4
Birkett Bank	F2
Birkett Street	F2-F3
Bishop Gate	B2
Bolton Street	E4
Brideman Terrace	B4
Brookhouse Street	D1-D2
Brown Street	B1-B2
Butler Street	D3
Cambridge Street	E2
Caroline Street	B1
Catherine Terrace	F3
Caunce Road	E4-E3-F3-F4
Cecil Street	F3
Chapel Lane	C1
Chapel Street	B1-C1
Chat Street	F2
Clarington Grove	F1-F2
Clayton Street	A2-B2
Coop Street	E4
Crompton Street	C3
Crook Street	A3
Darlington Street	C1-D1-E1-E2-F2
Dawber Street	A3-A2-B2
Dean Street	E2
Derby Terrace	D3
Dicconson Street	B4-C4
Dicconson Terrace	C4
Dorning Street	B2-B3
Durham Street	F4
Essex Street	E4
Florence Street	F3
Frog Lane	A3-B3
Gidlow Lane	A3
Gilroy Street	E3
Gordon Street	F2
Great George Street	A2-B2-B1
Greenough Street	D4-D3-E3
Haig Street	A1
Hallgate	B2-B3
Hardy Butts	D2-E2-F2
Harper Street	C2-F2
Harrogate Street	C2-D2-D1
Henry Park Street	F1-F2
Herbert Street	A1
Hey Street	A3
Hill Street	A4
Hilton Street	C4-D4
Hodson Street	B1
Hope Street	B4-B3-C3
Hunt Street	E2

Ivy Street	A2-A3
Johnson Street	E1
Kearsley Street	A4
Kendal Street	A3-A4
Kent Street	E1
King Street	C1-C2
King Street West	B2
Kirkless Street	F2-F3
Land Street	A3
Leader Street	F3
Leeds Street	A1-A2
Leigh Street	E1-E2
Library Street	C2
Lime Street	D3
Lorne Street	E3-F3
Lyon Street	B1-B2
Market Place	C2-C3
Market Street	B3-C3-C2
Markland Street	F2
Marton Street	C4
Mason Street	A1
Mesnes Street	B4-C4-C3
Millgate	C2-D2
Mill Meadow	D1-D2
Mill Street	B1-B2
Miry Lane	A1
Morris Street	D3
New Market Street	B3-B4
Northumberland Street	F4
Orchard Street	D3
Orrell Street	D1
Parsons Walk	A4-B4-B3
Peppermill Lane	D1
Pitt Street	B1
Platt Lane	F4
Prescott Street	A2-A3
Princess Street	B1-C1
Pottery Road	A1-B1
Powell Street	C4
Queen Street	B1-C1
Richmond Street	B3
River Way	D2-C2-C3-C4-D4
Rodney Street	C2
Rupert Street	E2
Scholes	D2-D3-E3-E4
Scholefield Lane	E3-E2-F2
School Lane	D2-D3
School Street	D3-D4
Scott Street	A3-A4
Sharp Street	A1
Silver Street	D2-E2
Soverign Road	D1
Spring Street	D2-E2-E1
Standishgate	C3-C4
Station Road	C2-C3
Sullivan Way	D4-E4
Swann Street	A1-A2
Taylor Street	E2
Teck Street	E2
Tic Street	A1
Turner Street	D4
Upper Dicconson Street	C4
Vauxhall Road	E2-E3
Wallgate	A1-B1-B2-C2
Warrington Lane	D2-D1-E1
Water Street	C3-C4
Watkin Street	C3
Wellington Street	D3-D2-E2
Wells Place	F4
Wiend	C2
Windermere Street	E4-F4
Windmill Close	D3
Woodcock Street	B3-C3

Wray Street	F2-F3
York Street	A2

Skelmersdale

Abbeystead	C1
Abbeywood	C1
Berry Street	C2
Birch Green Road	B4-C4
Church Road	A2-A3
Daniels Lane	C1-C2
Digmoor Road	C2
Elmers Green	C4
Elswick	C3
Eskbrook	C3
Eskbank	C2-C3
Eskdale	C2-C3
Findon	B4-C4
Firbeck	B3-C3-C4
Flamstead	C3-C4
Flaxton	C4
Flimby	C4
Flordon	C4
Garnett Place	B1
Gillibrands Road	A2-A1-B1-C1
Glebe Road	B1-B2
Glenburn Road	A1-B1-B2-A2-A3-A4
Greenhey Place	A2
Greetby Place	B1-B2
Grimrod Place	B1-B2
Grimshaw Road	B2-C2
Harsnips	C4
Hartshead	C4
Heathbrook	B4-C4
Helmsdale	C4
Heversham	C4
High Street	A2
Houghtons Road	A4-B4
Inglewhite	A4-B4
Inskip	A4-B4
Irwell	A4-B4
Ivydale	B4
Mill Lane	A3
Northway	B4-B3-C3
Ormskirk Road	C2
Railway Road	A1-A2
Southway	B2-B3-C3
Spencers Lane	C1-C2
Tanfields	A3
Tanhouse Road	C2-C3
Tarlswood	A2-A3
Tawd Road	C2
White Ledge Road	B2-C2-C3
White Moss Road	A1
Wigan Road	A2
Willow Hey	A2
Windrows	A2
Yewdale	A3-A2-B2-B3

Leigh

Abbey Street	B3
Albion Street	B1-B2
Arthur Street	A1
Bengal Street	A2-B2
Bold Street	B2-C2-B3
Bond Street	B2-C2
Boughey Street	A2
Boydell Street	B4
Bradshawgate	B2-C2
Brakley Street	B1
Brookfield Street	C4

Brown Street	C1-C2
Brunswick Street	C1
Canal Street	A1
Catherine Street	B4-C4
Chadwick Street	A4-B4
Chapel Street	C1
Charles Street	C2-C3-C4
Chester Street	B3-C3
Church Street	B2-C2
Coniston Street	A2-A3
Cook Street	A1-B1-B2
Coral Grove	A1
Derby Street	B1-C1
Diamond Street	A1
Dorothy Grove	A1
Earl Street	C1-C2
Ellesmere Street	B1-B2
Etherstone	A1
Eyet Street	A2-A3
Fairhurst Street	A2
Farnham Close	B3-B4-C4-B4
Gas Streets	B2-C2-C1
Glebe Street	A3-A4
Gordon Street	A3-B3-B4
Hanover Street	C3-C4
Henrietta Street	B3-C3-C2
Henry Street	C1
High Street	C1-C2
Holden Road	B3-C3
Hope Street	B2-B3-B4
Irvine Street	B3
King Street	B1-B2
Langdale Street	A2-A3
Ledbury Street	B4
Leigh Road	B2-B3-B4
Lilford Street	A1
Lord Street	B2-C2
Market Street	B2
Mather Lane	C1
Milton Street	B4
Opal Grove	A1
Organ Street	A1
Oxford Street	B3-B4
Peel Street	A3
Platfold Street	C2-C3
Platt Street	B3
Poets Nook	A1
Prescott Street	A3-B3
Princess Street	C2
Railway Road	A2-B2
Ramsey Street	C1
Reeves Street	B4
Romford Avenue	C4
Ruby Grove	A1
Rydal Street	A1-A2
St Helens Road	A1-B1
Sefton Street	B3
Selwyn Street	B3-B4
Silk Street	B2
Smithy Street	A1-B1
Stringer Street	A2-B2
The Avenue	B3-C3-C4
Thirlmere Street	A2
Twist Lane	A2-A1-B1
Ulleswater Street	A1
Union Street	B2-B3
Vernon Street	B2-C2
Victoria Street	A4
Walmesley Road	A3-A2-B2
West Bridgewater Street	A1-B1
Wilkinson Street	A1-A2
Windermere Road	A3-B3

61

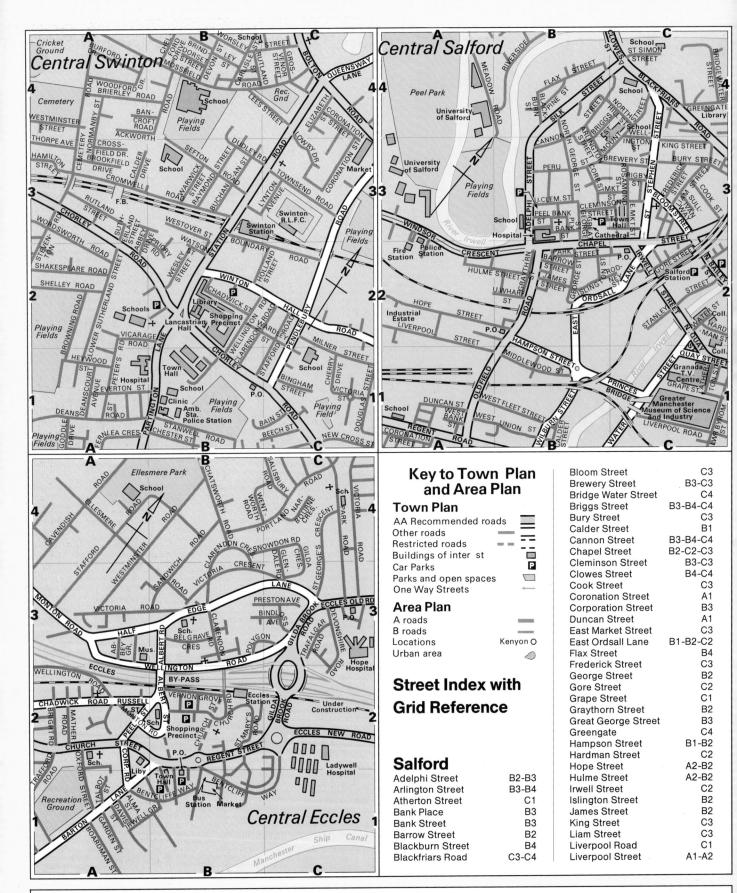

Key to Town Plan and Area Plan

Town Plan
AA Recommended roads
Other roads
Restricted roads
Buildings of inter st
Car Parks
Parks and open spaces
One Way Streets

Area Plan
A roads
B roads
Locations   Kenyon ○
Urban area

Street Index with Grid Reference

Salford
Adelphi Street	B2-B3
Arlington Street	B3-B4
Atherton Street	C1
Bank Place	B3
Bank Street	B3
Barrow Street	B2
Blackburn Street	B4
Blackfriars Road	C3-C4

Bloom Street	C3
Brewery Street	B3-C3
Bridge Water Street	C4
Briggs Street	B3-B4-C4
Bury Street	C3
Calder Street	B1
Cannon Street	B3-B4-C4
Chapel Street	B2-C2-C3
Cleminson Street	B3-C3
Clowes Street	B4-C4
Cook Street	C3
Coronation Street	A1
Corporation Street	B3
Duncan Street	A1
East Market Street	C3
East Ordsall Lane	B1-B2-C2
Flax Street	B4
Frederick Street	C3
George Street	B2
Gore Street	C2
Grape Street	C1
Graythorn Street	B2
Great George Street	B3
Greengate	C4
Hampson Street	B1-B2
Hardman Street	C2
Hope Street	A2-B2
Hulme Street	A2-B2
Irwell Street	C2
Islington Street	B2
James Street	B2
King Street	C3
Liam Street	C3
Liverpool Road	C1
Liverpool Street	A1-A2

Salford

Salford exploded into phenomenal growth with the Industrial Revolution — it was one of the fastest expanding places in the country, with vast areas of mills and poor quality housing. Much of this old Salford has disappeared, and the city now offers an interesting and lively blend of the industrial, commercial, rural and even maritime. It also boasts a fine university, and has been recorded for posterity in the paintings of L. S. Lowry, who knew it well. The Museum and Art Gallery has a collection of his work, and also of interest here is a Victorian street reconstruction. The Museum of Mining has two reproduction coalmines, and recalling a far older Salford is timber-framed Ordsall Hall's museum.

Swinton is said to owe its name to the unglamourous occupation of rearing pigs, but its more recent background is coal. An industrial area and residential district of Manchester, it has its own Civic Centre and a shopping precinct flanked by the attractive Victorian church of St Peter.

Eccles cakes first came from a shop in Church Street, where they are still being made to the original recipe. A busy area squeezed between the Manchester Ship Canal and the M62, this was once a group of medieval villages. Monk's Hall is Tudor and houses a museum. The Church of St Mary the Virgin dates from the 12th century.

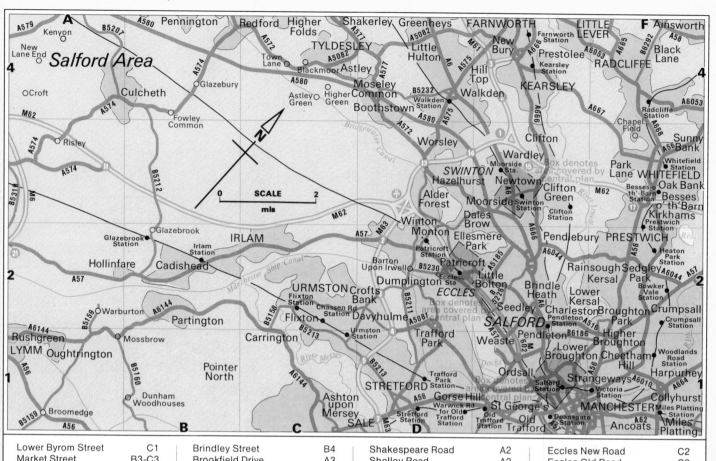

Lower Byrom Street	C1	Brindley Street	B4	Shakespeare Road	A2	Eccles New Road	C2
Market Street	B3-C3	Brookfield Drive	A3	Shelley Road	A2	Eccles Old Road	C3
Meadow Road	A4-B4	Browning Road	A1-A2	Stafford Road	B1-C1-C2	Ellesmere Road	A4-A3-B3
Middlewood Street	B1	Buchanan Street	B3	Stanwell Road	B1	Garden Street	A1
Mount Street	B3-C3-C4	Burford Drive	A4	Station Road	B2-B3-C3-C4	Gilda Brook Road	C2-C3
North Bailey Street	C2	Calder Drive	A3	Steventon Road	A2-A3	Gilda Crescent	C3-C4
North George Street	B3-B4	Carlisle Street	B4	Sutherland Street	A3	Glendale Road	C3-C4
North Hill Street	B4-C4	Cemetery Road	A3-A4	Thorpe Avenue	A3	Half Edge Lane	A3-B3-C3
North Quay Street	C1-C2	Chadwick Street	B2	Townsend Road	C3	Irwell Grove	A1-B1
Oldfield Road	A1-B1-B2	Chelford Drive	B4	Vicarage Road	A2-B2	Mather Road	A2
Park Street	B2-C2	Cherry Drive	C1	Victoria Street	C1	Monton Road	A3
Peel Street	B3	Chester Street	B1	Wardley Street	B2-C2	Monton Road	A2-B2
Peru Street	B3	Chorley Road	A3-A2-B2-B1-C1	Warwick Street	B3	Narbourne Crescent	C4
Pine Street	B4	Clarendon Road	B1-B2-C2	Watson Street	B2	Oxford Street	A1-A2
Princes Bridge	B1-C1	Coronation Street	C3-C4	Wellington Road	B1-B2	Park Road	C3-C4
Quay Street	C1	Cromwell Road	A3-B3	Wesley Street	B2	Peel Street	A2
Regent Road	A1-B1	Crossfield Drive	A3	Westminster Street	A4	Polygon	B3-C3
Rigby Street	C3	Deanscourt Avenue	A1	Westover Street	B2-B3	Portland Road	B4-C4
Riverside	B4	Deans Road	A1	Winton Hall Road	B2-C2	Preston Avenue	B3-C3
Rodney Street	B2-C2	Devon Street	B4	Woodford Drive	A4	Regent Street	B2
Rosamond Street	C3	Dorset Street	B4	Wordsworth Road	A2-A3	Russel Street	A2
St Simon Street	C4	Douglas Street	C1	Worsley Street	B4-C4	St George's Crescent	C3-C4
St Stephen Street	C3-C4	Dudley Road	B4-B3-C3			St Mary's Road	B2
Silk Street	B4-C4	Elizabeth Street	C4			Salisbury Road	C4
Stanley Street	C2	Everton Street	A1-B1	**Eccles**		Sandwich Road	B3-B4
Sullivan Way	C3	Fernlea Crescent	A1	Abbey Grove	A3	Snowdon Road	B4-C4
Upper Cleminson Street	B3	Goddle Drive	A1	Albert Road	B3	Stafford Road	A3-A4-B4
Upper Wharf Street	B2	Grosvenor Street	C4	Albert Street	B2	Talbot Street	A1
Water Street	B1-C1-C2	Hamilton Street	A3	Alma Street	A1	Trafalgar Road	C3
Wellington Street	C3-C4	Heywood Street	B2	Barton Lane	A1-A2-B2	Trafford Road	A1-A2
West Bank Street	A1	Holland Street	B2-C2	Belgrave Crescent	B3	Vernon Grove	B2
West Fleet Street	A1-B1	Lees Street	B4-C4	Bentcliffe Way		Victoria Crescent	B3-C3
West Union Street	A1-B1	Lower Sutherland Street	A1-A2	A1-B1-B2-B1-C1-C2		Victoria Road	A3-B3
Wilburn Street	B1	Lowry Drive	C3-C4	Bindloss Avenue	B3-C3	Victoria Road	C3-C4
Windsor Crescent	A3-A2-B2	Lynton Avenue	B3-C3	Boardman Street	A1	Wellington Road	A2-A3
		Milner Street	C1-C2	Bright Road	A2	Wellington Road	
		Mossfield Road	A4-B4-C4	Cavendish Road	A3-A4	A3-A2-B2-B3-C3	
Swinton		New Cross Street	C1	Chadwick Road	A2	Wentworth Road	B4-C4
Abbey Drive	A2-A3-B3	Normanby Street	A3-A4	Chatsworth Road	B4	Westminster Road	A3-A4-B4
Ackworth Road	A4-B4	Partington Lane	A1-B1-B2	Church Road	B2		
Bain Street	B1-C1	Pendlebury Road	C1-C2-C3	Church Street	A2-B2		
Bancroft Road	A4-B4	Priory Road	A3-B3-B2	Clarendon Crescent	B3-B4-B3		
Beech Street	B1-C1	Queensway Lane	C4	Clarendon Road	B3		
Bingham Street	C1	Raymond Street	B3	Corporation Road	A1-A2		
Bolton Road	C4	Rutland Street	B4-C4	Davis Street	A1		
Boundary Road	B3-B2-C2	Rutland Street	A3	Devonshire Road	C2-C3		
Brierley Road	A4-B4	St Peter's Road	A1-A2	Eccles By-pass	A3-A2-B2-C2		
		Sefton Road	B3-B4				

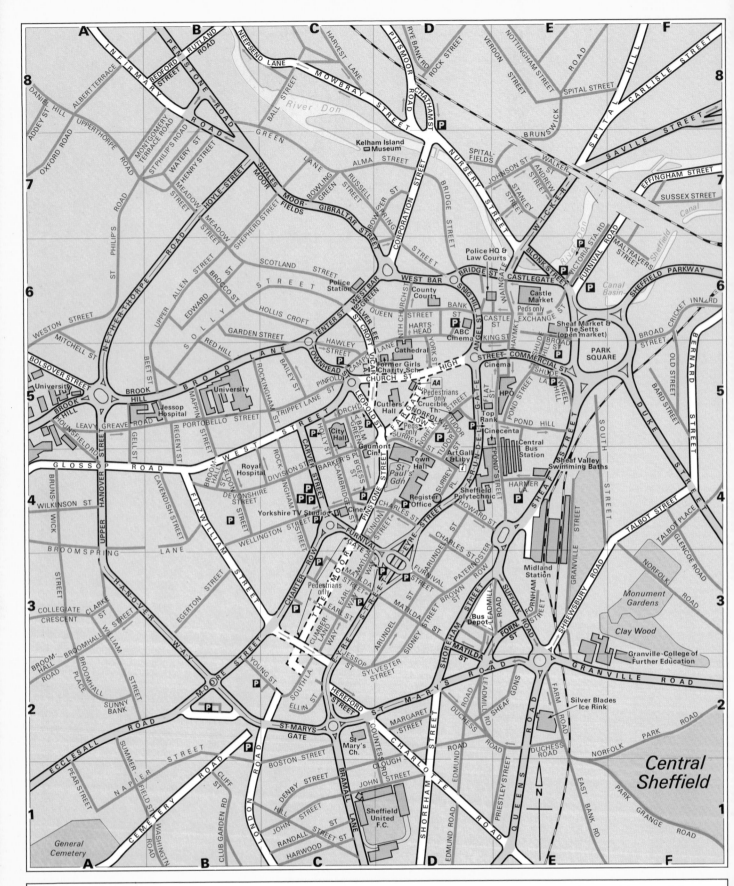

Sheffield

Cutlery – which has made the name of Sheffield famous throughout the world – has been manufactured here since at least as early as the time of Chaucer. The god of blacksmiths, Vulcan, is the symbol of the city's industry, and he crowns the town hall, which was opened in 1897 by Queen Victoria. At the centre of the industry, however, is Cutlers' Hall, the headquarters of the Company of Cutlers. This society was founded in 1624 and has the right to grant trade marks to articles of a sufficiently high standard. In the hall is the company's collection of silver, with examples of craftsmanship dating back every year to 1773. A really large collection of cutlery is kept in the city museum. Steel production, a vital component of the industry, was greatly improved when the crucible process was invented here in 1740. At Abbeydale Industrial Hamlet, 3½ miles south-west of the city centre, is a complete restored site open as a museum and showing 18th-century methods of steel production. Sheffield's centre, transformed since World War II, is one of the finest and most modern in Europe. There are no soot-grimed industrial eyesores here, for the city has stringent pollution controls and its buildings are carefully planned and set within excellent landscaping projects. Many parks are set in and around the city, and the Pennines are within easy reach.

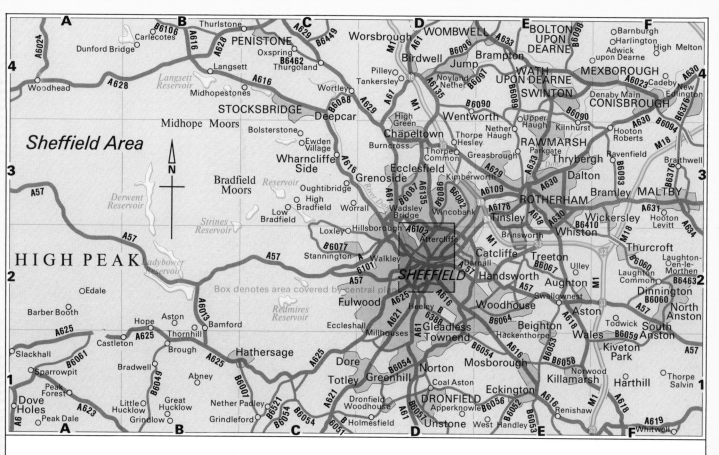

LEGEND

Town Plan
AA Recommended roads
Other roads
Restricted roads
Buildings of interest
One Way Streets
Car Parks   P
Parks and open spaces

Area Plan
A roads
B roads
Locations   Oakworth O
Urban area

Street Index with grid reference

Sheffield

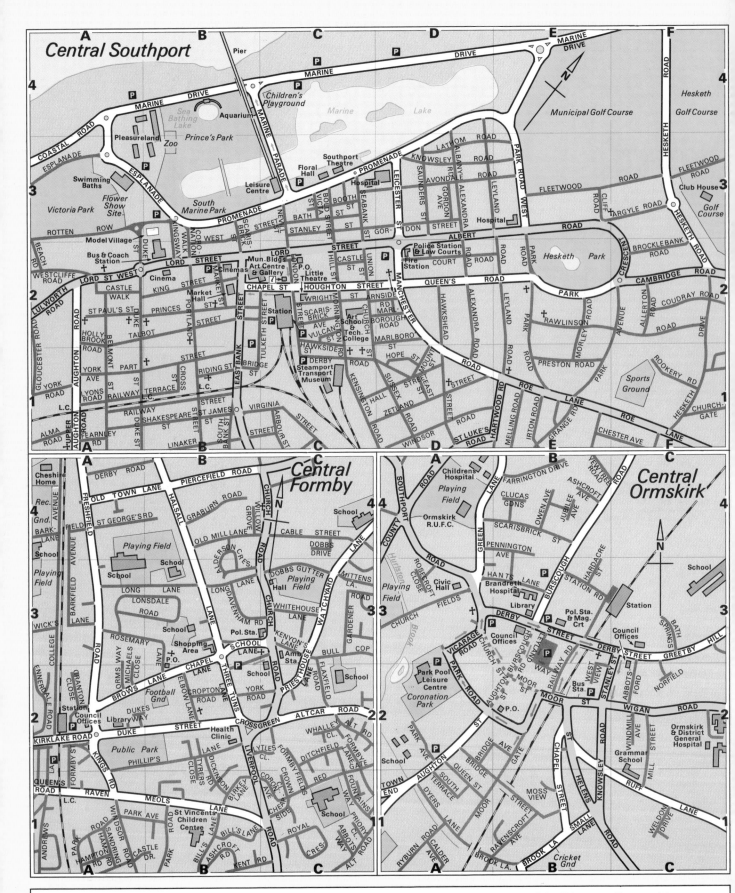

Southport

Seven miles of firm beaches and a ¾-mile long pier are just two of the attractions of Southport, which has been a popular resort since the 18th century. The elegant Victorian buildings of Lord Street run parallel with the Promenade, designated a conservation area, and in Lord Street itself, Atkinson Gallery houses a collection of 19th- and 20th-century art. The town also enjoys the distinction of having its own Botanic Gardens, and here the exhibits of the Botanic Gardens Museum include a collection of 18th- and 19th-century china. By way of contrast, Southport also offers the delights of such different areas of interest as the Steam Transport Museum, a model village and a model railway. Also to be seen are the birds and animals of Southport Zoo, which stretches over 1½ acres of land.

Formby people were farmers and seafarers right up until the 19th century. Unsuccessful attempts were made then to turn the town into a resort, and the National Trust now controls some 400 acres of the foreshore and sand dunes that lie to the west.

Ormskirk Granted a Royal Charter in 1670, Ormskirk's market has been the focal point of the town ever since. Standing at the junction of two trunk roads, this is still very much a market town, even though it has seen expansion in its industries and its residential areas.

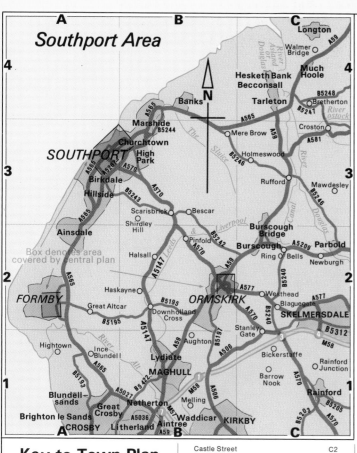

Southport Area

Longton
Walmer Bridge
Hesketh Bank
Becconsall
Much Hoole
Tarleton
Bretherton
Banks
Croston
Marshside
Churchtown
High Park
SOUTHPORT
Birkdale
Hillside
Mere Brow
Holmeswood
Rufford
Mawdesley
Scarisbrick
Bescar
Shirdley Hill
Ainsdale
Burscough Bridge
Burscough
Parbold
Newburgh
Ring O' Bells
Halsall
Pinfold
FORMBY
Haskayne
Great Altcar
Downholland Cross
ORMSKIRK
Westhead
Blaguegate
SKELMERSDALE
Hightown
Ince Blundell
Aughton
Stanley Gate
Bickerstaffe
Rainford Junction
Lydiate
MAGHULL
Barrow Nook
Rainford
Blundellsands
Netherton
Melling
Brighton le Sands
Great Crosby
Waddicar
KIRKBY
CROSBY
Litherland
Aintree

Box denotes area covered by central plan

Key to Town Plan and Area Plan

Town Plan
AA Recommended roads
Other roads
Restricted roads
Buildings of inter   University
Car Parks
Parks and open spaces
One Way Streets

Area Plan
A roads
B roads
Locations   Brasted ○
Urban area

Street Index with Grid Reference

Southport

Albany Road	D3-D4
Albert Road	D2-D3-E3
Alexandra Road	D1-D2-D3
Allerton Road	F2
Alma Road	A1
Arbour Street	C1
Argyle Road	E3-F3
Arnside Road	C2-D2
Aughton Road	A1-A2
Avondale Road	D3-E3
Bath Street	C3
Beach Road	A2-A3
Belmont Street	A1-A2
Bold Street	C2-C3
Booth Street	C3
Bridge Street	B1
Brocklebank Road	F2
Cambridge Road	F2
Castle Street	C2
Castle Walk	A2
Chapel Street	B2-C2
Chester Avenue	E1-F1
Churchgate	F1
Church Street	C1-C2
Cliff Road	E3
Coastal Road	A3-A4
Coronation Walk	B2-B3
Coudray Road	F2
Court Road	D2-E2
Cross Street	B1
Derby Road	C1
Duke Street	A1-A2-A3
East Street	D1
Eastbank Street	B1-B2
Esplanade	A3-B3
Fearnley Road	A1
Fleetwood Road	E3-F3
Gloucester Road	A1-A2
Gordon Avenue	D3
Gordon Street	C3-D3
Grange Road	E1
Hall Street	C1-D1
Hartwood Road	D1-E1
Hawkshead Street	D1-D2
Hawkside Street	C1-C2
Hesketh Drive	F1-F2
Hesketh Road	F2-F3-F4
Hill Street	C2
Hollybrook Road	A2
Hope Street	D1
Houghton Street	C2-D2
Irton Road	E1
Kensington Road	C1-D1
King Street	A2-B2
Kingsway	B2-B3
Knowsley Road	D3-E3
Lathom Road	D3-E3
Leicester Street	D3
Leyland Road	D4-D3-E3-E2-E1
Linaker Street	B1-C1
London Street	C1-C2
Lord Street	B2-C2-D2
Lord Street West	A2
Lulworth Road	A2
Lyons Road	A1
Manchester Road	D2-D1-E1
Marine Drive	A4-B4-C4-D4-E4-F4
Marine Parade	B4-C4-C3
Market Street	B2
Marlborough Road	C2-D2
Marlborough Street	C2-D2
Melling Road	E1

Morley Road	E1-E2
Mornington Road	C1-C2
Mount Street	D1
Nevill Street	C2-C3
Park Avenue	E1-E2-F2
Park Crescent	E2-F2-F3-E3
Park Road	E1-E2-E3
Park Road West	E3-E4
Part Street	A1-B1
Portland Street	B1-B2
Preston Road	E1
Princes Street	A2-B2
Promenade	B3-C3-D3-D4-E4
Queen's Road	D2-E2
Railway Street	A1-B1
Railway Terrace	A1-B1
Rawlinson Road	E2-F2
Riding Street	B1
Roe Lane	E1-F1
Rookery Road	F1
Rotten Row	A3
St James Street	B1
St Luke's Road	D1
St Paul's Street	A2
Saunders Street	D3
Scarisbrick Avenue	C2
Scarisbrick Street	B2-B3
Seabank Road	C2-C3
Shakespeare Street	A1-B1
South Bank Street	B1
Stanley Street	C3
Sussex Road	C1-D1
Talbot Street	A2-B2
Tulketh Street	B1-B2-C2
Union Street	C3
Upper Aughton Road	A1
Victa Street	C3
Virginia Street	B1-C1
Vulcan Street	C2
Westcliffe Road	A2
West Street	B2-B3-C3
Windsor Road	D1
Wright Street	C2
York Avenue	A1
York Road	A1
Zetland Street	C1-D1

Park Road	A1-B1
Phillip's Lane	A1-A2-B2
Piercefield Road	B4
Priesthouse Lane	C2-C3
Priory Close	C1
Queen's Road	A1
Raven Meols Lane	A1-B1-C1
Red Gate	C1-C2
Rosemary Lane	A3-B3-B2
Royal Crescent	C1
St George's Road	A4-B4
Sandringham Road	A1
School Lane	B3-C3
Three Tuns Lane	B2-B3
Tyrers Close	B1-B2
Watchyard Lane	C3-C4
Whalley Close	C2
Whitehouse Lane	C3
Wick's Lane	A3
Willow Grove	B4
Windsor Road	A1
York Road	B2-C2

Ormskirk

Abbotsford	C2-C3
Ashcroft Avenue	B4
Aughton Street	A1-A2-B2
Bath Springs	C3
Bridge Avenue	A2-B2
Bridge Street	A2-A1-B1
Brook Lane	A1-B1
Burscough Road	B3-B4-C4
Burscough Street	B2-B3-B4
Calder Avenue	A1
Chapel Street	B1-B2
Church Fields	A3
Church Street	A3-B3-B2
Clucas Gardens	B4
County Road	A3-A4
Derby Street	A3-B3-C3
Dyers Lane	A1
Farrington Drive	B4
Green Lane	A3-A4-B4
Greetby Hill	C3
Hants Lane	A3-B3
Hardacre Street	B3
Jubilee Avenue	B4
Knowsley Road	B1-B2
Leyland Way	B2-B3
Mill Street	C1-C2
Moor Gate	A1-B1-B2
Moor Street	B2
Moss View	B1
Norfield	C2-C3
Owen Avenue	B4
Park Avenue	A2
Park Road	A2-A3
Pennington Avenue	A4-B4
Queen Street	A1-A2
Railway Road	B2-B3
Ravenscroft Avenue	B1
Rosecroft Close	A3
Ruff Lane	B2-B1-C1
Ryburn Road	A1
St Helens Road	B2-B1-C1
Scarisbrick Street	A4-B4
Small Lane	B1
Southport Road	A3-A4
South Terrace	C1
Stanley Street	B2-C2-C3
Station Road	B3
Town End	A1
Vicarage Road	A3
Weldon Drive	C1
West View	B2
Wigan Road	B2-C2
Windmill Avenue	C2
Yew Tree Road	B4-C4

Formby

Abbots Way	C1
Alderson Crescent	B3-B4
Alt Road	C1-C2
Altcar Road	C2
Andrews Lane	A1-A2
Ashcroft Road	B1
Barkfield Avenue	A3-A4
Barkfield Lane	A4
Bill's Lane	B1-C1
Birkey Lane	B1
Brows Lane	A2-B2
Bull Cop	C3
Cable Street	C4
Castle Drive	A1-B1
Chapel Lane	B2-B3
Cheapside	C1
Church Road	C2-C3-B3-B4-C4
College Avenue	A2-A3-A4
Coronation Avenue	B1-C1
Cropton Road	B2
Crossgreen	B2-C2
Crown Close	C1
Davenham Road	B3-C3
Derby Road	A4-B4
Dickinson Road	B1-B2
Ditchfield	C2
Dobbs Drive	C4
Dobbs Gutter	C3
Duke Street	A2-B2
Dukes Way	A2
Elbow Lane	B2
Ennerdale Road	A2
Flaxfield Road	C2-C3
Formby Fields	C1-C2
Formby Lane	C2
Formby Street	A1-A2
Fountains Way	C1
Freshfield Road	A2-A3-A4
Gardener Road	C3
Graburn Road	B4
Granton Close	A2
Halsall Lane	B3-B4
Hampton Road	A1
Kent Road	B1-C1
Kenyon's Lane	C3
Kings Road	A1-A2
Kirklake Road	A2
Liverpool Road	B2-B1-C1
Long Lane	A3-B3
Lonsdale Road	A3-B3
Lytles Close	B2-C2
Michaels Close	A2-A3
Mittens Lane	C3
Old Mill Lane	B4
Old Town Lane	A4-B4
Orms Way	A2-A3
Park Avenue	A1-B1

SOUTHPORT
Retreating seas and a growing expanse of sands inspired the creation in the late 19th century of the 86-acre Marine Lake — a boating lake spanned by Princes Park Bridge and flanked by attractive gardens.

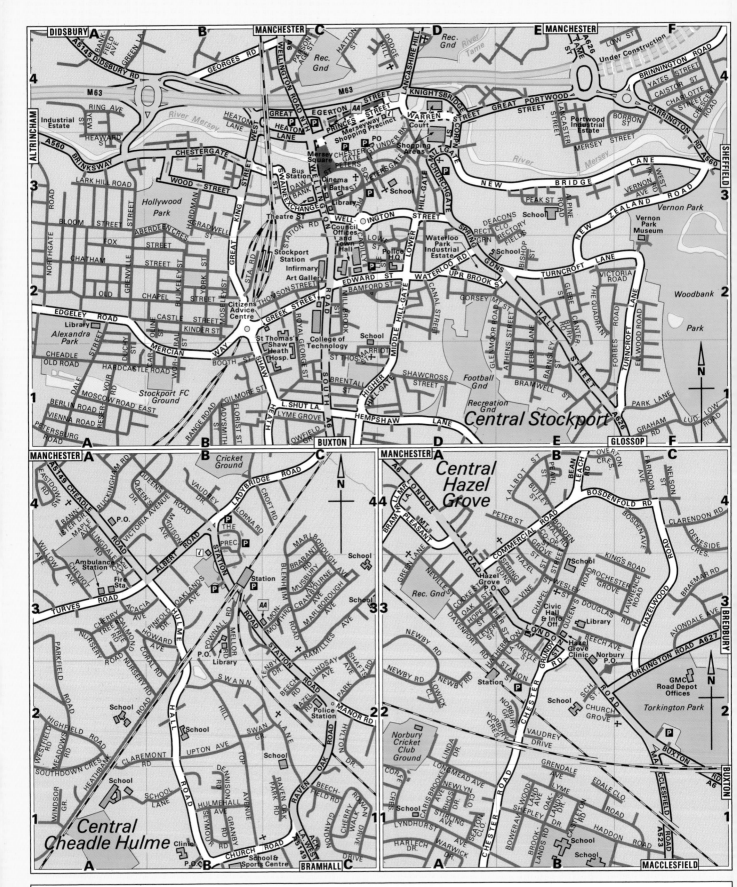

Stockport

The cafes, bandstand and open air travelators of the Merseyway Shopping Precinct stand in direct contrast with the narrow cobbled streets that run close to Stockport's old established traditional market, and the lively mixture must have contributed to making the town the popular destination for shoppers that it is today. Standing on the River Mersey, this was once a

textile town, and today its good road and rail connections with the rest of the country have helped to keep it busy in its new role as commercial and industrial centre. It has a museum at Vernon Park and professional football is provided by Stockport County, currently in the Fourth Division of the Canon League.

Cheadle Hulme has become a popular place to live, with its good facilities for shopping and for recreation. It can also boast the lovely

Bramhall Hall among its places of interest: this black and white half-timbered mansion dates from the 14th century and lies to the south-east in a pleasantly landscaped park.

Hazel Grove is a relatively new name for this settlement. In its old days as a village, it was called simply Bullock Smithy, and only switched to the less earthy Hazel Grove in the mid-19th century. Today it can offer a wide variety of water sports at extensive Torkington Park.

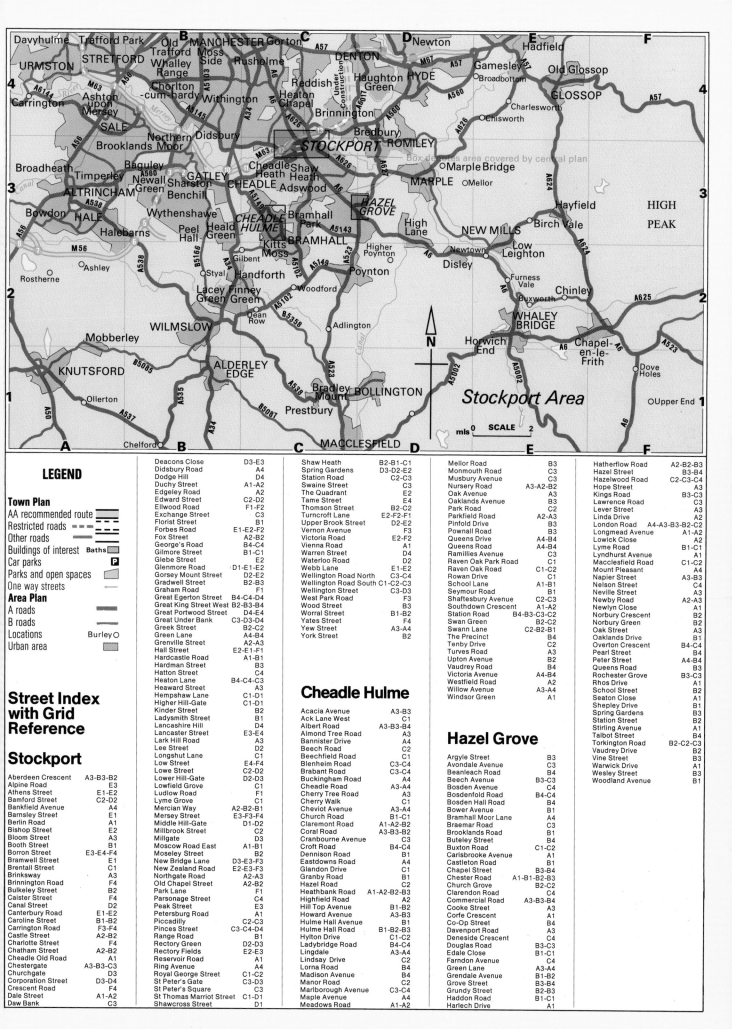

LEGEND

Town Plan
AA recommended route
Restricted roads
Other roads
Buildings of interest — Baths
Car parks — P
Parks and open spaces
One way streets

Area Plan
A roads
B roads
Locations — Burley O
Urban area

Street Index with Grid Reference

Stockport

Street	Grid
Aberdeen Crescent	A3-B3-B2
Alpine Road	E3
Athens Street	E1-E2
Bamford Street	C2-D2
Bankfield Avenue	A4
Barnsley Street	E1
Berlin Road	A1
Bishop Street	E2
Bloom Street	A3
Booth Street	B1
Borron Street	E3-E4-F4
Bramwell Street	E1
Brentall Street	C1
Brinksway	A3
Brinnington Road	F4
Bulkeley Street	B2
Caister Street	F4
Canal Street	D2
Canterbury Road	E1-E2
Caroline Street	B1-B2
Carrington Road	F3-F4
Castle Street	A2-B2
Charlotte Street	F4
Chatham Street	A2-B2
Cheadle Old Road	A1
Chestergate	A3-B3-C3
Churchgate	D3
Corporation Street	D3-D4
Crescent Road	C1
Dale Street	A1-A2
Daw Bank	C3
Deacons Close	D3-E3
Didsbury Road	A4
Dodge Hill	D4
Duchy Street	A1-A2
Edgeley Road	A2
Edward Street	C2-D2
Ellwood Road	F1-F2
Exchange Street	C3
Florist Street	B1
Forbes Road	E1-E2-F2
Fox Street	A2-B2
George's Road	B4-C4
Gilmore Street	B1-C1
Glebe Street	E2
Glenmore Road	D1-E1-F1
Gorsey Mount Street	D2-E2
Gradwell Street	B2-B3
Graham Road	F1
Great Egerton Street	B4-C4-D4
Great King Street West	B2-B3-B4
Great Portwood Street	D4-E4
Great Under Bank	C3-D3-D4
Greek Street	B2-C2
Green Lane	A4-B4
Grenville Street	A2-A3
Hall Street	E2-E1-F1
Hardcastle Road	A1-B1
Hardman Street	B3
Hatton Street	C4
Heaton Lane	B4-C4-C3
Heaward Street	A3
Hempshaw Lane	C1-D1
Higher Hill-Gate	C1-D1
Kinder Street	B2
Ladysmith Street	B1
Lancashire Hill	D4
Lancaster Street	E3-E4
Lark Hill Road	A3
Lee Street	D2
Longshut Lane	C1
Low Street	E4-F4
Lowe Street	C2-D2
Lower Hill-Gate	D2-D3
Lowfield Grove	C1
Ludlow Road	F1
Lyme Grove	C1
Mercian Way	A2-B2-B1
Mersey Street	E3-F3-F4
Middle Hill-Gate	D1-D2
Millbrook Street	C2
Millgate	D3
Moscow Road East	A1-B1
Moseley Street	B2
New Bridge Lane	D3-E3-F3
New Zealand Road	E2-E3-F3
Northgate Road	A2-A3
Old Chapel Street	A2-B2
Park Lane	F1
Parsonage Street	C4
Peak Street	E3
Petersburg Road	A1
Piccadilly	C2-C3
Pinces Street	C3-C4-D4
Range Road	B1
Rectory Green	D2-D3
Rectory Fields	E2-E3
Reservoir Road	A1
Ring Avenue	A4
Royal George Street	C1-C2
St Peter's Gate	C3-D3
St Peter's Square	C3
St Thomas Marriot Street	C1-D1
Shawcross Street	D1
Shaw Heath	B2-B1-C1
Spring Gardens	D3-D2-E2
Station Road	C2-C3
Swaine Street	C3
The Quadrant	E2
Tame Street	E4
Thomson Street	B2-C2
Turncroft Lane	E2-F2-F1
Upper Brook Street	D2-E2
Vernon Avenue	F3
Victoria Road	E2-F2
Vienna Road	A1
Warren Street	D4
Waterloo Road	D2
Webb Lane	E1-E2
Wellington Road North	C3-C4
Wellington Road South	C1-C2-C3
Wellington Street	C3-D3
West Park Road	F3
Wood Street	B3
Worral Street	B1-B2
Yates Street	F4
Yew Street	A3-A4
York Street	B2

Cheadle Hulme

Acacia Avenue	A3-B3
Ack Lane West	C1
Albert Road	A3-B3-B4
Almond Tree Road	A3
Bannister Drive	A4
Beech Road	C2
Beechfield Road	C1
Blenheim Road	C3-C4
Brabant Road	C3-C4
Buckingham Road	A4
Cheadle Road	A3-A4
Cherry Tree Road	A3
Cherry Walk	C1
Cheviot Avenue	A3-A4
Church Road	B1-C1
Claremont Road	A1-A2-B2
Coral Road	A3-B3-B2
Cranbourne Avenue	C3
Croft Road	B4-C4
Dennison Road	B1
Eastdowns Road	A4
Glandon Drive	C1
Granby Road	B1
Hazel Road	C2
Heathbank Road	A1-A2-B2-B3
Highfield Road	A2
Hill Top Avenue	B1-B2
Howard Avenue	A3-B3
Hulme Hall Avenue	B1
Hulme Hall Road	B1-B2-B3
Hylton Drive	C1-C2
Ladybridge Road	B4-C4
Lingdale	A3-A4
Lindsay Drive	C2
Lorna Road	B4
Madison Avenue	B4
Manor Road	C2
Marlborough Avenue	C3-C4
Maple Avenue	A4
Meadows Road	A1-A2
Mellor Road	B3
Monmouth Road	C3
Musbury Avenue	C3
Nursery Road	A3-A2-B2
Oak Avenue	A3
Oaklands Avenue	B3
Park Road	C2
Parkfield Road	A2-A3
Pinfold Drive	B3
Pownall Road	B3
Queens Drive	A4-B4
Queens Road	A4-B4
Ramillies Avenue	C3
Raven Oak Park Road	C1
Raven Oak Road	C1-C2
Rowan Drive	C1
School Lane	A1-B1
Seymour Road	B1
Shaftesbury Avenue	C2-C3
Southdown Crescent	A1-A2
Station Road	B4-B3-C3-C2
Swan Green	B2-C2
Swann Lane	C2-B2-B1
The Precinct	B4
Tenby Drive	C2
Turves Road	A3
Upton Avenue	B2
Vaudrey Road	B4
Victoria Avenue	A4-B4
Westfield Road	A2
Willow Avenue	A3-A4
Windsor Green	A1

Hazel Grove

Argyle Street	B3
Avondale Avenue	C3
Beanleach Road	B4
Beech Avenue	B3-C3
Bosden Avenue	C4
Bosdenfold Road	B4-C4
Bosden Hall Road	B4
Bower Avenue	B1
Bramhall Moor Lane	A4
Braemar Road	C3
Brooklands Road	B1
Buteley Street	B4
Buxton Road	C1-C2
Carisbrooke Avenue	A1
Castleton Road	B1
Chapel Street	B3-B4
Chester Road	A1-B1-B2-B3
Church Grove	B2-C2
Clarendon Road	C4
Commercial Road	A3-B3-B4
Cooke Street	A3
Corfe Crescent	A1
Co-Op Street	B4
Davenport Road	A3
Deneside Crescent	C4
Douglas Road	B3-C3
Edale Close	B1-C1
Farndon Avenue	C4
Green Lane	A3-A4
Grendale Avenue	B1-B2
Grove Street	B3-B4
Grundy Street	B2-B3
Haddon Road	B1-C1
Harlech Drive	A1
Hatherflow Road	A2-B2-B3
Hazel Street	B3-B4
Hazelwood Road	C2-C3-C4
Hope Street	A3
Kings Road	B3-C3
Lawrence Road	C3
Lever Street	A3
Linda Drive	A2
London Road	A4-A3-B3-B2-C2
Longmead Avenue	A1-A2
Lowick Close	A2
Lyme Road	B1-C1
Lyndhurst Avenue	A1
Macclesfield Road	C1-C2
Mount Pleasant	A4
Napier Street	A3-B3
Nelson Street	C4
Neville Street	A3
Newby Road	A2-A3
Newlyn Close	A1
Norbury Crescent	B2
Norbury Green	B2
Oak Street	A3
Oaklands Drive	B1
Overton Crescent	B4-C4
Pearl Street	B4
Peter Street	A4-B4
Queens Road	B3
Rochester Grove	B3-C3
Rhos Drive	A1
School Street	B2
Seaton Close	A1
Shepley Drive	B1
Spring Gardens	B3
Station Street	B2
Stirling Avenue	A1
Talbot Street	B4
Torkington Road	B2-C2-C3
Vaudrey Drive	B2
Vine Street	B3
Warwick Drive	A1
Wesley Street	B3
Woodland Avenue	B1

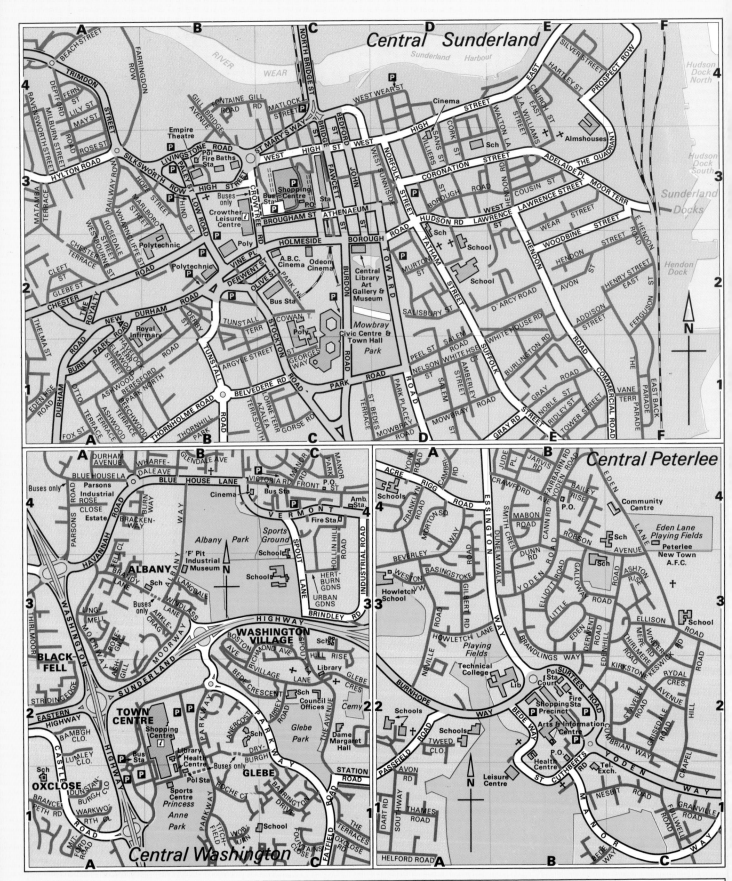

Sunderland

Renowned for its shipbuilding industry, Sunderland is also an important coal port. Its name is derived from the fact that it was 'sundered' from a monastery founded on the far bank of the River Wear in 674. Wearmouth Bridge, originally built in 1796, but replaced in 1929, was one of the first cast-iron bridges in the country. A modern Civic Centre and three museums feature among the town's amenities. Nearby are the fine beaches of Roker and Seaburn.

Peterlee, built to attract industry in the 1950s, is one of Durham's most successful New Towns. It is named after Peter Lee, who started work down the mines at the age of ten, and rose to become president of the Miners' Union. An unexpected but welcome feature of the town is Castle Eden Dene – a three-mile stretch of natural woodland kept as a nature reserve.

Washington is another New Town burgeoning in this industrial corner of north-east England. In the original village stands 17th-century Washington Old Hall, the former home of George Washington's ancestors. Now in the care of the National Trust, it has been fully restored in period style. Another far cry from industry is the Wildfowl Trust's 103-acre park on the north bank of the Wear, where visitors can observe a comprehensive collection of the world's waterfowl in landscaped surroundings.

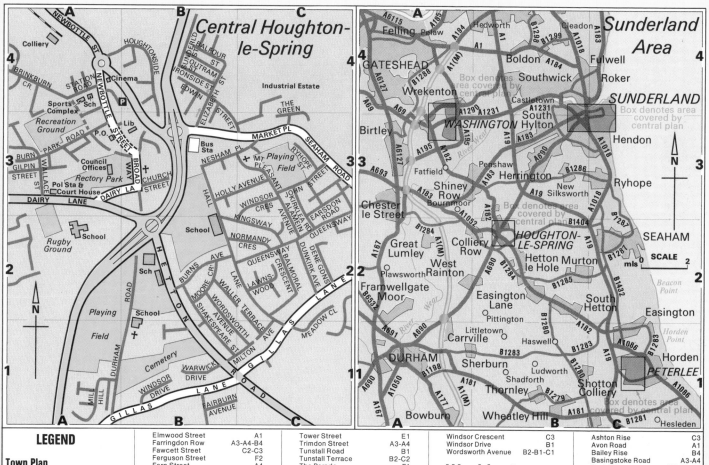

Central Houghton-le-Spring

Industrial Estate

Sunderland Area

SCALE mls

LEGEND

Town Plan
- AA recommended route
- Restricted roads
- Other roads
- Buildings of interest — Cinema
- Car parks — P
- Parks and open spaces
- One way streets

Area Plan
- A roads
- B roads
- Locations — Haswell O
- Urban area

Street Index with Grid Reference

Sunderland

Addison Street	E2-F2
Adelaide Place	E3
Amberley Street	A1
Argyle Street	B1-C1
Ashwood Road	A1-B1-B2
Ashwood Terrace	A1
Athenaeum	C3-D3
Avon Street	E2
Azalea Terrace South	B1-C1
Beach Street	A4
Beechwood Terrace	A1-B1
Bedford Street	C3-C4
Belvedere Road	B1-C1
Beresford Park North	A1-B1
Borough Road	C2-D2-D3-E3
Bridge Street	C3-C4
Brougham Street	C3
Burdon Road	C1-C2
Burlington Road	E1
Burn Park Road	A1-A2
Chester Road	A2-B2
Chester Street	A2
Church Street East	E3-E4
Cleft Street	A2
Commercial Road	E1-F1
Cork Street	D3-D4
Coronation Street	D3-E3
Cousin Street	E3
Cowan Terrace	C2
Crowtree Road	B3-C3-C2
D'Arcy Road	D2-E2
Deptford Road	A3-A4
Derby Street	B2
Derwent Street	B2-C2
Durham Road	A1-A2
East Back Parade	F1
East Hendon Road	F2-F3
Eden House Road	A1

Elmwood Street	A1
Farringdon Row	A3-A4-B4
Fawcett Street	C2-C3
Ferguson Street	F2
Fern Street	A4
Fontaine Road	B4
Fox Street	A1
Gill Bridge Avenue	B3-B4
Gill Road	B4-C4
Glebe Street	A2
Gorse Road	C1
Gray Road	D1-E1
Hartley Street	E4
Havelock Terrace	A2-A1-B1
Hendon Road	E1-E2-E3
Hendon Road	E2-F2
Henry Street East	F2
High Street East	D3-D4-E4
High Street West	B3-C3-D3
Hind Street	B2-B3
Holmeside	C2
Hope Street	A3-B3
Hudson Road	D3
Hylton Road	A3
J. A. Williams Street	E3-E4
John Street	C2-C3
Lawrence Street	E3
Lily Street	A4
Livingstone Road	B3
Lorne Terrace	C1
Low Road	B2-B3
Matamba Terrace	A3
Marlborough Street	A3-B3
Matlock Street	C4
May Street	A3-A4
Milburn Street	A3-A4
Moor Terrace	E3-F3
Mowbray Road	D1-E1
Murton Street	D2
Nelson Street	D1
New Durham Road	A2-B2
Noble Street	E1
Norfolk Street	D3
North Bridge Street	C4
Olive Street	B2-C2
Otto Terrace	A1
Paley Street	B3
Park Lane	C2
Park Road	C1-D1
Park Place	D1
Peel Street	D1
Prospect Row	E4-F4
Railway Row	A3
Ravensworth Street	A3-A4
Ridley Street	E1
Rosedale Street	A2-A3
Rose Street	A3
St Bedes Terrace	C1-D1
St George's Way	C1
St Mary's Way	C3-C4
Salisbury Street	D2
Sans Street	D3-D4
Salem Road	D1-D2
Salem Street	D1
Silksworth Row	A3-B3
Silver Street	E4-F4
Stockton Road	B2-C2-C1
Suffolk Street	D1-E1
Tatham Street	D2-D3
Thelma Street	A1-A2
Thornhill Park	B1
Thornholme Road	B1
Toward Road	D1-D2

Tower Street	E1
Trimdon Street	A3-A4
Tunstall Road	B1
Tunstall Terrace	B2-C2
The Parade	F1
The Royalty	A1
The Quadrant	E3-F3-F4-E4
Vane Terrace	F1
Villiers Street	D3
Vine Place	B2-C2
Walton Lane	E3-E4
Wear Street	E3
Westbourne Street	A2-A3
West Lawrence Street	D3-E3
West Sunniside	D3
West Wear Street	C4-D4
Wharncliffe Street	A2-A3
White House Court	D1
White House Road	D1-E1-E2
Woodbine Street	E2-E3-F3

Houghton-le-Spring

Alamein Avenue	C2-C3
Balfour Street	B4
Balmoral Crescent	C2
Brinkburn Crescent	A4
Broadway	B3
Burn Park Road	A3
Burns Avenue	B2
Church Street	B2
Dairy Lane	A3-B3
Dene Gardens	C2
Dunkirk Avenue	C2
Durham Road	A1-B1-B2
Earsdon Road	C3
Edwin Street	B4-B3-C3
Elizabeth Street	B3-B4
Fairburn Avenue	B1
Gillas Lane	A1-B1-C1-C2
Gilpin Street	A3
Hall Lane	B3-B2-C2
Hetton Road	B2-B1-C1
Holly Avenue	B3-C3
Houghtonside	A4-B4
Ironside Street	B4
John Street	C3
Kingsway	C3
Kirklea Road	C2-C3
Lawnswood	C2
Market Place	C3
Meadow Close	C1-C2
Mill Hill	A1
Milton Avenue	B1-C1
Moore Crescent	B2
Mount Pleasant	C3
Nesham Place	B3-C3
Newbottle Street	A4-A3-B3
Normandy Crescent	B2-C2
Outram Street	B4
Queensway	B2-C2-C3
Ryhope Street	C3
Seaham Road	C3
Shakespeare Street	B1-B2
Station Road	A4
Sunderland Street	B4
The Green	C3-C4
Wallace Street	B2
Waller Terrace	B2-C2
Warwick Drive	B1

Windsor Crescent	C3
Windsor Drive	B1
Wordsworth Avenue	B2-B1-C1

Washington

Abbey Road	C2
Albany Way	B3-B4
Arklecrag	B3
Ashgill	A2
Bamborough Close	A2
Barrington Drive	C1
Bede Crescent	B3-B2-C2
Blue House Lane	A4-B4
Boston Avenue	B2-B3
Bracken Way	A4
Brancepeth Road	A1
Brandy Lane	A3
Brindley Road	C1
Burn Way	A4-B4
Castle Road	A1-A2
Dryburgh	B2-C2
Dunstanburgh Close	A1
Durham Avenue	A4
Eastern Highway	A2
Fatfield Road	C1
Fell Close	A3-A4
Fountains Close	C1
Front Street	C4
Glebe Crescent	C2
Glendale Avenue	B4
Havannah Road	A3-A4
Hertburn Gardens	C3
Hill Rise	C2
Hollin Hill Road	C3-C4
Industrial Road	C3-C4
Lanercost	B2
Langdale	B3
Lingmell	A3
Lumley Close	A2
Manor Park	C4
Manor Road	C4
Mitford Road	A1
Moorway	A3-A2-B2-B3
Oxclose Road	C1
Parkway	B1-B2-C2-C1
Parsons Road	A3-A4
Richmond Avenue	B2-B3-C3
Roche Court	B1
Rose Close	A4
Rosegill	A3
Spout Lane	C2-C3-C4
Station Road	C1
Stridingedge	A2
Sunderland Highway	A2-B2-B3-C3
The Avenue	C1-C2
The Terraces	C1
Thirlmoor	A3
Titchfield	B1
Urban Gardens	C3
Vermont	B4-C4
Victoria Road	B4-C4
Village Lane	B2-C2
Warkworth Close	A1
Washington Highway	A1-A2-A3-A4
Wharfedale Avenue	A4
Windlass Lane	B3
Woburn	B1

Peterlee

Acre Rigg Road	A4

Ashton Rise	C3
Avon Road	A1
Bailey Rise	B4
Basingstoke Road	A3-A4
Bede Way	B2, B1-C1
Beverley Way	A3-A4
Brandlings Way	B3
Burnhope Way	A2-A3-B2
Cambridge Road	A4
Cann Road	B2
Chapel Hill Road	C1-C2-C3
Crawford Avenue	B4
Cumbrian Way	B2-C2-C1
Dart Road	A1
Derwent Road	B3
Dunelm Walk	B3-B4
Dunn Road	B3-B4
Edenhill Road	C2-C3
Eden Lane	B4-C4-C3
Elliot Road	B3
Ellison Road	C2
Essington Way	A4-B4-A3-B3-B2
Fairbairn Road	B4
Franklyn Road	A4
Fullwell Road	C1
Galloway Road	B4-B3-C3
Gilbert Road	A3
Granville Road	C1
Grisedale Road	C2
Helford Road	A1
Howletch Lane	A3-B3
Jarvis Road	B4
Jude Place	B4
Keswick Road	C2-C3
Kirkstone Avenue	C2
Little Eden	B3
Mabon Road	B4
Manor Way	B1-C1
Morton Square	A4
Nesbit Road	B1-C1
Neville Road	A2-A3
Passfield Road	A1-A2
Robson Avenue	B4-B3-C3
Rydal Crescent	C2
St Cuthberts Road	B1-B2
Smith Crescent	B4
Southway	A1
Staveley Road	C2
Surtees Road	B2
Thames Road	A1
Thirlmere Road	C2-C3
Tweed Close	A2
Weston View	A3
Windermere Road	A2
Yoden Road	B3-B4
Yoden Way	B2-C2-C1
York Road	A4

71

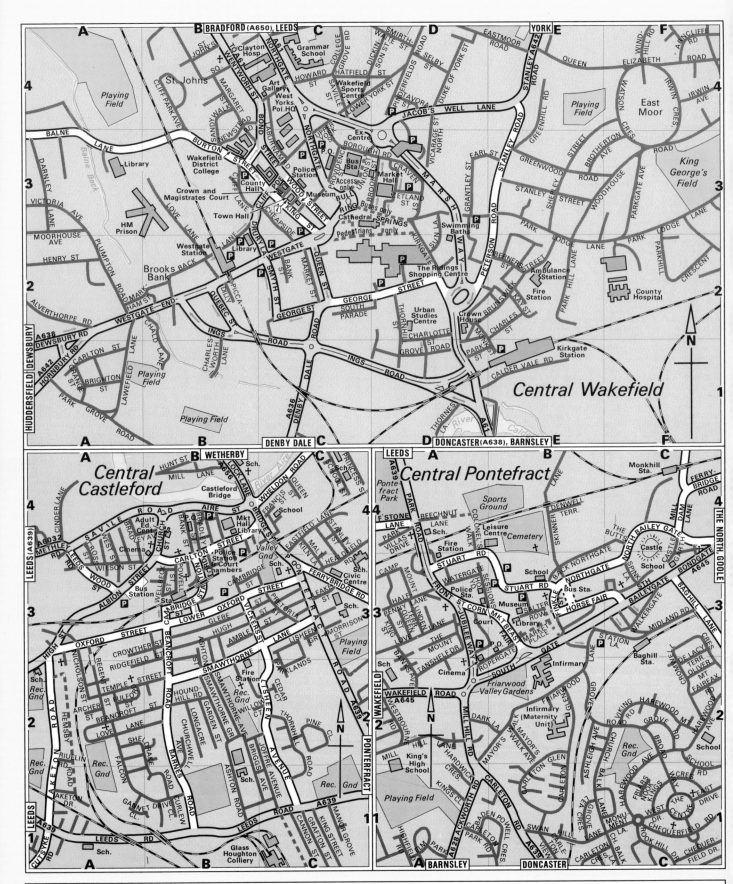

Wakefield

Towers and turrets unfolding over the hillsides greet the visitor to Wakefield, and the 247-ft spire of the Cathedral Church of All Saints has been a landmark for over 500 years. Today the spire looms over the Bull Ring pedestrian precinct which is part of a town centre development, and even older is the stone-built, nine-arched Old Bridge, site of the 14th-century Chapel of St

Mary. This was among the finest of the bridge chapels — perhaps because even in the 13th century, Wakefield was an important weaving and dyeing centre (coal mining and a growing reputation as an international industrial centre are more important today). The excellent art gallery has an enterprising collection of modern sculpture and paintings.

Castleford Birthplace of Henry Moore in 1898, this mining and bottlemaking town is on the site

of a Roman station. The Castleford Library Museum Room shows late 18th-century Castleford pottery.

Pontefract has been making Pontefract cakes for over 200 years, although today imported, not home-grown, liquorice is used. Its castle was one of the strongest in the north in medieval times and a bloody place of execution in the Wars of the Roses; of Pontefract's 18th- and 19th-century buildings, the Town Hall has the plaster casts used for the panel's at Nelson's Column's base.

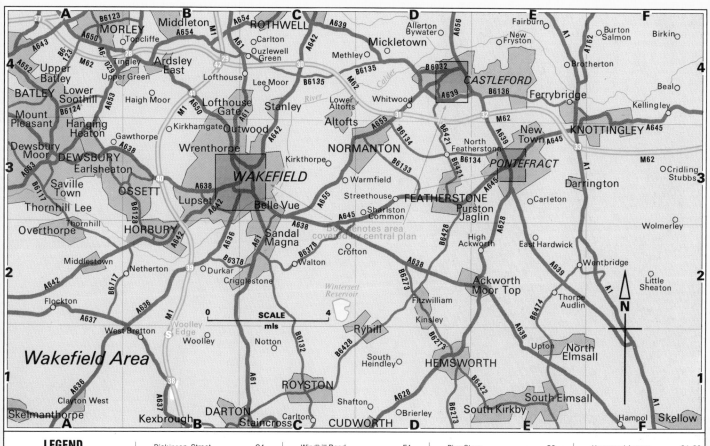

LEGEND

Town Plan

- AA Recommended route
- Restricted roads
- Other roads
- Buildings of interest
- Car parks   P
- Parks and open spaces
- One way streets

Area Plan

- A roads
- B roads
- Locations   ○
- Urban area

Street Index with grid Reference

Wakefield

Alverthorpe Road	A2
Arncliffe Road	F4
Back Lane	B2-B3
Balne Lane	A3-A4-B3
Bank Street	C2
Berners Street	E2
Bond Street	C3-C4
Borough Road	C3-D3
Brighton Street	A1
Brook Street	C3-D3
Brotherton Avenue	E3-F3
Brunswick Street	D2-E2
Bull Ring	C3
Burton Street	B3-C3
Calder Vale Road	D1-E1
Carlton Street	A1
Chald Lane	B1-B2
Charles Street	E2
Charlesworth Lane	B1-B2
Charlotte Street	D1-D2
Cheapside	C2-C3
Cliff Lane	B3
Cliff Parade	B3-C3
Cliff Park Avenue	C4
College Grove Road	C4
Craven Street	D3
Darnley Lane	A3
Denby Dale Road	C1-C2
Dewsbury Road	A1-A2
Dickinson Street	C4
Drury Lane	C3-B3-B2-C2
Duke of York Street	D4
Earl Street	D3-E3
Eastmoor Road	D4-E4
George Street	C2-D2
Grange Street	A1
Grantley Street	D3
Greenhill Road	E3-E4
Greenwood Road	E3-F3
Grove Road	D1
Hatfield Street	C4-D4
Henry Street	A2
Hornbury Road	A1-A2
Howard Street	C4
Ings Road	B2-B1-C2-C1-D1
Irwin Avenue	F4
Irwin Crescent	F3-F4
Jacob's Well Lane	D4-E4
Kay Street	E2
King Street	C3
Kirkgate	D2-D3
Laburnam Road	C3-C4
Lawefield Lane	A1-A2
Love Lane	B2-B3
Lower York Street	C4-D4
Margaret Street	B4
Market Street	C2
Markham Street	A2-B2
Marsh Way	D2-D3
Monk Street	D2-E2-E1
Moorhouse Avenue	A3
Newstead Road	B3-B4
Northgate	C3-C4
Park Street	D1-E1
Parkgate Avenue	F2-F3
Park Grove Road	A1-B1
Parkhill Crescent	F2-F3
Park Hill Lane	E2
Park Lodge Lane	D3-E3-E2-F2-F3
Peterson Road	D2-E2-E3
Piccadily	B2
Pinderfields Road	D4
Plumpton Road	A2-A3
Providence Street	C3
Quebec Street	B2
Queen Street	C2
Queen Elizabeth Road	E4-F4
St John's Square	B4
Sandy Walk	B3-B4
Saville Street	C4
Selby Street	D4
Shepley Street	E3-E4-F4
Smirthwaite Street	D4
Smyth Street	C2
South Parade	C2-D2
Springs	D3
Stanley Road	E3-E4
Stanley Street	E3
Sun Lane	D2-D3
Tavora Street	D4
Thornes Lane	D1
Thornhill Street	D1-D2
Union Street	C3
Upper York Street	C3-C4
Vicarage Street North	D3-D4
Victoria Avenue	A3
Watson Street	F3-F4
Wentworth Street	B4
Westgate	C2-C3
Westgate End	A1-A2-B2
Windhill Road	F4
Wood Street	C3
Woodhouse Road	E2-E3-F3-F4
Zetland Street	D3

Castleford

Aire Street	B4
Aketon Drive	A1
Aketon Road	A1-A2-A3
Albion Street	A3-B3
Amble Street	B3-C3
Archer Street	A2
Ashton Road	B1-B2
Ashton Street	B2-B3
Bank Street	B4
Barnes Road	B1-B2
Beancroft Road	B2-B3
Beancroft Street	A2-B2
Bradley Avenue	A4-B4
Bradley Street	B4
Bridge Street	B4-C4
Briggs Avenue	B2-B1-C1
Cambridge Street	B3-C3
Cannon Street	C1
Carlton Street	B3-B4
Cedar Court	C2
Church Street	B4
Churchwell Avenue	B1-B2
Cinder Lane	A4
Cross Street	A3-A4
Crowther Street	A3-B3
Curlew Close	B1
Cutsyke Road	A1
Eastfield Lane	C4
Falcon Drive	A2-A1-B1
Ferrybridge Road	C3
Francis Street	C4
Fulford Street	A2
Gannet Close	A1-B1
Garden Street	B2
Glebe Street	B3-C3
Grafton Street	C1
Healdfield Road	C3-C4
Hemsby Road	A1-A2
High Street	A2-A3
Houndhill Road	B2
Hugh Street	B3-C3
Hunt Street	B4
Joffre Avenue	B2-C2-C1
King Street	C1
Leake Street	C3
Leeds Road	A3-A4
Leeds Road	A1-B1-C1
Lisheen Avenue	C1-C2-C3
Lisheen Grove	C3
Lock Lane	B4
Longacre	B2
Love Lane	A2-B2
Lower Oxford Street	B3-C3
Maltkiln Lane	C3-C4
Manor Grove	C1
Methley Road	A3-A4
Mill Lane	B4
Morrison Street	C3
Nicholson Street	A2-A3
Oxford Street	A3-B3
Parklands	C2-C3

Castleford (continued)

Pine Close	C2
Pontefract Road	C2-C3-C4
Powell Street	B3
Pretoria Street	C3
Princess Street	C4
Queen Street	C4
Regent Street	A2-A3
Ridgefield Street	A2-B2-B3
Riuelin Road	A2
Savile Road	A4-B4
School Street	C4
Sheldrake Road	A2-B2-B1
Smawthorne Avenue	B2
Smawthorne Grove	B2
Smawthorne Lane	B2-B3-C3
Stanley Street	C4
Station Road	B3
Temple Street	A2-B2
Thornhill Road	C1-C2
Vickers Street	B3-C3
Wellbeck Street	B3
West Street	A3-A4
Wheldon Road	B4-C4
Willow Court	B2-C2
Wilson Street	A3
Wood Street	A3

Pontefract

Ackworth Road	A1
Ashleigh Avenue	B1-B2
Back Northgate	B3-B4-C4
Baden Powell Crescent	A1-B1
Baghill Lane	C3
Banks Avenue	A2-A3
Beast Fair	B3
Beechnut Lane	A4
Bondgate	C3-C4
Broad Way	C1-C2
Camp Mount	A3
Carleton Crescent	B1-C1
Carleton Glen	B1-B2
Carleton Road	A1-B1
Carleton View	B1
Carleton Park Road	A1-B1
Castlegarth	C3-C4
Chequerfield Drive	C1
Chequerfield Road	C1
Church Balk Lane	B1-B2-C1-C2
Colonel's Walk	A4
Corn Market	A3-B3
Cromwell Crescent	C2-C3
Dark Lane	A2-B2
De Lacy Terrace	C2-C3
Denwell Terrace	B4
East Drive	C1
Elm Park	A1
Fairfax Road	C2
Featherstone Lane	A4
Ferrybridge Road	C4
Finkel Street	B3
Friars Nook	C1
Friarwood Lane	B2-B3
Front Street	A3
Grove Road	B2-C2
Grove Lea Crescent	C1
Half Penny Lane	A3
Hardwick Crescent	A1

Pontefract (continued)

Harewood Avenue	C1-C2
Harewood Mount	C2
Highfield Road	A1
Horse Fair	B3-C3
Jubilee Way	A2-A3
King Street	A3
Kings Close	A1
Kings Crescent	C1
Linden Terrace	A3
Love Lane	A3
Market Place	B3
Mayor's Walk	A2-B2
Mayor's Walk Avenue	B2
Midland Road	C3
Mill Dam Lane	C4
Mill Hill Lane	A2
Mill Hill Road	A1-A2
Monument Lane	C1
North Bailey Gate	C3-C4
Northgate	B3-C3
Oliver Mount	C2
Park Road	A3-A4
Park Villas Drive	A4
Queen Street	A3
Rook Hill Drive	C1
Ropergate	A2-A3-B3
Salter Row	B3
School Road	C1-C2
Sessions House Yard	A3
Skinner Lane	B3-B4
South Baileygate	C3
South Gate	A2-B2-B3
Spink Lane	C3
Station Lane	B3-C3
Stuart Road	A3-A4-B3-B4
Swan Hill Lane	B1
Tanshelf Drive	A2-A3
The Butts	C4
The Centre	C1
The Mount	A3
Viking Road	C2
Wakefield Road	A2
Walkergate	C3
Watergate	A3
West Drive	C1
Westbourne Road	A2

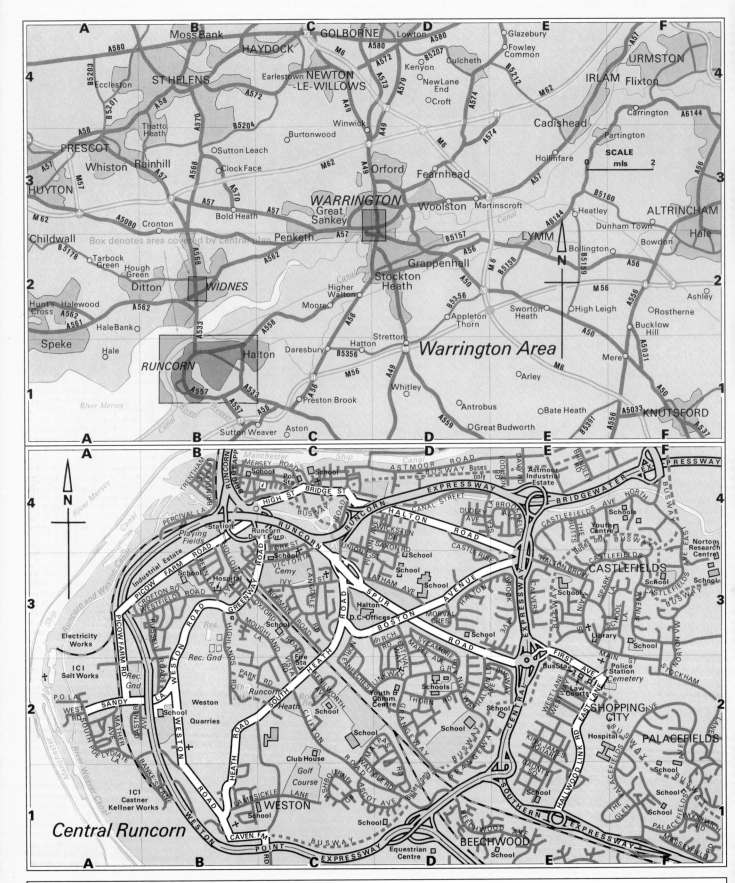

Warrington

This industrial town, situated near the Manchester Ship Canal, has been designated a New Town and is therefore expanding rapidly. Its traditional industry was clock-making, but in recent years this has given way to light industry, chemical production, metal casting and engineering. A few old houses can still be seen in the town, including the half-timbered Barley Mow inn.

Runcorn, on the River Mersey, is another industrial centre and has extensive petrochemical works. However, Norton Priory on the eastern edge of the town is of particular interest. Set in seven acres of landscaped woodland, the remains of the priory include a 12th-century undercroft notable for its beautiful carved passage. Excavation of the site in 1978 won the National Archaeological Award and the museum here, as well as containing various finds from the priory, has one of the best

exhibitions on medieval monastic life in Britain.

Widnes was just a collection of scattered villages before the Runcorn Gap and St Helen's Railway Company built the world's first railway, canal and dock complex here in the mid-19th century. Chemical and alkali works began to develop and the area rapidly grew into an industrial town with large housing estates. Today Widnes is linked to Runcorn by the railway bridge of 1868 and a road bridge which was built in 1961.

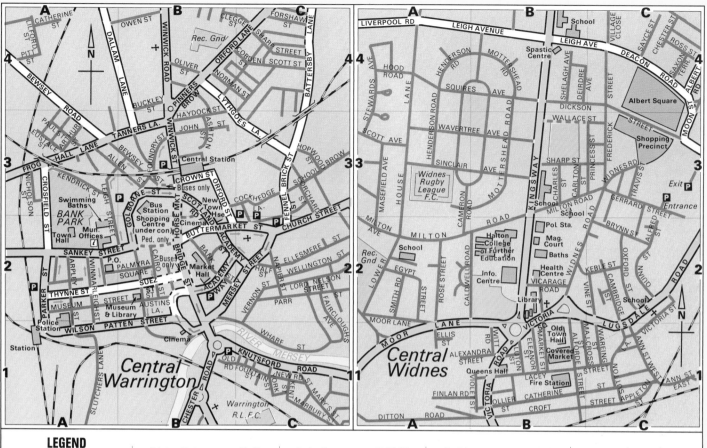

LEGEND

Town Plan

AA recommended route
Restricted roads
Other roads
Buildings of interest   Club
Car parks   P
Parks and open spaces
One way streets

Area Plan

A roads
B roads
Locations   Grittleton O
Urban area

Street Index with Grid Reference

Warrington

Academy Street	B2-C2
Academy Way	B2
Allen Street	A3-B3
Arpley Street	A1-A2
Arthur Street	A3
Ashton Street	B3
Austins Lane	B2
Bank Street	B2
Battersby Lane	C3-C4
Bewsey Road	A3-A4
Bewsey Street	A3-B3
Brick Street	C3
Bridge Street	B2
Buckley Street	B4
Buttermarket Street	B2-C2
Cairo Street	B2
Catherine Street	A4
Chester Road	B1
Church Street	C2-C3
Clegge Street	B4-C4
Cobden Street	B4-C4
Cockhedge Lane	B3-C3
Crossfield Street	A2-A3
Crown Street	B3
Dallam Lane	A4-B4-B3
Ellesmere Street	C2
Eustace Street	A3
Fairclough's Avenue	C1-C2
Fennel Street	C2-C3
Forshaw Street	C4
Foundry Street	B3
Fountain Street	C1
Froghall Lane	A3
Golborne Street	B2-B3
Half Street	C2
Haydock Street	B3-B4
Horse Market	B2-B3
Hopwood Street	C3
John Street	B3
Kendrick Street	A3
Kent Street	C1
Knutsford Road	B1-C1
Leigh Street	A3-A2-B2
Lilford Street	A4
Lord Nelson Street	C2
Lythgoes Lane	B4-B3-C3
Marbury Street	C1
Mersey Street	B1-B2-C2
Museum Street	A2-B2
Napier Street	C2
New Road	C1
Nicholson Street	A3
Norman Street	B4-C4
Old Road	B1
Oliver Street	B4
Orford Lane	B4-C4
Orford Street	B2-B3
Owen Street	A4-B4
Palmyra Square	A2-B2
Parker Street	A1-A2
Parr Street	C2
Paul Street	A3
Pinners Brow	B4
Pitt Street	A4
Richard Street	C3
St Mary's Street	C1
Sankey Street	A2-B2
School Brow	C3
Scotland Road	B2-B3
Scott Street	C4
Sharp Street	C4
Slutchers Lane	A1
Suez Street	B2
Tanners Lane	A3-B3
Thynne Street	A2
Vernon Street	C2
Wellington Street	C2
Wharf Street	B1-B2-C2-C1
Wilson Patten Street	A1-B1-B2
Winmarleigh Street	A1-A2
Winwick Road	B4
Winwick Street	B3
York Street	C1

Runcorn

Ascot Avenue	C1-D1
Ashbourne Road	C1
Astmoor Road	C4-D4-E4
Banke's Lane	A2-A1-B1
Beechwood Avenue	D1-E1
Birch Road	C3-D3
Boston Avenue	C3-D3-E3
Bridge Street	C4
Bridgewater Expressway	E4-F4
Brindley Road	E4
Brindley Street	B4
Brookfield Avenue	E4
Calvers	E3
Canal Street	C4-D4
Castner Avenue	A2
Castle Rise	D4-D3-E3
Castlefields Avenue	E3-F3
Castlefields Avenue East	F3-F4
Castlefields Avenue North	E3-E4-F4
Cavendish Farm Road	B1-C1
Central Expressway	E1-E2-E3-E4
Clifton Road	C2-C1-D1
Crofton Road	B3
Davy Road	E4
Dudley Avenue	D4
East Lane	E2
Eddison Road	E4
Festival Way	D2-D3
First Avenue	E2-E3
Gaunts Square	E1-E2
Grangeway	D1-D2
Greenway Road	B3-C3-C4
Hallwood Link Road	E1-E2
Halton Brook Avenue	D3-E3
Halton Brow	E3
Halton Lodge Avenue	D2
Halton Road	C4-D4-E4
Heath Road	C2-C3-C4
Heath Road South	B1-B2-C2
High Street	B4-C4
Highlands Road	B2-B3
Hollow Way	B3-B4
Ivy Street	C3
Kenilworth Avenue	C2
King James Square	C2
Lambsickle Lane	B1-C1
Langdale Road	C3
Latham Avenue	C3-D3
Linkway	D2
Lydiate Lane	A2-B2
Main Street	E3-F3-F2
Malpas Road	C1-C2-D2-D1
Maple Avenue	D2-D3
Masseyfield Road	F1
Mather Avenue	A2
Mersey Road	B4-C4
Morval Crescent	D3
Moughland Lane	B3-B4
Norleane Crescent	C2-C3
Norman Road	C3
Norton View	F2-F3
Oxford Road	B3-C3-C2
Palacefields Avenue	F1-F2
Park Road	B2-C2
Penn Lane	B3
Percival Lane	B4
Picow Farm Road	A2-A3-B3-B4
Picton Avenue	C3-C4-B4
Post Office Lane	A2
Runcorn Bridge Approach	B4
Runcorn Expressway	C4-D4-E4
Runcorn Spur Road	B4-C4-C3-D3-E3-E2
Russell Road	B2-B3
Sandy Lane	A2-B2
Saxon Road	C4-D4
School Lane	E3-F3
Sea Lane	D4
South Parade	A2
Southern Expressway	E1-F1
Spark Lane	E3-F3
Stockham Lane	F2-F3
Sycamore Road	D2-D3
The Butts	E4
The Glen	E1-F1
Thorn Road	D2
Trentham Street	B4
Union Street	C4-D4-D3
Victoria Road	C3-C4
Vista Road	C2-C3
Walpole Road	C2-C1-D1
West Lane	E2
West Road	A2
Westfield Road	A3-B3
Weston Road	B2-B3
Weston Point Expressway	B4-B3-A3-B3-B2-B1-C1-D1
Westway	E2
Wicksten Drive	C4-D4
Woodhatch Road	F1
York Street	C3-C4

Widnes

Albert Road	C4
Alexandra Street	A1-B1
Alforde Street	B1-B2
Alfred Street	C2
Ann Street East	C1
Ann Street West	C1
Appleton Street	C1
Brynn Street	C2
Caldwell Road	A2-B2
Cambridge Street	C2
Cameron Road	A2-A3
Carlton Street	B3
Catherine Street	B1-C1
Charles Street	B3
Chester Street	C4
Croft Street	B1-C1
Deacon Road	C4
Deidre Avenue	B4
Dickson Street	B4-C4-C3
Ditton Road	A1-B1
Egypt Street	A2
Eleanor Street	B1
Ellis Street	A1
Finlan Road	A1-B1
Frederick Street	C3-C4
Gerrard Street	C3
Henderson Road	A3-A4-B4
Hood Road	A4
Keble Street	B2-C2
Kingsway	B2-B3-B4
Lacey Street	B1-C1
Leigh Avenue	A4-B4-C4
Liverpool Road	A4
Lower House Lane	A2-A3-A4
Lugsdale Road	B2-C2-C1-C2
Luton Street	B1
Major Cross Street	B2-B1-C1
Market Street	B1-B2
Masefield Avenue	A2-A3
Milton Avenue	A2
Milton Road	A2-B2-B3-C3
Moor Lane	A1-A2-B2-B1
Moon Street	C3-C4
Mottershead Road	A3-B3-B4
Ollier Street	B1
Oxford Street	C2
Princess Street	C3
Quinn Street	C2
Rose Street	A2
Ross Street	C4
Saxon Terrace	C4
Sayce Street	C4
Scott Avenue	A3
Sharp Street	B3-C3
Shelagh Avenue	B4
Sinclair Avenue	A3-B3
Smith Road	A2
Squires Avenue	A4-B4
Stewards Avenue	A3-A4
Sutton Lane	C1
Travis Street	C3
Vicarage Road	B2
Victoria Road	B1
Victoria Square	B1-B2
Victoria Street	C1-C2
Village Close	C4
Vine Street	C2
Violet Street	B1
Wallace Street	B3-C3
Wavertree Avenue	A3-B3
Widnes Road	B2-C2-C3
Witt Road	B1

75

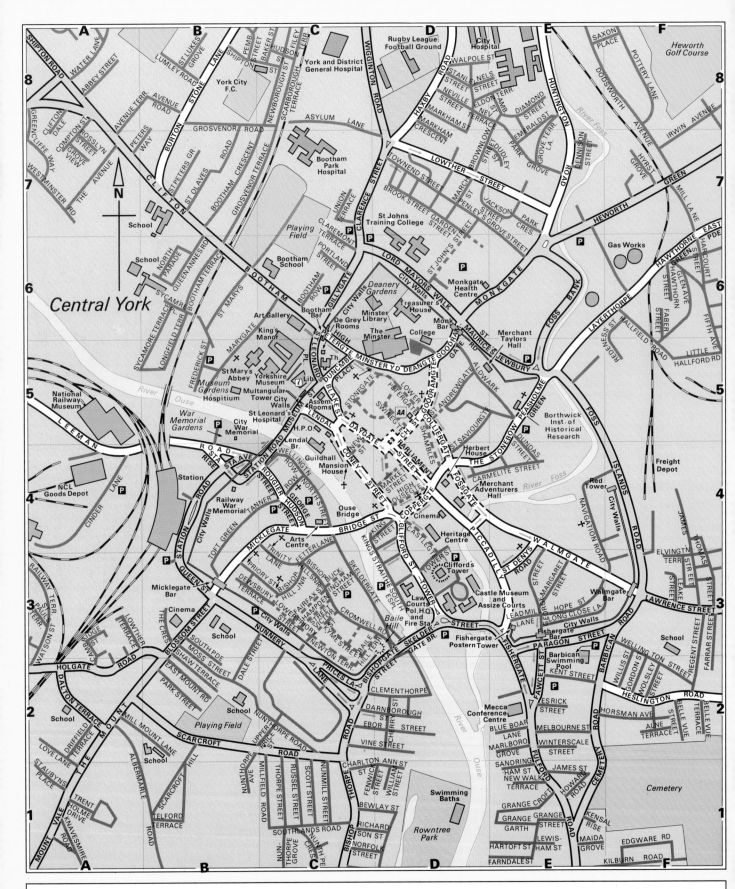

York

York Minster, unquestionably the city's outstanding glory, is considered to be one of the greatest cathedral churches in Europe. It is especially famous for its lovely windows which contain more than half the medieval stained glass in England.

Great medieval walls enclose the historic city centre and their three-mile circuit offers magnificent views of the Minster, York's numerous fine buildings, churches and the River Ouse. The ancient streets consist of a maze of alleys and lanes, some of them so narrow that the overhanging upper storeys of the houses almost touch. The most famous of these picturesque streets is The Shambles, formerly the butchers' quarter of the city, but now colonised by antique and tourist shops. York flourished throughout Tudor, Georgian and Victorian times and handsome buildings from these periods also feature throughout the city.

The Castle Museum gives a fascinating picture of York as it used to be and the Heritage Centre interprets the social and architectural history of the city. Other places of exceptional note in this city of riches include the Merchant Adventurer's Hall; the Treasurer's House, now owned by the National Trust and filled with fine paintings and furniture; the Jorvik Viking Centre, where there is an exciting restoration of the original Viking settlement at York, and the National Railway Museum.

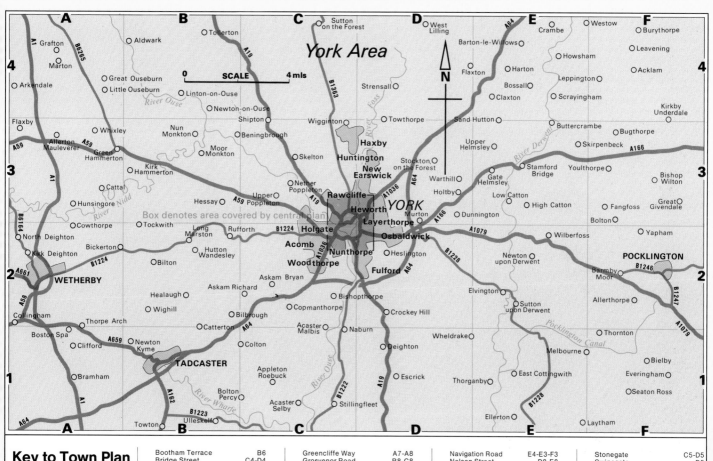

York Area

Key to Town Plan and Area Plan

Town Plan

AA Recommended roads
Other roads
Restricted roads
Buildings of interest   Station
Churches
Car Parks
Parks and open spaces
AA Service Centre   AA
One Way Streets

Area Plan

A roads
B roads
Locations   Fangfoss
Urban area

Street Index with Grid Reference

York

Abbey Street	A8
Albermarle Road	A2-A1-B1
Aldwark	D5-E5
Alne Terrace	F2
Amber Street	E8
Ann Street	D1
Asylum Lane	C8-C7-D7
Avenue Road	B8
Avenue Terrace	A7-A8-B8
Baile Hill Terrace	C2-C3-D3
Baker Street	C8
Barbican Road	E2-F2-F3-E3
Belle Vue Street	F2
Belle Vue Terrace	F2
Bewlay Street	C1-D1
Bishopgate Street	C2-D2-D3
Bishophill Junior	C3
Bishophill Senior	C3
Bishop Thorpe Road	C1-C2
Blake Street	C5
Blossom Street	B2-B3
Blue Boar Lane	E2
Bootham	B6-C6
Bootham Crescent	B7-C7-C8
Bootham Row	C6
Bootham Terrace	B6
Bridge Street	C4-D4
Brook Street	D7
Brownlow Street	D7-E7-E8
Buckingham Street	C3
Burton Stone Lane	B7-B8
Cambridge Street	A2-A3
Carmelite Street	D4-E4
Castlegate	D3-D4
Cemetery Road	E1-E2
Charlton Street	C1-D1
Cherry Street	D2
Church Street	D5
Cinder Lane	A4
Claremont Terrace	C6-C7
Clarence Street	C6-C7-D7
Clementhorpe	C2-D2
Clifford Street	D3-D4
Clifton	A8-A7-B7
Clifton Dale	A7-A8
Colliergate	D4-D5
Compton Street	A7-A8
Coppergate	D4
Cromwell Road	C3-D3
Dale Street	B2-B3
Dalton Terrace	A2
Darnborough Street	C2-D2
Daygate	C5-C4-D4-D5
Deangate	D5
Dennison Street	E7
Dewsbury Terrace	B3-C3
Diamond Street	E8
Dodsworth Avenue	E8-F8-F7
Driffield Terrace	A2
Dudley Street	D7-E7
Duncombe Place	C5
Dundas Street	E4-E5
East Parade	F6-F7
East Mount Road	B2
Ebor Street	C2-D2
Edgware Road	F1
Eldon Terrace	D8-E8
Elvington Terrace	F3
Emerald Street	E7-E8
Escrick Street	E2
Faber Street	F6
Fairfax Street	C3
Farndale Street	E1
Farrar Street	F2-F3
Fawcett Street	E2-E3
Fenwick Street	C1-D1
Fetter Lane	C3-C4
Fifth Avenue	F5-F6
Filey Terrace	C8
Fishergate	E2-E3
Foss Bank	E5-E6
Fossgate	D4
Foss Islands Road	E4-E5-F5-F4
Frederick Street	B5
Fulford Road	E1-E2
Garden Street	D7
George Hudson Street	C4
George Street	E3-E4
Gillygate	C6
Glen Avenue	F6
Goodramgate	D5-D6
Gordon Street	F2
Grange Croft	E1
Grange Garth	E1
Grange Street	E1

Greencliffe Way	A7-A8
Grosvenor Road	B8-C8
Grosvenor Terrace	B6-B7-C7-C8
Grove Terrace Lane	E7-E8
Grove View	A7
Hallfield Road	F5-F6
Hampden Street	C3
Harcourt Street	F6
Harloft Street	E1
Hawthorne Green	F6
Hawthorn Street	F6
Haxby Road	D7-D8
Heslington Road	E2-F2
Heworth Green	E6-E7-F7
High Ousegate	D4
High Petergate	C5-C6
Holgate Road	A2-A3-B3
Hope Street	E3
Horsman Avenue	E2-F2
Howard Road	E1
Hudson Street	C8
Huntington Road	E6-E7-E8
Hyrst Grove	F7
Irwin Avenue	F7-F8
Jackson Street	D7-E7
James Street	E1
James Street	F3-F4
Jewbury	E5
Kensal Rise	E1
Kent Street	E2
Kilburn Road	E1-F1
Kings Straithe	C4-D4-D3
King Street	C4-D4
Knavesmire Road	A1
Kyme Street	C3
Lawrence Street	F3
Layerthorpe	E5-E6-F6
Lead Mill Lane	E3
Leake Street	F3
Leeman Road	A5-A4-B5-B4
Lendal Coney Street	C5-C4-D4
Lewisham Street	E1
Little Hallford Road	F5
Long Close Lane	E3-F3
Longfield Terrace	B5-B6
Lord Mayors Walk	C6-D6
Lumley Road	B8
Love Lane	A1-A2
Lower Petergate	D5
Lower Priory Street	C3
Lowther Street	D7-E7
Lowther Terrace	A3
Maida Grove	E1
March Street	D7
Margaret Street	E3
Market Street	D4
Markham Crescent	D7-D8
Markham Street	D7-D8
Marlborough Grove	E2
Marygate	B5-B6-C6
Melbourne Street	E2
Micklegate	B3-B4-C4
Millfield Road	C1-C2
Mill Lane	F7
Mill Mount Lane	A2-B2
Minster Yard	C5-D5
Monkgate	D6-E6
Moss Street	B2-B3
Mount Vale	A1
Museum Street	C5

Navigation Road	E4-E3-F3
Nelson Street	D8-E8
Neville Street	D8
Neville Terrace	D8-E8
Newborough Street	C8
New Street	C4-C5
Newton Terrace	C2-C3
New Walk Terrace	E1
Norfolk Street	C1-D1
North Parade	B6
North Street	C4
Nunmill Street	C1-C2
Nunnery Lane	B3-C3-C2
Nunthorpe Avenue	B1-B2
Nunthorpe Grove	C1
Nunthorpe Road	B2-C2
Paragon Street	E3-F3
Park Crescent	E7
Park Grove	E7-E8
Park Street	B2
Parliament Street	D4-D5
Peasholme Green	E5
Pembroke Street	B8
Penley's Grove Street	D7-E7-E6
Peters Way	A7-B7-B8
Piccadilly	D4-D3-E3-E4
Portland Street	C6
Pottery Lane	F8
Prices Lane	C2
Priory Street	B3-C3
Queen Annes Road	B6
Queen Street	B3
Railway Terrace	A3
Redness Street	F5-F6
Regent Street	F2-F3
Richardson Street	C1-D1
Rosslyn Street	A7
Rougier Street	C4
Russel Street	C1-C2
St Andrewgate	D5
St Aubyns Place	A1
St Denys Road	E3-E4
St Johns Street	D6-D7
St Leonards Place	D5-D6
St Lukes Grove	B8
St Marys	B6
St Maurices	D6-D5-E5
St Olaves Road	B7-B8
St Pauls Terrace	A3
St Peters Grove	B7
St Saviourgate	D4-D5-E5
Sandringham Street	E8-F8
Saxon Place	E8
Scarborough Terrace	C8
Scarcroft Hill	B1-B2
Scarcroft Road	A2-B2-C2-C1
Scott Street	C1-C2
Shambles	D4-D5
Shaw Terrace	B2-B3
Shipton Road	A8
Shipton Street	B8-C8
Skeldergate	C4-C3-D3
Skeldergate Bridge	D3
South Esplanade	D3
Southlands Road	C1
South Parade	B2-B3
Stanley Street	D8
Station Avenue	B4
Station Rise	B4
Station Road	B3-B4-C4-C5

Stonegate	C5-D5
Swinegate	D5
Sycamore Place	B6
Sycamore Terrace	A5-B5-B6
Tanner Row	B4-C4
Telford Terrace	B1
The Avenue	A7
The Crescent	B3
The Mount	A1-A2-B2
The Stonebow	D4-E4-E5
Thomas Street	F3-F4
Thorpe Street	C1-C2
Toft Green	B3-B4
Tower Street	D4-D3-E3
Townend Street	D7
Trent Holme Drive	A1
Trinity Lane	C3-C4
Union Terrace	C7
Upper Price Street	B2-C2
Victor Street	C3
Vine Street	C2-D2
Walmgate	D4-E4-E3-F3
Walpole Street	D8-E8
Water Lane	A8
Watson Street	A2-A3
Wellington Row	C4
Wellington Street	F2-F3
Westminster Road	A7
William Street	D1
Willis Street	F2-F3
Winterscale Street	E2
Wolsley Street	F2

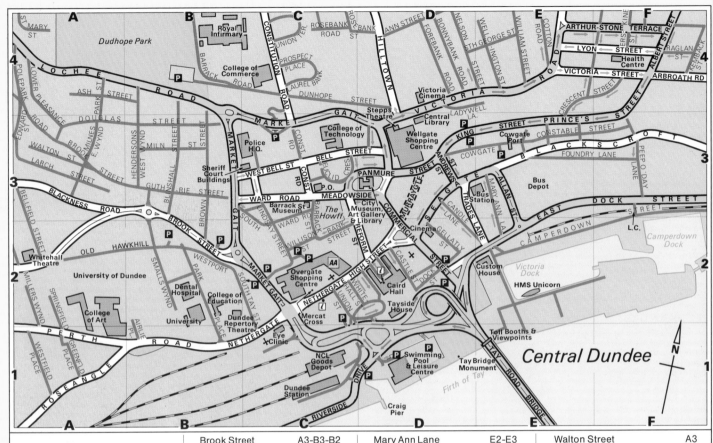

Central Dundee

Dundee Third largest city of Scotland and capital of Tayside, Dundee is a major port with a long and colourful maritime history, and it was also central to the 19th-century textile boom. But with its setting of moors, lochs and mountains, Dundee has become a centre for tourists. The city has a fine landmark in St Mary Tower, also known as Old Steeple, and the Mills Observatory has a refracting telescope and other displays dealing with astronomy and space exploration. Two top-flight football teams are based in the city and complement its fine sports facilities.

Inverness has long been called the 'Capital of the Highlands' and stands at the eastern end of the Great Glen, on the banks of the River Ness. Amongst the many places of interest that draw visitors to the town, Aberstaff House dates from the 16th century and has a rare, good example of an old turnpike stair. St Andrew's Cathedral has fine carved columns.

Perth Sir Walter Scott's 'Fair Maid of Perth' lived in a 14th-century house which still stands in this historic old Tayside town. St John's Kirk is a magnificent example of 16th-century Gothic architecture and notable as the scene of John Knox's fiery sermon against church idolatry in 1599 — a sermon which is now regarded as one of the major milestones of the Reformation. Also of interest are the Caithness Glass Factory (open to visitors) and the Perth Museum and Art Gallery.

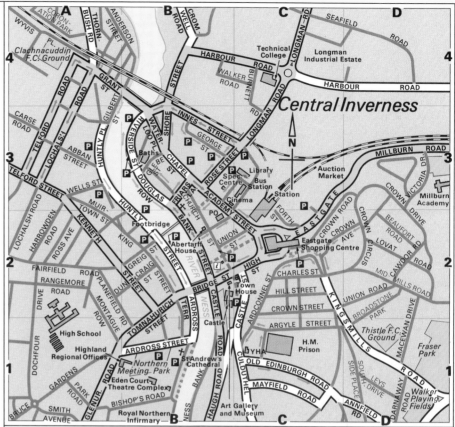

Central Inverness

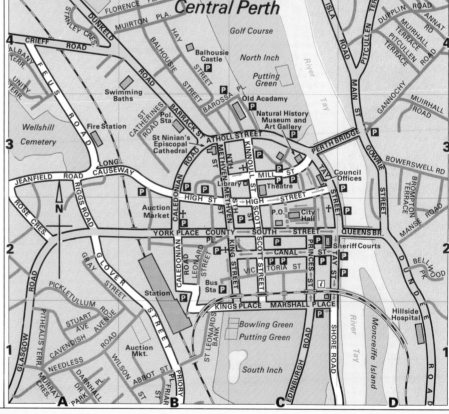

Central Perth

INVERNESS
Crowding the skyline with its battlements and towers, Inverness Castle commands an imposing site above the town — but was only built in the last century.

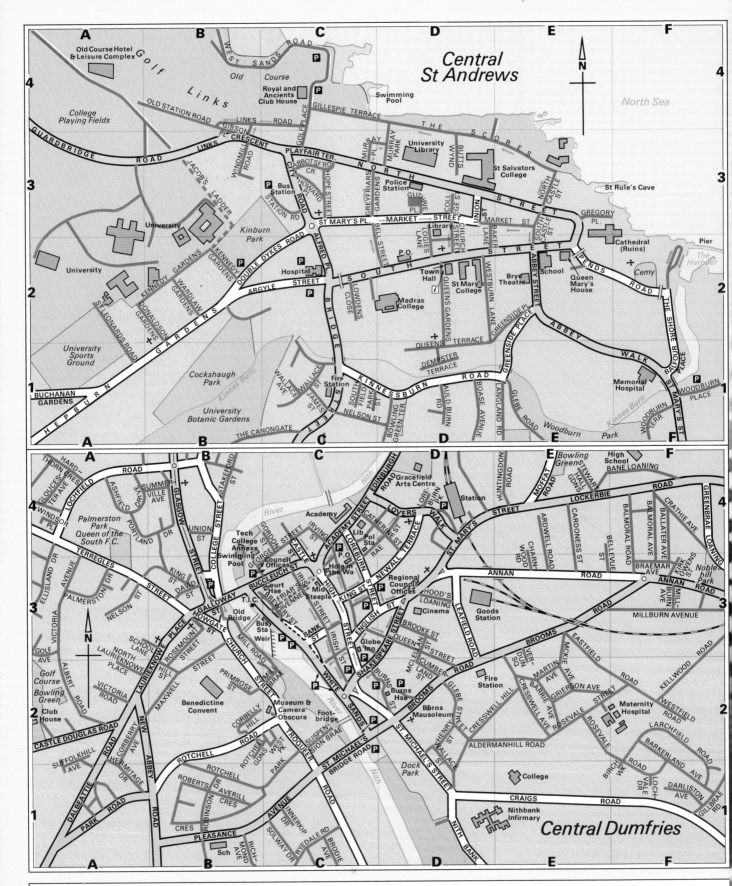

Central St Andrews

Central Dumfries

St Andrews is synonymous with golf. There are no less than 15 golf courses in the vicinity, and the Royal and Ancient Golf Club, founded in the 18th century, has come to be regarded as the international headquarters of the game. But the town's links with the past go back even further: it has a distinguished university which was founded in 1411, its castle is 13th-century and the cathedral dates from the 12th century.

Stirling lies just north of Bannockburn, where Robert the Bruce inflicted a swingeing defeat on the armies of England in 1314, and twelve years later he held his first parliament in the town's Cambuskenneth Abbey, which can still be seen. The castle dates back to the 13th century and its Landmark Centre provides an exciting audio-visual display. The Wallace Memorial offers fine views.

Oban has been a popular desination for tourists since the 19th century, not least because of its ferry links with the Hebrides. Visitors can see paperweights being made at the local glassworks, and other attractions are the fine views of the town and its surroundings to be seen from McCaig's Tower and Pulpit Hill.

Dumfries is Walter Scott's 'Queen of the South': a fine country town and market centre of old sandstone and spacious parks. Robert Burns spent the last years of his life here, and Burns House, where he died in 1796, is now a museum. His Mausoleum stands in St Michael's Churchyard.

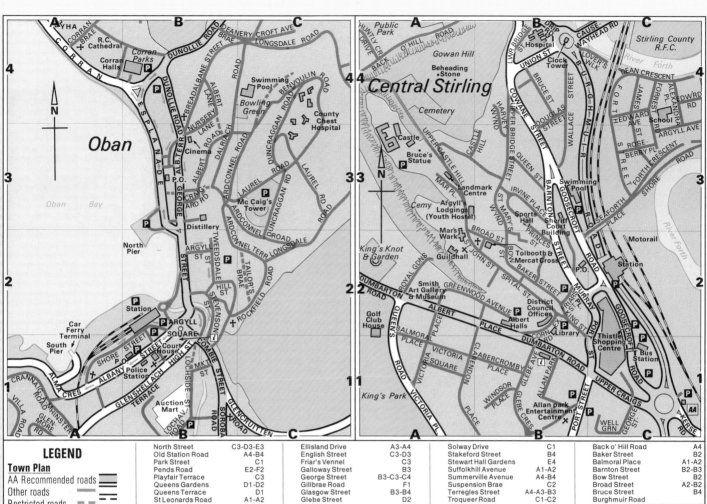

LEGEND

Town Plan

AA Recommended roads

Other roads

Restricted roads

Buildings of interest   Station 🏢

Churches   ✝

Car parks   🅿

Parks and open spaces

One way streets   →

Street Index with Grid Reference

St Andrews

Abbey Street	E2
Abbey Walk	E2-E1-F1
Abbotsford Crescent	C3
Alfred Place	C2-C3
Argyle Street	B2-C2
Auld Burn Road	D1
Baker Lane	D2-D3
Balfour Place	F1
Bell Street	C3-C2-D2
Boase Avenue	D1
Bowling Green Terrace	D1
Bridge Street	C1-C2
Buchanan Gardens	A1
Butts Wynd	D3
Church Street	D2-D3
City Road	C3
College Street	D3
Dempster Terrace	D1
Donaldson Gardens	A2-B2
Double Dykes Road	B2-C2-C3
Gibson Place	B3-B4
Gillespie Terrace	C4-D4
Glebe Road	E1
Golf Place	C3-C4
Greenside Place	D1-D2-E2-E1
Gregory Place	E3
Greyfriars Gardens	C3
Guardbridge Road	A4-A3-B3
Guthrie Place	D3
Hepburn Gardens	A1-B1-B2
Hope Street	C3
Howard Place	C3
Jacob's Ladder	B3
James Street	C1
Kennedy Gardens	A2-B2
Kinnessburn Road	C1-D1-E1
Langland Street	E1
Links Crescent	B3-C3
Links Road	B4-C4
Logies Lane	D2-D3
Lowdens Close	C2
Market Street	D3-E3
Murray Park	D3-D4
Murray Place	C3-D3
Nelson Street	C1-D1
North Castle Street	E3
North Street	C3-D3-E3
Old Station Road	A4-B4
Park Street	C1
Pends Road	E2-F2
Playfair Terrace	C3
Queens Gardens	D1-D2
Queens Terrace	D1
St Leonards Road	A1-A2
St Mary's Place	C3
St Mary's Street	F1
South Castle Street	E2-E3
South Field	C1
South Street	C2-D2-E2
Station Road	C3
The Canongate	B1-C1
The Scores	D4-D3-E3
The Shore	F1-F2
Union Street	D3
Wallace Avenue	C1
Wallace Street	C1
Wardlaw Gardens	B2
Westburn Lane	D1-D2
West Sands Road	B4-C4
Windmill Road	B3
Woodburn Place	F1
Woodburn Terrace	F1

Dumfries

Academy Street	C3-C4
Albert Road	A2-A3
Aldermanhill Road	D2-E2
Annan Road	D3-E3-F3
Ardwall Road	E3-E4
Ashfield Drive	A4
Averill Crescent	B1
Ballater Avenue	F3-F4
Balmoral Avenue	F3-F4
Balmoral Road	F3-F4
Ban Loaning	E4-F4
Bank Street	C3
Barkerland Avenue	F1-F2
Barrie Avenue	E2
Bellevue Street	E3-E4
Birch Walk	F1
Braemar Avenue	F3
Brewery Street	B3-C3
Brodie Avenue	C1
Brooke Street	D3
Brooms Road	D2-D3-E3-F3
Buccleuch Street	B3-C3
Burns Street	C2-D2
Cardoness Street	E3-E4
Castle Douglas Road	A2
Castle Street	C3-C4
Catherine Street	C4-D4
Charnwood Road	E3-E4
Chuch Street	B3-B2-C2
College Street	B3-B4
Corbelly Hill	B2
Corberry Avenue	A1-A2
Craigs Road	D1-E1-F1
Crathie Avenue	F4
Cresswell Avenue	E2
Cresswell Hill	D2-E2
Cumberland Street	D2
Dalbeattie Road	A1-A2
Darliston Avenue	F1
David Street	B3
Eastfield Road	E3-E2-F2
Edinburgh Road	C4-D4
Ellisland Drive	A3-A4
English Street	C3-D3
Friar's Vennel	C3
Galloway Street	B3
George Street	B3-C3-C4
Gillbrae Road	F1
Glasgow Street	B3-B4
Glebe Street	D2
Gloucester Avenue	A4
Golf Avenue	A3
Gordon Street	C4
Greenbrae Loaning	F3-F4
Grierson Avenue	E2
Hardthorn Crescent	A4
Henry Street	D2
Hermitage Drive	A1-A2
High Street	C2-C3
Hill Street	B2
Hood's Loaning	D3
Howgate Street	B3
Huntingdon Road	E4
Innerkip Drive	C1
Irish Street	C2-C3
Irving Street	C4
Kellwood Road	F2-F3
King Street	B3
King Street	C3
Kirkowens Street	F3
Larchfield Road	F1-F2
Laurieknowe Place	A2-B2-B3
Leafield Road	D3
Lochfield Road	A4-B4
Lochvale Drive	F1
Lockerbie Road	E4-F4
Loreburn Park	D4
Loreburn Street	C4-C3-D3
Lovers Walk	C4-D4
Martin Avenue	E2
Maxwell Street	A2-B2-B3
McLellan Street	D2-D3
Mickie Avenue	E2-E3
Mill Brae	C2
Millburn Avenue	E3-F3
Mill Road	B3-C3-C2
Moffat Road	E4
Nelson Street	A3
New Abbey Road	A2-B2-B1
Newall Terrace	C3-D3-D4
North Bank	D1
North Laurieknowe Place	A2
Palmerston Drive	A3
Park Road	A1
Pleasance Avenue	B1-C1
Portland Drive	A4-B4
Primrose Street	B2
Queen Street	D2-D3
Rae Street	C3-C4-D4
Richmond Avenue	B1
Roberts Crescent	B1
Robinson Drive	B1
Rosemount Street	B2-B3
Rosevale Street	E2-F2-F1
Rosevale Street	E2-F2
Rotchell Gardens	B2-C2
Rotchell Park	B1-C1-C2
Rotchell Road	B1-B2-C2
Ryedale Road	C1
St Michael's Bridge Road	C1-C2-D2
St Michael's Street	D1-D2
St Mary's Street	D3-D4-E4
School Lane	A3-B3
Shakespeare Street	C2-D2-D3
Solway Drive	C1
Stakeford Street	B4
Stewart Hall Gardens	E4
Suffolkhill Avenue	A1-A2
Summerville Avenue	A4-B4
Suspension Brae	C2
Terregles Street	A4-A3-B3
Troqueer Road	C1-C2
Union Street	B4
Verdun Square	E2-E3
Victoria Avenue	A3
Victoria Road	A2
Wallace Street	D1-D2
Westfield Road	F2
West Park	C2
White Sands	C2
Windsor Place	A4

Oban

Albany Street	A1-B1-B2
Albert Lane	B4
Albert Road	B3
Albert Terrace	B3
Alma Crescent	A4
Ardconnel Road	C3-B3-C3-C2
Ardconnel Terrace	B3-B2-C2
Argyll Square	B1-B2
Argyll Street	B2
Benvoulin Road	C3-C4
Breadalbane Street	B3-B4-C4
Combie Street	B1
Corran Brae	A4
Corran Esplanade	A4-B4-B3
Craigard Road	B3
Crannaig-a-Mhinster Road	A1
Croft Avenue	C4
Dalriach Road	B3-B4-C4
Deanery Brae	B4-C4
Duncraggan Road	C2-C3-C4
Dunolie Road	B3-B4
George Street	B2-B3
Glencruitten Road	B1-C1
Glenmore Road	A1
Glenshellach Terrace	A1-B1
High Street	B1
Hill Street	B2
Laurel Road	B3-C3
Lochavillin Road	B1
Lochside Street	B1
Longsdale Road	C2-C3
Longsdale Road	C4
Market Street	B1
Nursery Lane	B3-B4
Rockfield Road	B2-C2
Shore Street	A1-B1-B2
Soroba Road	B1
Stevenson Street	B1-B2
Tailor's Brae	C2
Tweedsdale Street	B2
Villa Road	A1

Stirling

Abercromy Place	A1-B1
Albert Place	A2-B2
Alexandra Place	C4
Allan Park	B1
Argyll Avenue	C3-C4
Back o' Hill Road	A4
Baker Street	B2
Balmoral Place	A1-A2
Barnton Street	B2-B3
Bow Street	B2
Broad Street	A2-B2
Bruce Street	B4
Burghmuir Road	B4-C4-C3-B3-C3-C2
Castle Hill	A3-B3
Causewayhead Road	B4-C4
Clarendon Place	B2-B1-A1-B1
Corn Exchange Road	B2
Cowane Street	B3-B4
Dean Crescent	C4
Douglas Street	B3-B4
Drip Road	B4
Dumberton Road	A2, B2-B1
Edward Avenue	C4
Edward Road	C4
Forrest Road	C3-C4
Forth Crescent	C3
Forth Street	C3-C4
Friar's Street	B2
George Street	C1
Glebe Avenue	B1
Glebe Crescent	B1
Goosecroft Road	B3-B2-C2-C1
Greenwood Avenue	A2-B2
Harvey Wynd	B3-B4
Huntley Crescent Drive	A4
Irvine Road	B3
James Street	C3-C4
Kerse Road	C1
King Street	B2
Lover's Walk	B4-C4
Lower Bridge Street	B4
Mar Place	A3
Murray Place	B2-C2
Port Street	B1-C1-C2
Princes Street	B2-B3
Queen's Road	A1-A2
Queen Street	B3
Roseberry Place	C3
Royal Gardens	A2
St John Street	A2-B2
St Mary's Wynd	B2-B3
Seaforth Place	B2-C2-C3
Shore Road	C3
Spital Street	B2
Union Street	B4
Upper Bridge Street	B3-B4
Upper Castle Hill	A3-A4
Upper Craigs	C1
Victoria Place	A1-A2
Victoria Square	A2
Wallace Street	B3-B4
Well Green	C1
Windsor Place	B1

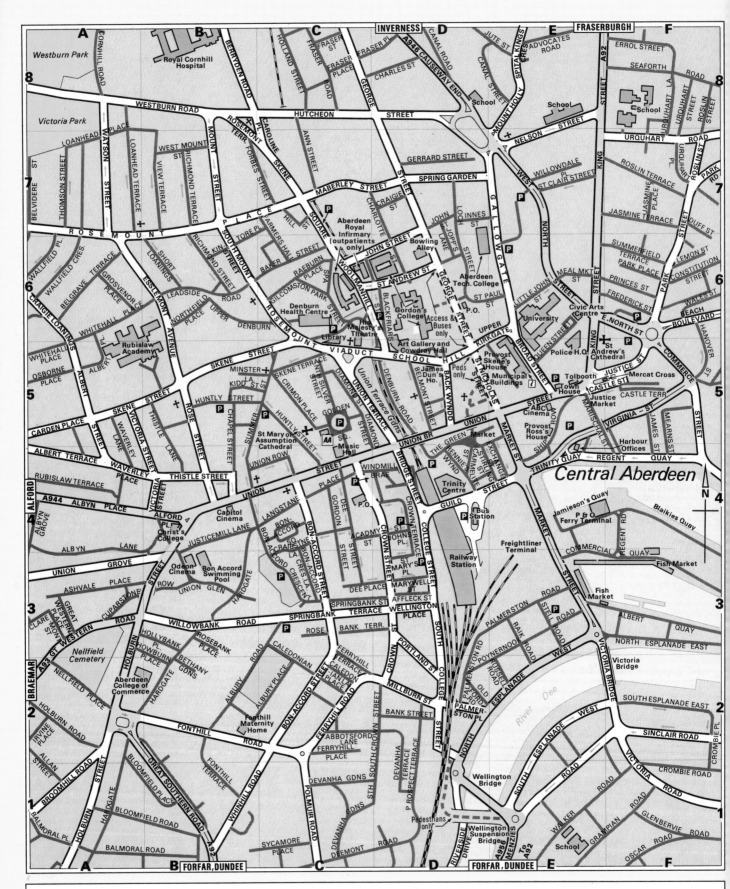

Aberdeen

Granite gives Aberdeen its especial character; but this is not to say that the city is a grim or a grey place, the granites used are of many hues – white, blue, pink and grey. Although the most imposing buildings date from the 19th century, granite has been used to dramatic effect since at least as early as the 15th century. From that time dates St Machar's Cathedral, originally founded in AD580,

but rebuilt several times, especially after a devasting fire started on the orders of Edward III of England in 1336. St Machar's is in Old Aberdeen, traditionally the ecclesiastical and educational hub of the city, while 'New' Aberdeen (actually no newer) has always been the commercial centre. Even that definition is deceptive, for although Old Aberdeen has King's College, founded in 1494, New Aberdeen has Marischal College, founded almost exactly a century later (but rebuilt in 1844)

and every bit as distinguished as a seat of learning. Both establishments functioned as independent universities until they were merged in 1860 to form Aberdeen University. The North Sea oil boom has brought many changes to the city, some of which threatened its character. But even though high-rise buildings are now common, the stately façades, towers and pillars of granite still reign supreme and Union Street remains one of the best thoroughfares in Britain.

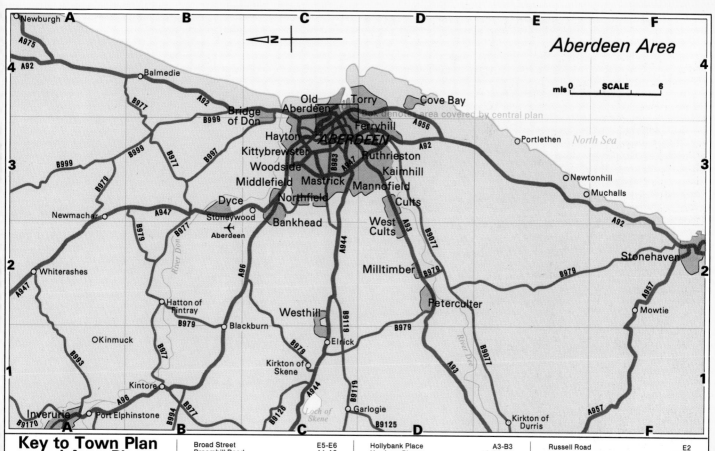

Key to Town Plan and Area Plan

Town Plan

A A Recommended roads
Other roads
Restricted roads
Buildings of interest   Cinema
Car Parks   P
Parks and open spaces
One Way Streets
Churches   +

Area Plan

A roads
B roads
Locations   Hattoncrook O
Urban area

Street Index with Grid Reference

Aberdeen

Abbotsford Lane	C2-D2
Academy Street	C4-D4
Advocates Road	E8
Affleck Street	D3
Albert Quay	E3-F3
Albert Place	A5-A6
Albert Street	A4-A5
Albert Terrace	A4-A5
Albyn Grove	A4
Albyn Lane	A4-A3-B3-B4
Albyn Place	A4-B4
Alford Place	B4
Allan Street	A1-A2
Ann Street	C7-C8
Ashvale Place	A3-B3
Back Wynnd	D5
Baker Street	B6-C6
Balmoral Place	A1
Balmoral Road	A1-B1
Bank Street	D2
Beach Boulevard	F6
Belgrave Terrace	A6
Belmont Street	D5
Belvidere Street	A7
Berryden Road	B8-C8
Bethany Gardens	B2
Blackfriars Street	D6
Bloomfield Place	A2-A1-B1
Bloomfield Road	A1-B1
Bon-Accord Crescent	B4-C4-C3
Bon-Accord Crescent Lane	C3-C4
Bon-Accord Square	C4
Bon-Accord Street	C2-C3-C4
Bridge Place	D4

Broad Street	E5-E6
Broomhill Road	A1-A2
Caledonian Lane	C2
Caledonian Place	C2-C3
Canal Road	D8
Canal Street	D8-E8
Carden Place	A5
Carmelite Street	D4
Caroline Place	B8-B7-C7-C8
Castle Street	E5-F5
Castle Terrace	E5-F5
Causeway End	D8
Chapel Street	B4-B5
Charles Street	C8-D8
Charlotte Street	C7-D7-D6
Claremont Street	A3
College Street	D3-D4
Commerce Street	F4-F5
Commercial Quay	E3-F3
Constitution Street	F6
Cornhill Road	A8
Craibstone Lane	C3-C4
Craigie Loanings	A5-A6
Craigie Street	D7
Crimon Street	C5
Crombie Place	F1-F2
Crombie Road	F1
Crown Street	D2-D3-D4-C4
Crown Terrace	D3-D4
Cuparstone Row	A3-B3
Dee Place	C3-D3
Dee Street	C3-C4
Deemont road	C1-D1
Denburn Road	D5
Devanha Gardens	C1
Devanha Terrace	D1-D2
Diamond Street	C4-D4-C5
Duff Street	F6-F7
East North Street	E6-F6
Errol Street	F8
Esslemont Avenue	A6-B6-B5
Exchange Street	E4-E5
Farmers Hill	C6-C7
Ferryhill Place	C2
Ferryhill Road	C2-D2
Ferryhill Terrace	C2-D2
Fonthill Road	A2-B2-C2
Fonthill Terrace	B1-B2
Forbes Street	B7-C7
Fraser Place	C8-D8
Fraser Road	C8
Fraser Street	C8
Frederick Street	E6-F6
Gallowgate	D7-E7-E6
George Street	C8-D8-D7-D6-D5
Gerrard Street	D7
Gilcomston Park	C6
Glenbervie Road	F1
Golden Square	C5
Gordon Street	C3-C4
Grampian Road	E1-F1
Great Southern Road	A1-B2-B1
Great Western Place	A3
Great Western Road	A2-A3
Grosvenor Place	A6
Guild Street	D4-E4
Hanover Street	F5-F6
Hardgate	A1-A2-B2-B3-B4
Hill Street	C7
Holburn Road	A2
Holburn Street	A1-A2-A3-B3-B4
Holland Street	C8

Hollybank Place	A3-B3
Howburn Place	A3-B3-B2
Huntly Street	B5-C5-C4
Hutcheon Street	B8-C8-D8
Innes Street	D7-E7
Irvine Place	A2
James Street	F4-F5
Jasmine Place	F7
Jasmine Terrace	E7-F7
John Street	C6-D6-D7
Jopp's Lane	D6-D7
Justice Street	E5-F5-F6
Justice Mill Lane	B3-B4
Jute Street	D8-E8
Kidd Street	B5-C5
King Street	E5-E6-E7-E8-F8
Kintore Place	B6-B7-C7
Langstone Place	C4
Leadside Road	B6
Lemon Street	F6
Little John Street	E6
Loanhead Place	A7-A8-B8
Loanhead Terrace	A7
Loch Street	D6-D7
Maberley Street	C7-D7
Marischal Street	E5-F5-F4
Market Street	E3-E4-E5
Marywell Street	D3
Meal Market Street	E6
Mearns Street	F4-F5
Menzies Road	E1-E2-F2
Millburn Street	D2
Minster Holly	B5-C5
Mount Holly	E7-E8
Mount Street	B7-B8
Nellfield Place	A2
Nelson Street	E7-E8
North Esplanade East	E3-F3
North Esplanade West	D1-D2-E2-E3
North Silver Street	C5
Northfield Place	B6
Old Ford Road	D2
Osborne Place	A5
Oscar Road	F1
Palmerston Place	D2
Palmerston Road	D2-D3-D3-E3
Park Place	F6
Park Road	F7
Park Street	F6-F7
Polmuir Road	C1-C2
Portland Street	D2-D3
Poynernook Road	D2-E2-E3
Princes Street	E6-F6
Prospect Terrace	D1-D2
Queen Street	E5-E6
Raeburn Place	C6
Raik Road	E2-E3
Regent Road	F3-F4
Regent Quay	E5-F5
Rennies Wyndd	D4
Richmond Street	B6-B7
Richmond Terrace	B7
Riverside Drive	D1
Rose Street	B4-B5
Rosebank Place	B3
Rosebank Terrace	C3-D3
Rosemount Place	A7-A6-B6-B7-C7
Rosemount Terrace	B7-B8
Rosemount Viaduct	B6-C6-C5
Roslin Street	F7-F8
Roslin Terrace	E7-F7
Rubislaw Terrace	A4

Russell Road	E2
St Andrew Street	C6-D6
St Clair Street	E7
St John's Place	D4
St Mary's Place	D3
St Nicholas Street	D5-E5
St Paul Street	D6-E6
School Hill	D5
Seaforth Road	F8
Ship Row	E4-E5
Short Loanings	B6
Sinclair Road	F2
Skene Square	C6-C7
Skene Street	A5-B5-C5
Skene Terrace	C5
South College Street	D2-D3
South Crown Street	C1-D1-D2
South Esplanade East	F2
South Esplanade West	E1-E2
South Mount Street	B6-B7
Spa Street	C6
Spital Kings Crescent	E8
Spring Garden	D7
Spring Bank Street	C3-D3
Spring Bank Terrace	C3-D3
Stell Road	E3
Stirling Street	D4-E4
Summer Street	B4-B5-C5
Summerfield Terrace	E6-F6
Sycamore Place	B1-C1
The Green	D4-D5
Thistle Lane	B4-B5
Thistle Street	B4
Thomson Street	A7
Trinity Quay	E4
Upper Denburn	B6-C6
Upper Kirkgate	D5-D6-E5-E6
Urquhart Lane	F7-F8
Urquhart Place	F7
Urquhart Road	F7
Urquhart Street	F7-F8
Union Bridge	D4-D5
Union Glen	B3
Union Grove	A3-B3
Union Row	B4-C4
Union Street	B4-C4-D4-D5-E5
Union Terrace	C5-D5
Victoria Bridge	E3-E2-F2
Victoria Road	F1-F2
Victoria Street	A5-B4-B5
View Terrace	B7
Virginia Street	E5-F5
Wales Street	F6
Walker Road	E1-F1
Wallfield Crescent	A6
Wallfield Place	A6-A7
Watson Street	A7-A8
Waverley Lane	A4-A5
Waverley Place	A4-B4
Wellington Place	D3
West Mount Street	B7
West North Street	E6-E7-E8
Westburn Road	A8-B8
Whinhill Road	B1-C1-C2
Whitehall Place	A5-A6-B6
Willow Bank Road	B3-C3
Willowdale Place	E7
Windmill Brae	C4-D4
Woolmanhill	C6-D6-D5

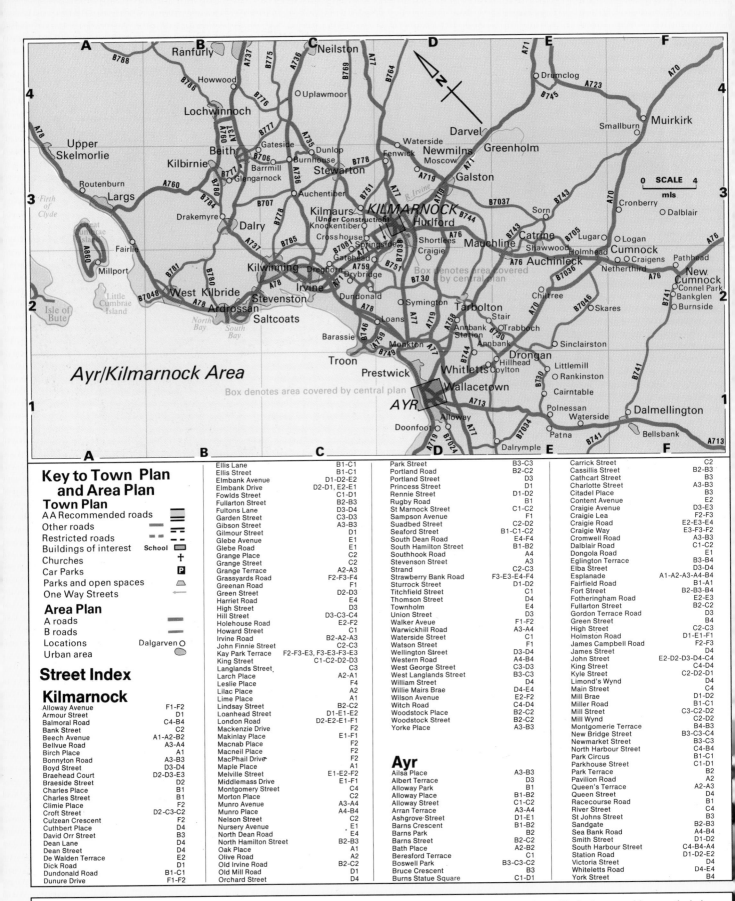

Key to Town Plan and Area Plan

Town Plan

AA Recommended roads	
Other roads	
Restricted roads	
Buildings of interest	School
Churches	†
Car Parks	P
Parks and open spaces	
One Way Streets	

Area Plan

A roads	
B roads	
Locations	Dalgarven
Urban area	

Street Index

Kilmarnock

Alloway Avenue	F1-F2
Armour Street	D1
Balmoral Road	C4-B4
Bank Street	C2
Beech Avenue	A1-A2-B2
Bellvue Road	A3-A4
Birch Place	A1
Bonnyton Road	A3-B3
Boyd Street	D3-D4
Braehead Court	D2-D3-E3
Braeside Street	D2
Charles Place	B1
Charles Street	B1
Climie Place	F2
Croft Street	D2-C3-C2
Culzean Crescent	F2
Cuthbert Place	D4
David Orr Street	B3
Dean Lane	D4
Dean Street	D4
De Walden Terrace	E2
Dick Road	D1
Dundonald Road	B1-C1
Dunure Drive	F1-F2
Ellis Lane	B1-C1
Ellis Street	B1-C1
Elmbank Avenue	D1-D2-E2
Elmbank Drive	D2-D1, E2-E1
Fowlds Street	C1-D1
Fullarton Street	B2-B3
Fultons Lane	C3-D3
Garden Street	C3-D3
Gibson Street	A3-B3
Gilmour Street	D1
Glebe Avenue	E1
Glebe Road	E1
Grange Place	C2
Grange Street	C2
Grange Terrace	A2-A3
Grassyards Road	F2-F3-F4
Greenan Road	F1
Green Street	D2-D3
Harriet Road	E4
High Street	D3
Hill Street	D3-C3-C4
Holehouse Road	E2-F2
Howard Street	C1
Irvine Road	B2-A2-A3
John Finnie Street	C2-C3
Kay Park Terrace	F2-F3-E3, F3-E3-F3-E3
King Street	C1-C2-D2-D3
Langlands Street	C3
Larch Place	A2-A1
Leslie Place	F4
Lilac Place	A2
Lime Place	A1
Lindsay Street	B2-C2
Loanhead Street	D1-E1-E2
London Road	D2-E2-E1-F1
Mackenzie Drive	F2
Makinlay Place	E1-F1
Macnab Place	F2
Macneil Place	F2
MacPhail Drive	F2
Maple Place	A1
Melville Street	E1-E2-F2
Middlemass Drive	E1-F1
Montgomery Street	C4
Morton Place	C2
Munro Avenue	A3-A4
Munro Place	A4-A4
Nelson Street	C2
Nursery Avenue	E1
North Dean Road	E4
North Hamilton Street	B2-B3
Oak Place	A1
Olive Road	A2
Old Irvine Road	B2-C2
Old Mill Road	D1
Orchard Street	D4

Park Street	B3-C3
Portland Road	B2-C2
Portland Street	D3
Princess Street	D1
Rennie Street	D1-D2
Rugby Road	B1
St Marnock Street	C1-C2
Sampson Avenue	F1
Suadbed Street	C2-D2
Seaford Street	B1-C1-C2
South Dean Road	E4-F4
South Hamilton Street	B1-B2
Southhook Road	A4
Stevenson Street	A3
Strand	C2-C3
Strawberry Bank Road	F3-E3-E4-F4
Sturrock Street	D1-D2
Titchfield Street	C1
Thomson Street	D4
Townholm	E4
Union Street	D3
Walker Aveue	F1-F2
Warwickhill Road	A3-A4
Waterside Street	C1
Watson Street	F1
Wellington Street	D3-D4
Western Road	A4-B4
West George Street	C3-D3
West Langlands Street	B3-C3
William Street	D4
Willie Mairs Brae	D4-E4
Wilson Avenue	E2-F2
Witch Road	C4-D4
Woodstock Place	B2-C2
Woodstock Street	B2-C2
Yorke Place	A3-B3

Ayr

Ailsa Place	A3-B3
Albert Terrace	D3
Alloway Park	B1
Alloway Place	B1-B2
Alloway Street	C1-C2
Arran Terrace	A3-A4
Ashgrove Street	D1-E1
Barns Crescent	B1-B2
Barns Park	B2
Barns Street	B2-C2
Bath Place	A2-B2
Beresford Terrace	C1
Boswell Park	B3-C3-C2
Bruce Crescent	B3
Burns Statue Square	C1-D1

Carrick Street	C2
Cassillis Street	B2-B3
Cathcart Street	B3
Charlotte Street	A3-B3
Citadel Place	B3
Content Avenue	E2
Craigie Avenue	D3-E3
Craigie Lea	F2-F3
Craigie Road	E2-E3-E4
Craigie Way	E3-F3-F2
Cromwell Road	A3-B3
Dalblair Road	C1-C2
Dongola Road	E1
Eglinton Terrace	B3-B4
Elba Street	D3-D4
Esplanade	A1-A2-A3-A4-B4
Fairfield Road	B1-A1
Fort Street	B2-B3-B4
Fotheringham Road	E2-E3
Fullarton Street	B2-C2
Gordon Terrace Road	D3
Green Street	B4
High Street	C2-C3
Holmston Road	D1-E1-F1
James Campbell Road	F2-F3
James Street	D4
John Street	E2-D2-D3-D4-C4
King Street	C4-D4
Kyle Street	C2-D2-D1
Limond's Wynd	D4
Main Street	C4
Mill Brae	D1-D2
Miller Road	B1-C1
Mill Street	C3-C2-D2
Mill Wynd	C2-D2
Montgomerie Terrace	B4-B3
New Bridge Street	B3-C3-C4
Newmarket Street	B3-C3
North Harbour Street	C4-B4
Park Circus	B1-C1
Parkhouse Street	C1-D1
Park Terrace	B2
Pavilion Road	A2
Queen's Terrace	A2-A3
Queen Street	D4
Racecourse Road	B1
River Street	C4
St Johns Street	B3
Sandgate	B2-B3
Sea Bank Road	A4-B4
Smith Street	D1-D2
South Harbour Street	C4-B4-A4
Station Road	D1-D2-E2
Victoria Street	D4
Whiteletts Road	D4-E4
York Street	B4

Ayr

Set on the lovely coastline of the Firth of Clyde, Ayr enjoys a well-deserved reputation as one of Scotland's most attractive seaside resorts. Its fine natural assets of sandy beaches and pastoral river scenery have been augmented by extensive parks and gardens, as well as a host of leisure amenities.

However, some of Ayr's visitors are drawn to the town by its associations with Scotland's beloved national poet – Robert Burns. He was born at the nearby village of Alloway and many of the places immortalised in his poems can be seen in Ayr. These include the medieval Auld Brig, one of the famous 'twa brigs' that span the River Ayr. The thatched Tam O'Shanter Inn in the High Street, now a museum devoted to Burns, and an imposing statue, are further reminders that this was 'Rabbie's' town.

Ayr has been a prosperous fishing port for centuries and its harbour provides a particularly charming focal point to the town. Surprisingly, few buildings pre-date the 19th century, but one exception is Loudon Hall – a fine 16th-century town house now open to the public. Several handsome Georgian edifaces surround Wellington Square, overlooked by the soaring steeple of the Town Buildings. A statue here commemorates another son of Ayr, John Macadam, who invented the road surface that bears his name.

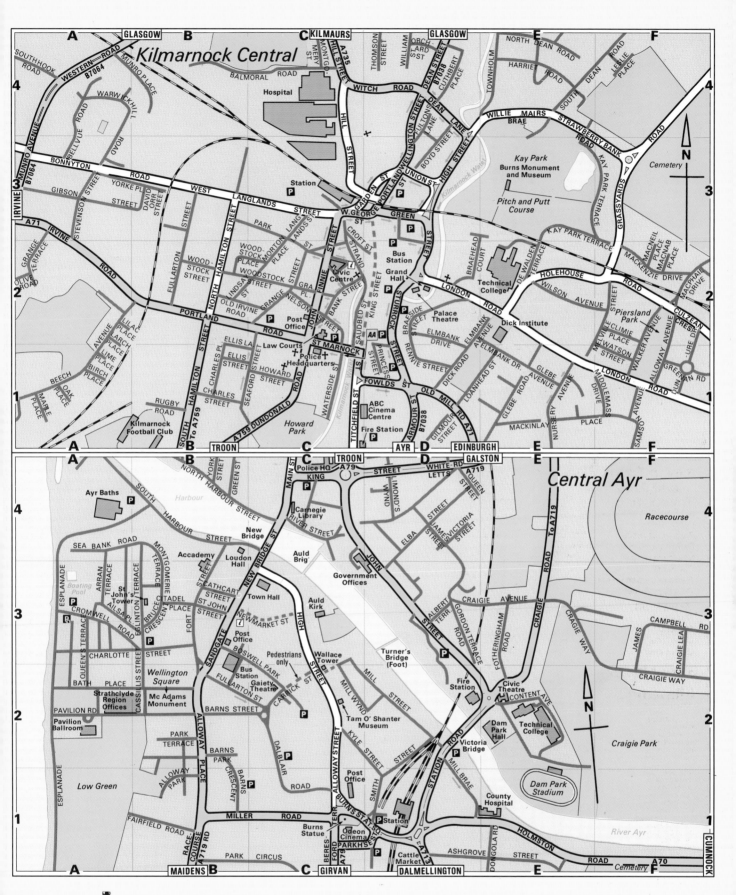

AYR
The town has been an important fishing port on the Firth of Clyde for several hundred years. Today, Ayr is a major seaside resort and tourist centre and the harbour is as busy as ever, with yachts and leisure craft.

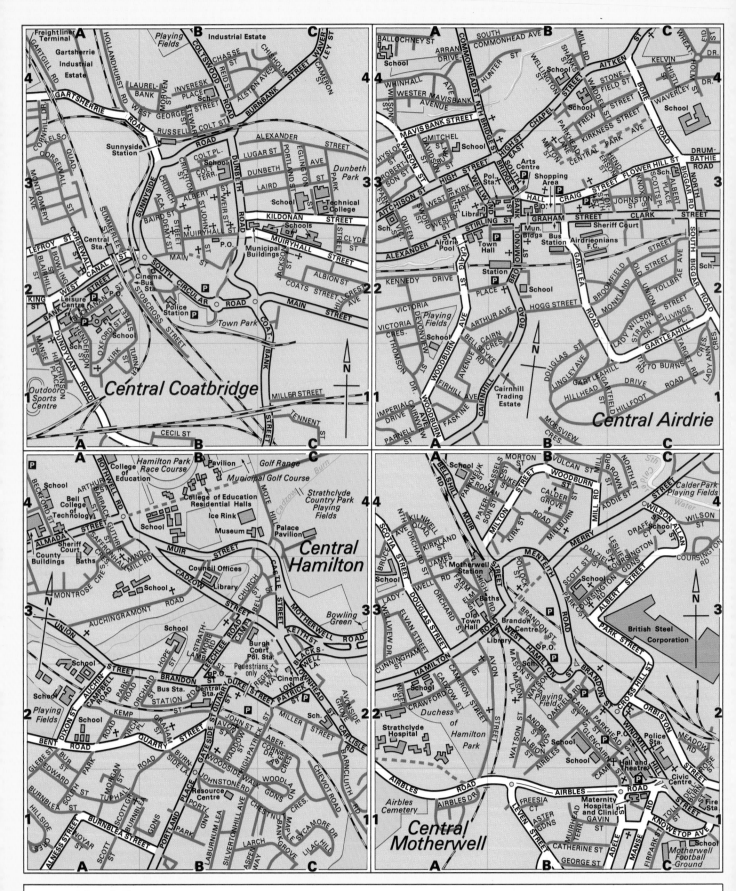

Coatbridge

Six villages went into the making of Coatbridge, a town whose iron and coal mining made it the centre of the Scottish iron industry. Scotland's first railway was here, but today Coatbridge achieves industrial prominence via its waterway, which gives it the largest inland port in Britain and is part of a major project to revitalise the entire town. Drumpellier Country Park nearby stands in fine wood and loch surroundings.

Airdrie Few industrial towns make such a pleasant first impression on the visitor as Airdrie, which, for all its industrial past, still has the air of a country market centre.

Motherwell Heartland of Scottish steelmaking, the place where the metal for the hulls of the *Queen Mary* and *Queen Elizabeth* was forged, Motherwell is a town where industry is heard and felt. But the town's name has gentler origins: it comes from a well — or pool — dedicated to the Virgin Mary, the site of which is marked by a plaque in Ladywell Road.

Hamilton's most notable landmark is the beautiful dome construction of Hamilton Mausoleum, noted for the six-second echo it produces. An industrial centre set in attractive surroundings, the town also enjoys a race course and an ice-rink, and in Strathclyde Park, it has excellent land and water sports facilities.

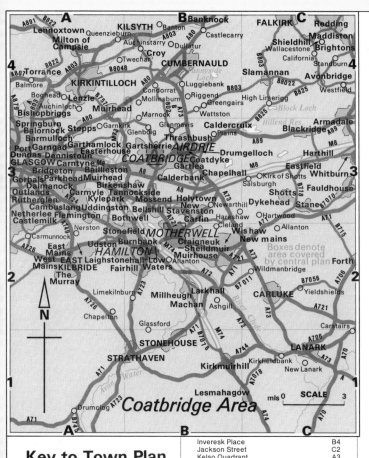

Coatbridge Area

Henderson Street	C3
High Street	A3
High Street East	B3
Hillfoot Road	C1
Hillhead Drive	B1-C1
Hogg Street	B2
Hunter Street	A4-B4
Hyslop Street	A3
Imperial Drive	A1
Johnston Street	C3
Kelvin Drive	C4
Kennedy Drive	A2
Kirkness Street	B3-B4-C4
Knox Street	C3
Lady Ann Crescent	C1-C2
Lady Wilson Street	C2
Lingley Avenue	B1
Livingstone Place	C2
Mavis Bank Street	A3-A4
Mill Road	B4
Milton Street	B3
Mitchel Street	A3
Monkland Street	B2-C2
Mossview Crescent	B1
North Biggar Road	C3
North Bridge Street	A3-A4-B3
Old Union Street	C3
Park Street	A3
Parkhead Lane	B3
Parnell Street	A1
Queen Victoria Street	A3
Reid Street	C4
Robertson Street	A3
Scotts Place	C3
Shanks Street	B4
South Biggar Road	C2-C3
South Bridge Street	B3
South Commonhead Avenue	A4-B4
Stirling Street	A3-B3
Stonefield Street	B4-C4
Strain Street	C2
Sword Street	A3
Target Road	C1-C2
Thomson Drive	A1-A2
Thistle Street	C4
Tinto Road	C1
Tollbrae Avenue	C2
Victoria Crescent	A2
Victoria Place	A2-B2
Waddell Street	B4-C4
Waverley Drive	C4
Wellington Street	B4
Wellwynd	A3-B3
Wesley Street	A3
West Kirk Street	A3
Western Mavisbank Avenue	A4
Wheatholm Street	C4
Wilson Street	A3-A4
Woodburn Avenue	A1-A2

Hamilton

Abercorn Crescent	C2
Abercorn Drive	C1
Almada Street	A4
Alness Street	A1
Arthur Street	A4
Aspen Way	B1
Auchincampbell Road	A2
Auchingramont Road	A3-B3
Avon Street	B2
Avonside Grove	C2
Barncluith Road	C1-C2
Barrack Street	A4
Beckford Street	A4
Bent Road	A2
Blackswell Lane	C3
Bothwell Road	A4
Brandon Street	B2
Burnblea Gardens	A1-B1
Burnblea Street	A1-B1
Burns Street	A1-A2
Burnside Lane	B2
Cadzow Street	B3-C3
Campbell Street	B3-C3
Carlisle Road	C2
Castle Street	C3
Chestnut Crescent	B1-C1
Cheviot Road	C1-C2
Church Street	B3-C3
Duke Street	B2-C2
Dixon Street	A2
Edward Street	A1
Gateside Street	B2
Glebe Street	A1-A2
Graham Street	B2
Guthrie Street	A4
Haddow Street	B2
High Patrick Street	B2-C2
Hillside Crescent	A1
Hope Street	B2-B3
John Street	B2
Johnstone Road	B1
Keith Street	C3
Kemp Street	A2-B2
Laburnum Lea	B1
Lamb Street	B2-B3
Larch Grove	B1-C1
Leechlee Road	B2-B3
Lilac Hill	C1
Low Patrick Street	C2
Maple Bank	C1
Miller Street	C2
Montrose Crescent	A3
Morgan Street	A1
Mote Hill	C4
Motherwell Road	C3
Muir Street	B4-C4
Noyar Street	A1
Orchard Place	A2
Orchard Street	B2
Park Road	A2
Portland Place	B1
Portland Place	B1
Quarry Street	A2-B2
Regent Way	C2
Saffronhall Crescent	A3-A4
Scott Grove	A1

Scott Street	A1
Silvertonhill Avenue	B1
Station Road	B2
Strathmore Road	B3
South Park Road	A1-A2
Sycamore Drive	C1
Townhead Street	C2
Tuphall Road	A1-B2
Union Street	A2-A3
Windmill Road	A3-B4
Woodland Gardens	C1
Woodside Walk	B1-B2

Motherwell

Addie Street	B4-C4
Adele Street	C1
Airbles Drive	A1
Airbles Road	A1-B1-C1
Airbles Street	B1
Albert Street	B3-C3
Albion Street	B2
Allan Street	C4
Anderson Street	B2
Aster Gardens	B1
Avon Street	A1-A2-B2-B3-A3
Bellshill Road	A4
Brandon Street	B2-B3-C2
Brown Street	B4-C4
Bruce Avenue	A3-A4
Cadzow Street	A2
Cairn Street	B2
Calder Grove	B4
Cameron Street	A2
Camp Street	B1-B2-C2
Cassels Street	B4
Catherine Street	B1
Coursington Gardens	C3
Coursington Road	B3-C3-C4
Crawford Street	A2
Cross Hill Street	C2
Cunningham Street	A2-A3
Dalziel Street	B3-B4
Dellburn Street	C1
Douglas Street	A3
Draffen Court	C4
Duke Street	B4
Elm Street	A3
Elvan Street	A3
Farm Street	A3
Firpark Street	C1
Freesia Court	B1
Gavin Street	B1-C1
George Street	B1
Glencairn Street	B2-C2-C1
Hamilton Road	A2-A3-B3
High Road	A3-B3
James Street	A3-A4
Kilnwell Quad	A4
Kirk Street	B4
Kirkland Street	A4
Knowetop Avenue	C1
Ladywell Road	A3
Leslie Street	C3-C4
Leven Street	B1
Manse Street	C1
Mason Lane	B2
Mason Street	B2-B3
Meadow Road	C2
Menteith Road	B3-B4
Merry Street	B4-C4
Mill Road	B4
Millburn Street	B4
Milton Street	A4-B4
Morton Street	B4
Muir Street	A4-B3
Muirhead Terrace	B1
Nigel Street	A2
North Street	C4
North Orchard Street	A3-A4
Oakfield Road	B2
Orbiston Street	C1-C2
Orchard Street	A3
Park Street	B3-C3
Parkhead Street	B2-C2
Parkneuk Street	A4
Paterson Street	A4-B4
Pollock Street	B3
Roman road	A4-B4
Rose Street	C2
Scotia Street	A3-A4
Scott Street	B3
Toll Street	C1
Vulcan Street	B4
Watson Street	B2
Wellview Drive	A3
West Hamilton Street	B2-B3
Wilson Street	B1
Windmill Hill Street	C1-C2
Woodburn Street	B4

Key to Town Plan and Area Plan

Town Plan

- A A Recommended roads
- Other roads
- Restricted roads
- Buildings of interest   Mill
- Car Parks   P
- Parks and open spaces

Area Plan

- A roads
- B roads
- Locations   Banton ○
- Urban Area

Street Index with Grid Reference

Coatbridge

Academy Street	B2-B3
Albert Street	B3
Albion Street	C2
Alexander Street	B3-C3
Alston Avenue	B4-C4
Baird Street	B3
Bank Street	A2
Blairhill Street	A2
Bowling Street	A2
Buchanan Street	A2
Burnbank Street	B4-C4
Cameron Street	C4
Cecil Street	B1
Chassels Street	B4
Chisholm Street	C4
Church Street	B2-B3
Clyde Street	C2
Coatbank Street	C1-C2
Coats Street	C2
Colt Place	B3
Colt Terrace	B3
Coltswood Road	B4
Cornhill Drive	A3-A4
Corsewall Street	A2-A3
Crichton Street	B3
Dunbeth Avenue	B3-C3
Dunbeth Road	B2-B3
Dundyvan Road	A1-A2
Eglinton Street	C3
Gartgill Road	A4
Gartsherrie Road	A4-B3-B4
Henderson Street	A1-A2
Hillcrest Avenue	C2
Hollandhurst Road	A4
Hutchinson Place	A1

Inveresk Place	B4
Jackson Street	C2
Kelso Quadrant	A3
Kildonan Street	C3
King Street	A2
Kirk Street	A1-A2
Laird Street	B3-C3
Laurelbank	A4-B4
Lefroy Street	A2
Lugar Street	B3-C3
Main Street	B2-C2
Manse Street	A1-A2
Miller Street	C1
Montgomery Avenue	A3
Morton Street	B4
Muiryhall Street	B2-B3-C2-C3
Oxford Street	A1-A2
Park Street	C2-C3
Portland Street	C3
Reid Street	B4
Russel Colt Street	B3-B4
St John Street	B2-B3
South Circular Road	B2
Stewart Street	B3-B4
Stobcross Street	A2-B1-B2
Summerlee Street	A2-A3
Sunnyside Road	A3-B3
Tennent Street	C1
Turner Street	A1
Waverley Street	C4
Weir Street	B3
West Canal Street	A2
West George Street	A4-B4

Airdrie

Aitchison Street	A3
Aitken Street	B4-C4
Albert Place	C3
Alexander Street	A2-A3
Arran Drive	A4
Arthur Avenue	A2-B2
Ballochney Street	A4
Bank Street	B3
Bell Street	A3
Bellsdyke Road	A1-A2-B1
Broomfield Street	B2-C2
Broomknoll Street	B2-B3
Bore Road	C3-C4
Burnbank Street	A3
Burns Crescent	C1-C2
Cairnhill Crescent	A1-B2
Cairnhill Road	A1-B1-B2
Cairnview	A1
Central Park Avenue	B3-C3-C4
Chapel Street	B4
Clark Street	C3
Commonhead Street	A4
Craig Street	A2
Davidson Street	A3
Devonview Street	A1-A2
Douglas Street	B1-B2
Drumbathie Road	C3
Faskine Avenue	A1
Firhill Avenue	A1
Flowerhill Street	C3
Forsyth Street	C3
Frew Street	B4-C4
Gartfield Street	B1
Gartlea Road	B1-B2-B3
Gartleahill	B1-C1-C2
Graham Street	B3
Hallcraig Street	B3-C3

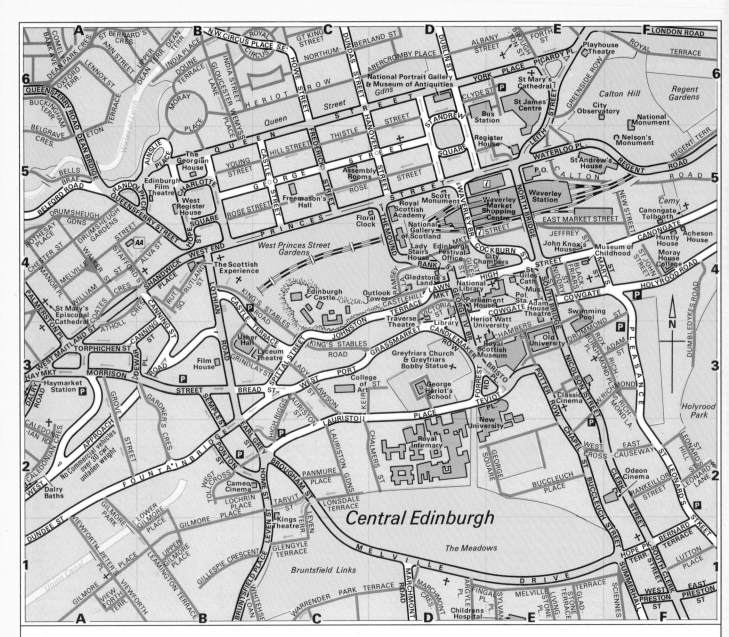

Key to Town Plan and Area Plan

Town Plan
A A Recommended roads
Other roads
Restricted roads
Buildings of intrest   Gallery
Car Parks   P
Parks and open spaces
One Way Streets
Churches   +

Area Plan
A roads
B roads
Locations   Newcraighall O
Urban area

Street Index with Grid Reference

Edinburgh

Edinburgh

Scotland's ancient capital, dubbed the "Athens of the North", is one of the most splendid cities in the whole of Europe. Its buildings, its history and its cultural life give it an international importance which is celebrated every year in its world-famous festival. The whole city is overshadowed by the craggy castle which seems to grow out of the rock itself. There has been a fortress here since the 7th

century and most of the great figures of Scottish history have been associated with it. The old town grew up around the base of Castle Rock within the boundaries of the defensive King's Wall and, unable to spread outwards, grew upwards in a maze of tenements. However, during the 18th century new prosperity from the shipping trade resulted in the building of the New Town and the regular, spacious layout of the Georgian development makes a striking contrast with the old

hotch-potch of streets. Princes Street is the main east-west thoroughfare with excellent shops on one side and Princes Street Gardens with their famous floral clock on the south side.

As befits such a splendid capital city there are numerous museums and art galleries packed with priceless treasures. Among these are the famous picture gallery in 16th-century Holyroodhouse, the present Royal Palace, and the fascinating and unusual Museum of Childhood.

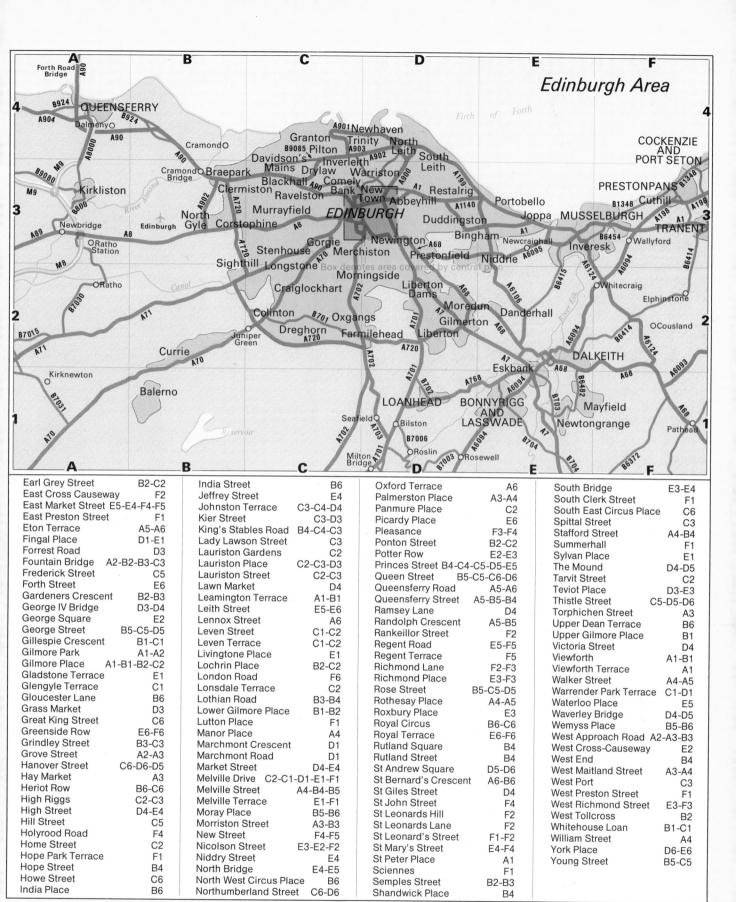

Edinburgh Area

Earl Grey Street	B2-C2
East Cross Causeway	F2
East Market Street	E5-E4-F4-F5
East Preston Street	F1
Eton Terrace	A5-A6
Fingal Place	D1-E1
Forrest Road	D3
Fountain Bridge	A2-B2-B3-C2
Frederick Street	C5
Forth Street	E6
Gardeners Crescent	B2-B3
George IV Bridge	D3-D4
George Square	E2
George Street	B5-C5-D5
Gillespie Crescent	B1-C1
Gilmore Park	A1-A2
Gilmore Place	A1-B1-B2-C2
Gladstone Terrace	E1
Glengyle Terrace	C1
Gloucester Lane	B6
Grass Market	D3
Great King Street	C6
Greenside Row	E6-F6
Grindley Street	B3-C3
Grove Street	A2-A3
Hanover Street	C6-D6-D5
Hay Market	A3
Heriot Row	B6-C6
High Riggs	C2-C3
High Street	D4-E4
Hill Street	C5
Holyrood Road	F4
Home Street	C2
Hope Park Terrace	F1
Hope Street	B4
Howe Street	C6
India Place	B6

India Street	B6
Jeffrey Street	E4
Johnston Terrace	C3-C4-D4
Kier Street	C3-D3
King's Stables Road	B4-C4-C3
Lady Lawson Street	C3
Lauriston Gardens	C2
Lauriston Place	C2-C3-D3
Lauriston Street	C2-C3
Lawn Market	D4
Leamington Terrace	A1-B1
Leith Street	E5-E6
Lennox Street	A6
Leven Street	C1-C2
Leven Terrace	C1-C2
Livingtone Place	E1
Lochrin Place	B2-C2
London Road	F6
Lonsdale Terrace	C2
Lothian Road	B3-B4
Lower Gilmore Place	B1-B2
Lutton Place	F1
Manor Place	A4
Marchmont Crescent	D1
Marchmont Road	D1
Market Street	D4-E4
Melville Drive	C2-C1-D1-E1-F1
Melville Street	A4-B4-B5
Melville Terrace	E1-F1
Moray Place	B5-B6
Morriston Street	A3-B3
New Street	F4-F5
Nicolson Street	E3-E2-F2
Niddry Street	E4
North Bridge	E4-E5
North West Circus Place	B6
Northumberland Street	C6-D6

Oxford Terrace	A6
Palmerston Place	A3-A4
Panmure Place	C2
Picardy Place	E6
Pleasance	F3-F4
Ponton Street	B2-C2
Potter Row	E2-E3
Princes Street	B4-C4-C5-D5-E5
Queen Street	B5-C5-C6-D6
Queensferry Road	A5-A6
Queensferry Street	A5-B5-B4
Ramsey Lane	D4
Randolph Crescent	A5-B5
Rankeillor Street	F2
Regent Road	E5-F5
Regent Terrace	F5
Richmond Lane	F2-F3
Richmond Place	E3-F3
Rose Street	B5-C5-D5
Rothesay Place	A4-A5
Roxbury Place	E3
Royal Circus	B6-C6
Royal Terrace	E6-F6
Rutland Square	B4
Rutland Street	B4
St Andrew Square	D5-D6
St Bernard's Crescent	A6-B6
St Giles Street	D4
St John Street	F4
St Leonards Hill	F2
St Leonards Lane	F2
St Leonard's Street	F1-F2
St Mary's Street	E4-F4
St Peter Place	A1
Sciennes	F1
Semples Street	B2-B3
Shandwick Place	B4

South Bridge	E3-E4
South Clerk Street	F1
South East Circus Place	C6
Spittal Street	C3
Stafford Street	A4-B4
Summerhall	F1
Sylvan Place	E1
The Mound	D4-D5
Tarvit Street	C2
Teviot Place	D3-E3
Thistle Street	C5-D5-D6
Torphichen Street	A3
Upper Dean Terrace	B6
Upper Gilmore Place	B1
Victoria Street	D4
Viewforth	A1-B1
Viewforth Terrace	A1
Walker Street	A4-A5
Warrender Park Terrace	C1-D1
Waterloo Place	E5
Waverley Bridge	D4-D5
Wemyss Place	B5-B6
West Approach Road	A2-A3-B3
West Cross-Causeway	E2
West End	B4
West Maitland Street	A3-A4
West Port	C3
West Preston Street	F1
West Richmond Street	E3-F3
West Tollcross	B2
Whitehouse Loan	B1-C1
William Street	A4
York Place	D6-E6
Young Street	B5-C5

EDINBURGH
Holyrood Palace orginated as a guest house for the Abbey
of Holyrood in the 16th century, but most of the present
building was built for Charles II. Mary Queen of Scots was
one of its most famous inhabitants.

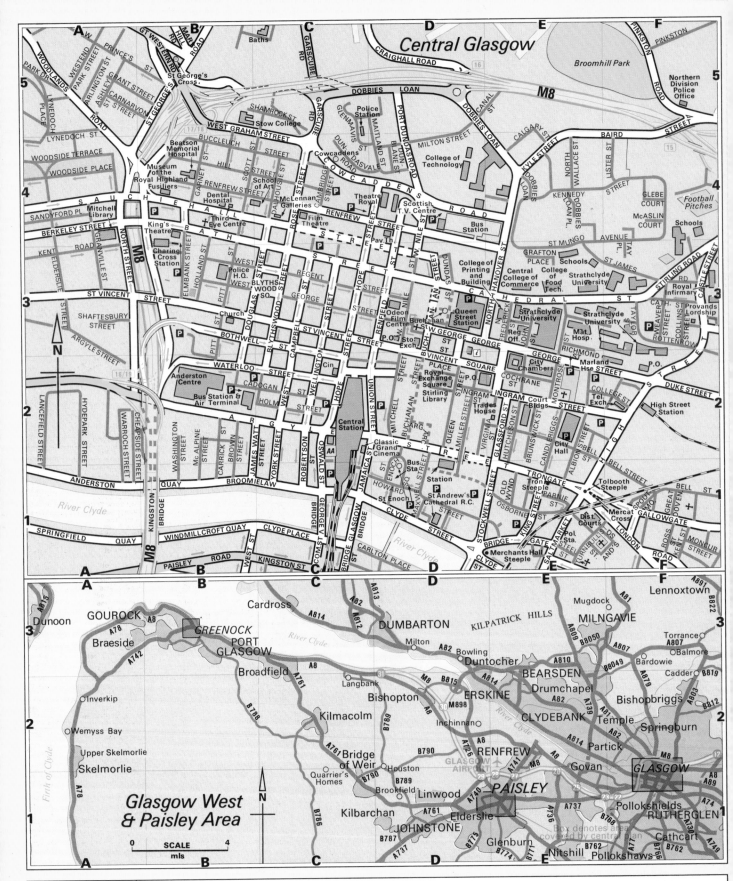

Glasgow

Although much of Glasgow is distinctly Victorian in character, its roots go back very many centuries. Best link with the past is the cathedral; founded in the 6th century, it has features from many succeeding centuries, including an exceptional 13th- century crypt. Nearby is Provand's Lordship, the city's oldest house. It dates from 1471 and is now a museum. Two much larger museums are to

be found a little out of the centre – the Art Gallery and Museum contains one of the finest collections of paintings in Britain, while the Hunterian Museum, attached to the University, covers geology, archaeology, ethnography and more general subjects. On Glasgow Green is People's Palace – a museum of city life. Most imposing of the Victorian buildings are the City Chambers and City Hall which was built in 1841 as a concert hall but now houses the Scottish National Orchestra.

Paisley is famous for the lovely fabric pattern to which it gives its name. It was taken from fabrics brought from the Near East in the early 19th century, and its manufacture, along with the production of thread, is still important.

Greenock has been an important port and shipbuilding centre since as early as the 16th century. Its most famous son is James Watt, the inventor of steam power, born here in 1736. The town has numerous memorials to the great man.

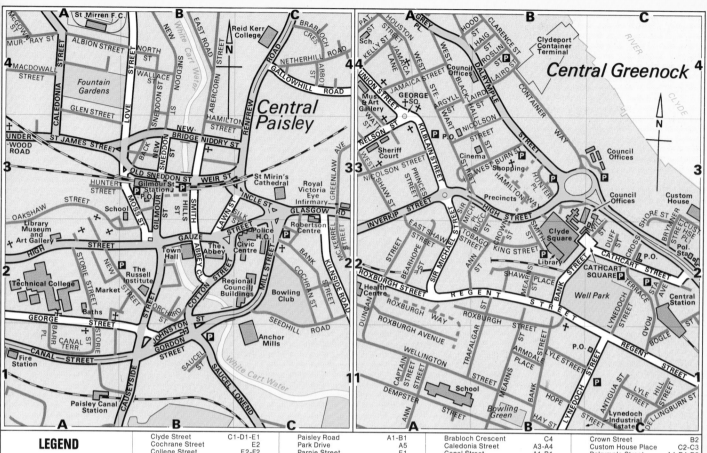

LEGEND

Town Plan

- AA recommended route
- Restricted roads
- Other roads
- Buildings of interest Station
- Car parks P
- Parks and open spaces
- One way streets

Area Plan

- A roads
- B roads
- Locations Garvock O
- Urban area

Street Index with grid reference

Glasgow

Albion Street	E1-E2
Anderston Quay	A2-A1-B1
Argyle Arcade	D1
Argyle Street	A3-A2-B2-C2-D2-D1-E1
Arlington Street	A5
Ashley Street	A5
Baird Street	E4-E5-F5-F4
Bath Street	B4-C4-C3-D3
Bell Street	E2-E1-F1
Berkeley Street	A4
Blythswood Square	B3-C3
Blythswood Street	C2-C3
Bothwell Street	B3-C3-C2
Bridgegate	D1-E1
Bridge Street	C1
Broomielaw	B1-C1
Brown Street	B1-B2
Brunswick Street	E2
Buccleuch Street	B4-C4
Buchannan Street	D3-D4
Cadogan Street	B2-C2
Calgary Street	E4-E5-E4
Canal Street	D5-E5
Candleriggs	E1-E2
Cambridge Street	C4
Carlton Place	C1-D1
Carnarvon Street	A5-B5
Carrick Street	B1-B2
Castle Street	F3
Cathedral Street	D3-E3-F3
Cheapside Street	A1-A2
Clyde Place	B1-C1
Clyde Street	C1-D1-E1
Cochrane Street	E2
College Street	E2-F2
Collins Street	F3
Commerce Street	C1
Cowcaddens Road	C4-D4-E4
Craighall Road	C5-D5
Dalhousie Street	C4
Dobbies Loan	C5-D5-E5-E4-D4
Dobbies Loan Place	E4
Douglas Street	B3-C3
Duke Street	F2
Dunblane Street	D4-D5
Dundas Street	D3
Dundasvale Road	C4-D4
Elderslie Street	A3-A4
Elmbank Street	B3-B4
Gallowgate	E1-F1
Garscube Road	C4-C5
Garnet Street	B4
George V Bridge	C1
George Square	D3-E3-E2-D2
George Street	E3-E2-F2
Glasgow Bridge	C1
Glassford Street	E2
Glebe Court	F4
Glenmavis Street	C5-C4-D4
Grafton Place	E3
Grant Street	A5-B5
Granville Street	A3-A4
Great Dovenhill	F1
Great Western Road	A5-B5
High Street	E1-E2-F2-F3
Hill Street	B4-C4-C4
Holland Street	B3-B4
Holm Street	C2
Hope Street	C2-C3-C4-C4
Howard Street	C1-D1
Hutcheson Street	E1-E2
Hyde Park Street	A1-A2
Ingram Street	D2-E2-F2
Jamaica Street	C1-C2-D2
James Watt Street	B1-B2-C2
John Street	E3
Kennedy Street	E4-F4
Kent Road	A3-A4
Kent Street	F1
King Street	E1
Kingston Bridge	B1
Kingston Street	B1-C1
Kyle Street	E4
Lancefield Street	A1-A2
Lister Street	F4
London Road	E1-F1
Lyndoch Place	A5
Lyndoch Street	A4-A5
McAlpine Street	B1-B2
McAslin Court	B1
Maitland Street	C5-D5-D4
Maryhill Road	B5
Maxwell Street	D1-D2
Miller Street	D2
Milton Street	D4-D5
Mitchell Street	D2
Moncur Street	F1
Montrose Street	E2-E3
North Street	A3-A4
North Frederick Street	E3
North Hannover Street	D3-E3-E4
North Wallace Street	E4
Old Wynd	E1
Osborne Street	E1
Oswald Street	C1-C2

Paisley Road	A1-B1
Park Drive	A5
Parnie Street	E1
Pinkston Drive	F5
Pinkston Road	F5
Pitt Street	B2-B3-B4
Port Dundas Road	D4-D5
Queen Street	D2
Renfield Street	D4-D3-C3-C2-D2
Renfrew Street	B4-C4-D4
Richmond Street	E3-E2-F2
Robertson Street	C1-C2
Rose Street	C3-C4
Ross Street	F1
Rottenrow	F3
St Andrew's Square	E1-F1
St Enoch Square	D1-D2
St George's Road	A4-B4-B5
St James Road	E3-F3
St Mungo Avenue	E3-E4-F4
St Vincent Place	D2-D3
St Vincent Street	A3-B3-C3-D3-D2
Saltmarket	E1
Sandyford Place	A4
Sauchiehall Street	A4-B4-C4-C3-D3
Scott Street	B4-C4
Shaftesbury Street	A3
Shamrock Street	B5-C5-C4
Spoutmouth	F1
Springfield Quay	A1
Steel Street	E1
Stirling Road	F3
Stockwell Street	D1-E1
Taylor Place	F4
Taylor Street	F3
Trongate	E1
Turnbull Street	E1
Union Street	C2-D2
Virginia Street	D2-E2
Warroch Street	A1-A2
Washington Street	B1-B2
Waterloo Street	B2-C2
Weaver Street	F3
Wellington Street	C2-C3
West Street	B1
West Campbell Street	C2-C3
West George Street	B3-C3-D3
West Graham Street	B5-C5-C4
West Nile Street	D3-D4
West Prince's Street	A5-B5
West Regent Street	B3-C3-D3
Westend Park Street	A5
Windmill Croft Quay	B1
Woodlands Road	A4-A5
Woodside Place	A4
Woodside Terrace	A4
York Street	C1-C2

Paisley

Abbey Close	B2
Abbot Street	C4
Abercorn Street	B3-B4
Albion Street	A4-B4
Back Sneddon Street	B3-B4
Bank Street	C2
Barr Place	A1

Brabloch Crescent	C4
Caledonia Street	A3-A4
Canal Street	A1-B1
Canal Terrace	A1
Causeyside Street	A1-B1-B2
Cochran Street	C2
Cotton Street	B2
East Road	B4
Gallowhill Road	C4
Gauze Street	B2-C2-C3
George Street	A1-B1-B2-A2
Gilmour Street	B2-B3
Glasgow Road	C3
Glen Street	A4-A3-B3
Gordon Street	B1
Greenlaw Avenue	C3
Hamilton Street	B3-C3
High Street	A2-B2
Hunter Street	A3-B3
Incle Street	C3
Johnston Street	B1-B2
Kilnside Road	C2-C3
Lawn Street	B2-B3-C3
Love Street	B3-B4
Macdowall Street	A4
McGown Street	A4
McKerrel Street	C2-C3
Mill Street	C2
Moss Street	B2-B3
Murray Street	A4
Netherhill Road	C4
Newbridge	B3
New Sneddon Street	B3-B4
New Street	A2-B2
Niddry Street	B3-C3
North Street	A4
Oakshaw Street	A2-A3-B2
Old Sneddon Street	B3
Orchard Street	B2
Renfrew Road	C3-C4
St James Street	A3
Saucel Lonend	B1-C1
Saucel Street	B1
Seedhill Road	C1-C2
Silk Street	B3-C3-C2
Smith Hills Street	B2-B3
Storie Street	A1-A2
Underwood Road	A3
Wallace Street	B4
Weir Street	B3-C3

Crown Street	B2
Custom House Place	C2-C3
Dalrymple Street	A4-B4-B3
Dellingburn Street	C1
Dempster Street	A1-B1
Duff Street	C2
Duncan Street	A1-A2
East Shaw Street	A2-A3
George Square	A3-A4
Grey Place	A4
Haig Street	B4
Hamilton Way	B3
Hay Street	B1
High Street	A3-B3-B2
Hill Street	C1
Hood Street	A4-B4
Hope Street	B1-C1
Houston Street	B1
Hunter Place	B3
Inverkip Street	A2-A3
Jamaica Lane	A4
Jamaica Street	A4
Kelly Street	A4
Kilblain Street	A3
King Street	B2
Laird Street	A4-B4
Lyle Street	B1-C1
Lynedoch Street	B1-C1-C2
Mearns Street	B1-B2
Nelson Street	A3
Nicolson Street	A3-B3
Patrick Street	A3
Princes Street	A3
Regent Street	A2-B2-C2-C1
Roslin Street	B4
Roxburgh Avenue	A1-A2
Roxburgh Street	A2-B2-B1
Roxburgh Way	A1-A2
Shaw Place	B2
Sir Michael Place	A2-A3
Sir Michael Street	A2-A3
Smith Street	B2
Station Avenue	C2
Terrace Road	C1-C2
Tobago Street	A2-B2
Trafalgar Street	A1-B1-B2
Union Street	A1
Watt Street	A3-A4
Wellington Street	A1-B1
West Blackhall Street	A4-A3-B3
West Burn Street	A3-B3
West Shaw Street	A3
West Stewart Street	A4-A3-B3
William Street	C2-C3

Greenock

Ann Street	A1
Ann Street	A2-B2
Antigua Street	C1
Argyll Street	A4
Armdale Place	B1
Bank Street	B1-B2-C2
Bearhope Street	A2
Bogle Street	C1-C2
Brymner Street	C2-C3
Buccleugh	B2-B3
Captain Street	A1
Cathcart Square	B2-C2
Cathcart Street	C2
Clarence Street	B4
Container Way	B3-B4
Cross Shore Street	C2-C3

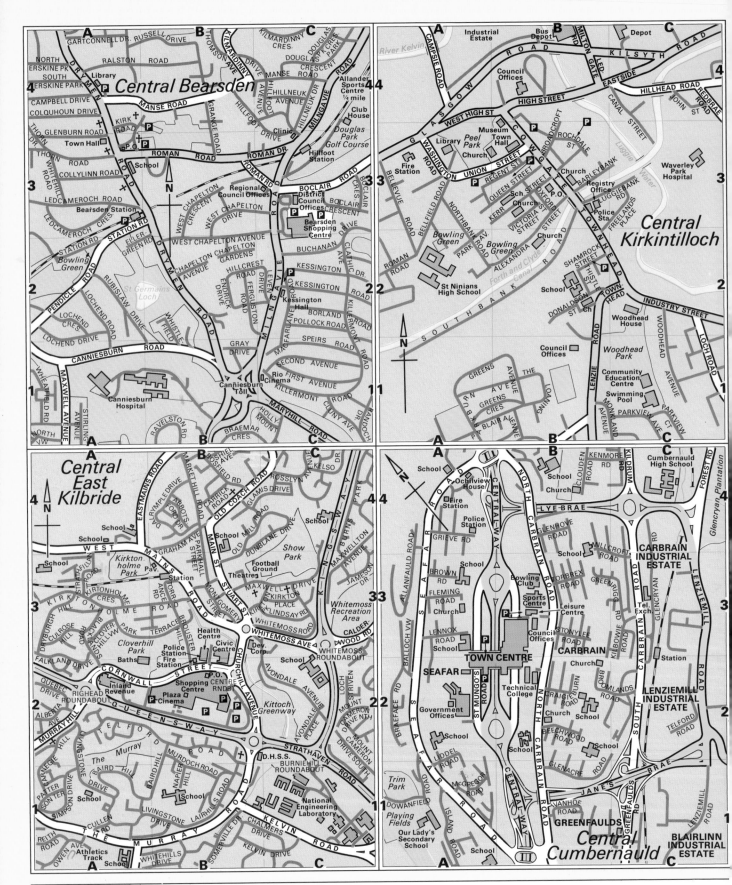

Glasgow environs

Cumbernauld is a New Town — built during the 1950s and '60s, it was specially designed to provide easy access for both motorists and pedestrians. A multi-level shopping area, a sports centre and a thriving local theatre are some of the amenities it enjoys, and amongst the many parks and open spaces in the area, Palacerigg Country Park (1 ½ miles to the south-east) covers over 600 acres.

Bearsden is noted for its public parks and woodland areas. It became established as a residential area in the 19th century, but a number of Georgian buildings are used by the community: Kilmardinny House, for instance, is an Arts Centre with a small theatre.

East Kilbride was well-known for its shoemaking and weaving in the 18th century. Its designation as a New Town shortly after the end of World War I boosted its expansion, and today, it is noted for

the good integration of new buildings with old. Popular attractions among the modern buildings are the arcaded shopping precinct and the Dollan Swimming Pool, lying beneath an unusually deep roof within the town's central park.

Kirkintilloch Once a station on the old Roman wall, Kirkintilloch in recent years has suffered from the decline of a good many local industries. The former Parish Church of St Mary has been converted into a local history museum.

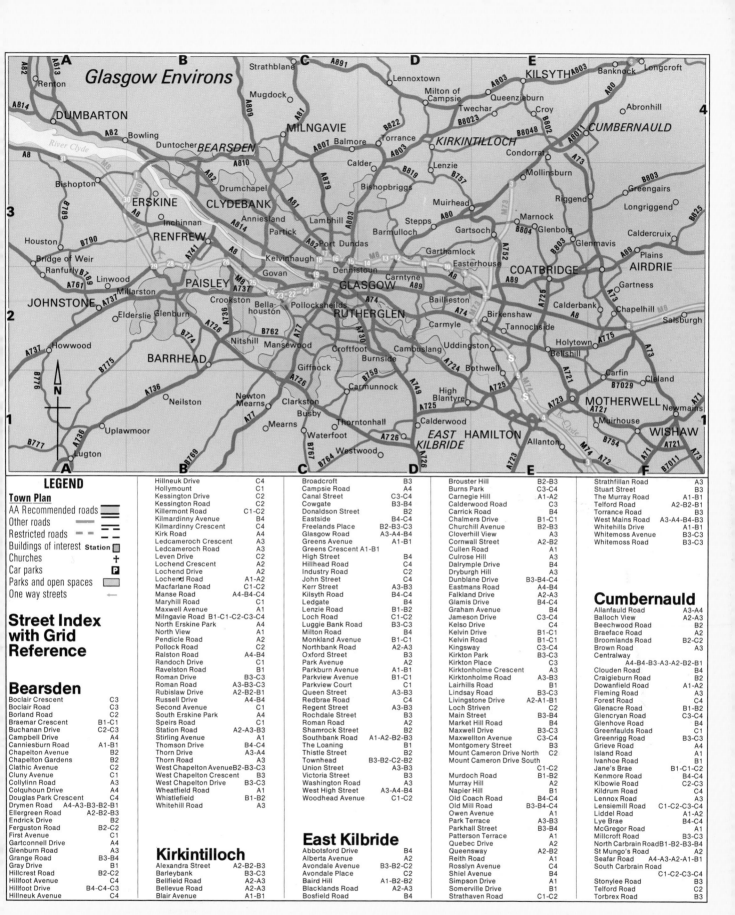

Glasgow Environs

LEGEND

Town Plan

- AA Recommended roads
- Other roads
- Restricted roads
- Buildings of interest — Station
- Churches — †
- Car parks — P
- Parks and open spaces
- One way streets

Street Index with Grid Reference

Bearsden

Boclair Crescent	C3
Boclair Road	C3
Borland Road	C2
Braemar Crescent	B1-C1
Buchanan Drive	C2-C3
Campbell Drive	A4
Canniesburn Road	A1-B1
Chapelton Avenue	B2
Chapelton Gardens	B2
Clathic Avenue	C2
Cluny Avenue	C1
Collylinn Road	A3
Colquhoun Drive	A4
Douglas Park Crescent	C4
Drymen Road	A4-A3-B3-B2-B1
Ellergreen Road	A2-B2-B3
Endrick Drive	B2
Ferguson Road	B2-C2
First Avenue	C1
Gartconnell Drive	A4
Glenburn Road	A3
Grange Road	B3-B4
Gray Drive	B1
Hillcrest Road	B2-C2
Hillfoot Avenue	C4
Hillfoot Drive	B4-C4-C3
Hillneuk Avenue	C4
Hillneuk Drive	C4
Hollymount	C1
Kessington Drive	C2
Kessington Road	C2
Killermont Road	C1-C2
Kilmardinny Avenue	B4
Kilmardinny Crescent	C4
Kirk Road	A4
Ledcameroch Crescent	A3
Ledcameroch Road	A3
Leven Drive	C2
Lochend Crescent	A2
Lochend Drive	A2
Lochend Road	A1-A2
Macfarlane Road	C1-C2
Manse Road	A4-B4-C4
Maryhill Road	C1
Maxwell Avenue	A1
Milngavie Road	B1-C1-C2-C3-C4
North Erskine Park	A4
North View	A1
Pendicle Road	A2
Pollock Road	C2
Ralston Road	A4-B4
Randoch Drive	C1
Ravelston Road	B1
Roman Drive	B3-C3
Roman Road	A3-B3-C3
Rubislaw Drive	A2-B2-B1
Russell Drive	A4-B4
Second Avenue	C1
South Erskine Park	A4
Speirs Road	C1
Station Road	A2-A3-B3
Stirling Avenue	A1
Thomson Drive	B4-C4
Thorn Drive	A3-A4
Thorn Road	A3-A4
West Chapelton Avenue	B2-B3-C3
West Chapelton Crescent	B3
West Chapelton Drive	B3-C3
Wheatfield Road	A1
Whistlefield	B1-B2
Whitehill Road	A3

Kirkintilloch

Alexandra Street	A2-B2-B3
Barleybank	B3-C3
Bellfield Road	A2-A3
Bellevue Road	A2-A3
Blair Avenue	A1-B1
Broadcroft	B3
Campsie Road	A4
Canal Street	C3-C4
Cowgate	B3-B4
Donaldson Street	B2
Eastside	B4-C4
Freelands Place	B2-B3-C3
Glasgow Road	A3-A4-B4
Greens Avenue	A1-B1
Greens Crescent	A1-B1
High Street	B4
Hillhead Road	C4
Industry Road	C2
John Street	C2
Kerr Street	A3-B3
Kilsyth Road	B4-C4
Ledgate	B4
Lenzie Road	B1-B2
Loch Road	C1-C2
Luggie Bank Road	B3-C3
Milton Road	B4
Monkland Avenue	B1-C1
Northbank Road	A2-A3
Oxford Street	B3
Park Avenue	A2
Parkburn Avenue	A1-B1
Parkview Avenue	B1-C1
Parkview Court	C1
Queen Street	A3-B3
Redbrae Road	C4
Regent Street	A3-B3
Rochdale Street	B3
Roman Road	A2
Shamrock Street	B2
Southbank Road	A1-A2-B2-B3
The Loaning	B1
Thistle Street	B2
Townhead	B3-B2-C2-B2
Union Street	A3-B3
Victoria Street	B3
Washington Road	A3
West High Street	A3-A4-B4
Woodhead Avenue	C1-C2

East Kilbride

Abbotsford Drive	B4
Alberta Avenue	A2
Avondale Avenue	B3-B2-C2
Avondale Place	B2
Baird Hill	A1-B2-B2
Blacklands Road	A2-A3
Bosfield Road	B4
Brouster Hill	B2-B3
Burns Park	C3-C4
Carnegie Hill	A1-A2
Calderwood Road	C3
Carrick Road	B4
Chalmers Drive	B1-C1
Churchill Avenue	B2-B3
Cloverhill View	A3
Cornwall Street	A2-B2
Cullen Road	A1
Culrose Hill	A3
Dalrymple Drive	B4
Dryburgh Hill	A3
Dunblane Drive	B3-B4-C4
Eastmans Road	A4-B4
Falkland Drive	A2-A3
Glamis Drive	B4-C4
Graham Avenue	B4
Jameson Drive	C3-C4
Kelso Drive	C4
Kelvin Drive	B1-C1
Kelvin Road	B1-C1
Kingsway	C3-C4
Kirkton Park	B3-C3
Kirkton Place	C3
Kirktonholme Crescent	A3
Kirktonholme Road	A3-B3
Lairhills Road	B1
Lindsay Road	B3-C3
Livingstone Drive	A2-A1-B1
Loch Striven	C2
Main Street	B3-B4
Market Hill Road	B4
Maxwell Drive	B4
Maxwellton Avenue	C3-C4
Montgomery Street	B3
Mount Cameron Drive North	C2
Mount Cameron Drive South	C1-C2
Murdoch Road	B1-B2
Murray Hill	A2
Napier Hill	B1
Old Coach Road	B4-C4
Old Mill Road	B3-B4-C4
Owen Avenue	A1
Park Terrace	A3-B3
Parkhall Street	B3-B4
Patterson Terrace	A1
Quebec Drive	A2
Queensway	A2-B2
Reith Road	A1
Rosslyn Avenue	C4
Shiel Avenue	B4
Simpson Drive	A1
Somerville Drive	B1
Strathaven Road	C1-C2
Strathfillan Road	A3
Stuart Street	B3
The Murray Road	A1-B1
Telford Road	A2-B2-B1
Torrance Road	B3
West Mains Road	A3-A4-B4-B3
Whitehills Drive	A1-B1
Whitemoss Avenue	B3-C3
Whitemoss Road	B3-C3

Cumbernauld

Allanfauld Road	A3-A4
Balloch View	A2-A3
Beechwood Road	B2
Braeface Road	A2
Broomlands Road	B2-C2
Brown Road	A3
Centralway	A4-B4-B3-A3-A2-B2-B1
Clouden Road	B4
Craigieburn Road	B2
Downfield Road	A1-A2
Fleming Road	A3
Forest Road	C4
Glenacre Road	B1-B2
Glencryan Road	C3-C4
Glenhove Road	B4
Greenfaulds Road	C1
Greenrigg Road	B3-C3
Grieve Road	A4
Island Road	A1
Ivanhoe Road	B1
Jane's Brae	B1-C1-C2
Kenmore Road	B4-C4
Kibowie Road	C2-C3
Kildrum Road	C4
Lennox Road	A3
Lensiemill Road	C1-C2-C3-C4
Liddel Road	A1-A2
Lye Brae	B4-C4
McGregor Road	A1
Millcroft Road	B3-C3
North Carbrain Road	B1-B2-B3-B4
St Mungo's Road	A2
Seafar Road	A4-A3-A2-A1-B1
South Carbrain Road	C1-C2-C3-C4
Stonylee Road	B3
Telford Road	C2
Torbrex Road	B3

EAST KILBRIDE
A fine modern Civic Centre symbolises the forward-looking approach of East Kilbride — an agricultural town of just 2,400 people in 1946, but now one of Britain's biggest new towns.

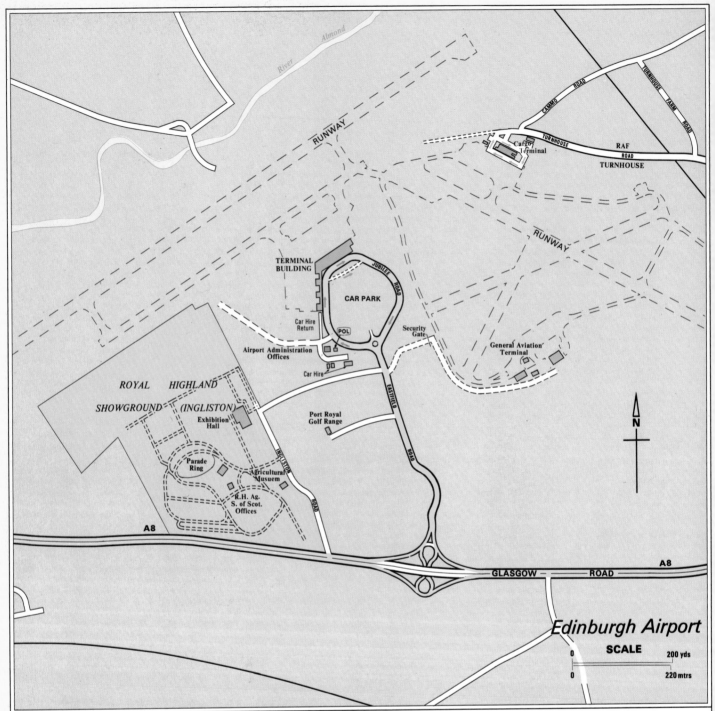

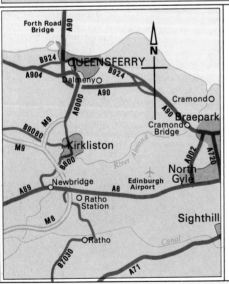

Edinburgh Airport

Charter flights to international holiday
destinations such as Spain, Italy, Corsica and
Portugal, business flights to Paris, Amsterdam
and Frankfurt and commuter links with the Leeds,
Humberside, East Midlands and Norwich Airports are
among the services offered by Edinburgh Airport.

Originally known as Turnhouse Aerodrome, it
was used by the Royal Flying Corps in World War I,
because its closeness to the railway allowed for
the delivery of aircraft by rail. The airport
remained under military control and in World War
II was a fighter station — a period commemorated
by the vintage Spitfire which is on display near
the cargo terminal.

Next came the very different years of
redevelopment, and the British Airports Authority
took control in 1971. A new runway and terminal
building had been added by 1977, the year in which
HM the Queen honoured Edinburgh Airport by coming
here to open the new building.

Available for the convenience of passengers and
other visitors to the airport today is the

Aerogrill on the first floor. Refreshments are
also supplied by the buffet on the ground floor.
Alongside each of these is a bar, and to
complement the service they provide, the
International Departure Lounge also offers the
facilities of a bar and buffet.

Ready to deal with any enquiries or problems
that arise is the Airport Information Desk, which
is situated on the main concourse of the Terminal,
and is open from 7am to 11pm.

For those wishing to watch the aeroplanes and
the airport at work, a spectators' viewing terrace
has been provided. This is accessible by lift and
is open to visitors during daylight hours. The
terrace runs along the northern side of the second
floor of the Terminal.

The airport can be reached by car via the A8
from Edinburgh, and open air car parking is
available for 1,025 vehicles. A regular coach
service operates between Edinburgh (Waverley
Bridge) and the airport, and the journey takes 25
minutes. There is also a coach service to link it
with Glasgow Airport, with a pick-up point on the A8
outside the airport.

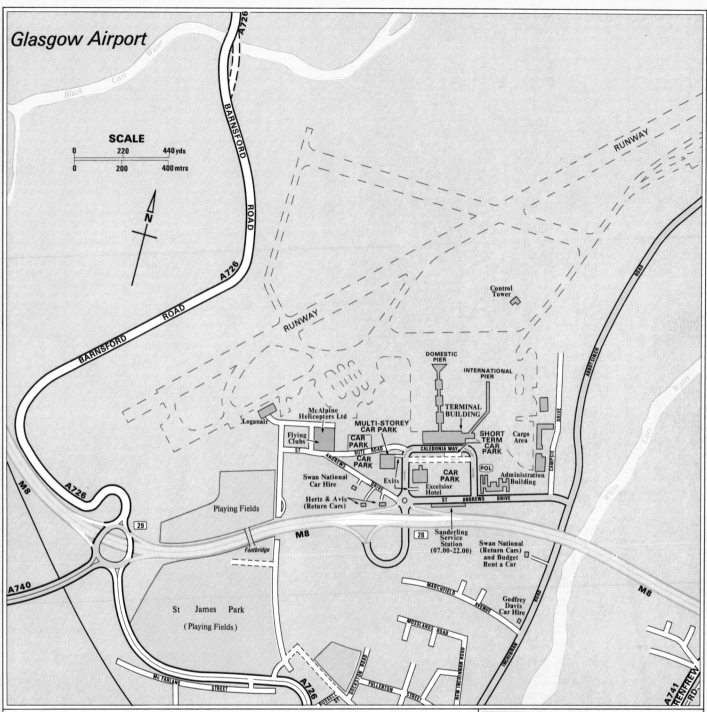

Glasgow Airport

Crucial as the fast link between Scotland's business community and the financial centre of London, this is Scotland's busiest international airport. Business flights have been calculated to make up approximately 40 per cent of Glasgow Airport's traffic, but it is also popular with other travellers — both scheduled and holiday flights are operated from here and go to a wide variety of destinations around the world.

The original site was known as Abbotsinch, and was used as an aerodrome by 602 Squadron of the Royal Auxiliary Air Force. During World War II it was converted into an RAF station, and was an important base at this time for the Fleet Air Arm. With the coming of peace and up until 1963, the airport became essentially a centre for repairs and for the fitting and testing of new aircraft.

By the early 1960s, however, it had been decided that the runway facilities at nearby Renfrew Airport were inadequate. Abbotsinch was selected as a more suitable site, and over the next three years the old aerodrome was to see a period of major redevelopment. Finally, it was renamed Glasgow Airport, and was officially opened as such by HM the Queen in 1966. Military connections of the past were remembered by the hanging in the main terminal of the crest and ship's bell of *HMS Sanderling,* which had operated from here during the war years.

In 1975, the ownership of the airport passed to the British Airports Authority. For car drivers, it lies eight miles west of Glasgow off the M8 at Junction 28. The airport is also accessible from the A8 west of Renfrew. Two car parks provide parking spaces under cover for 712 vehicles, and open air parking is provided for a further 1,164.

There are regular coach services direct from Central Glasgow, and coach services also operate between the airport and Edinburgh. Local buses run from Renfrew and Paisley.

For travellers and other visitors to the airport coming by British Rail, the nearest station is Paisley (Gilmour Street), which stands approximately one mile from the airport. Train connections are available to Ayrshire, Gourock, Glasgow and Wemyss Bay.

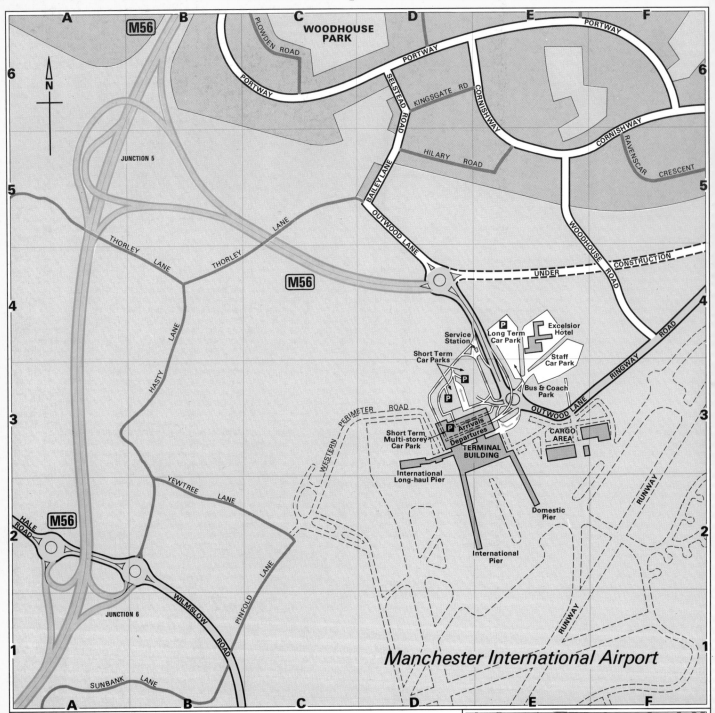

Manchester International Airport

Manchester International Airport

Nine miles south of the city of Manchester lies Manchester International Airport, operating flights to and from the Midlands, the north west, north east, Yorkshire and Wales. As well as flights within Britain, there are regular scheduled services operating to all the major business centres in Europe, the Far East and Australia. Charter and inclusive tour flights also operate from here to destinations world-wide.

The airport has been in use since just before World War II, and enjoys the distinction that its main buildings were opened by HRH Prince Philip. This was not until 1962, when the Prince became the first pilot to park an aircraft alongside the arrivals pier, and the first passenger to use the airport's facilities.

Today Manchester International has a spacious concourse area on the first floor of the terminal.

A bank, post office, bookstall, tobacconist and pharmacy are situated here. At the apron end of the concourse (and lying adjacent to the observation windows) is the Concourse Cafe, a self-service restaurant and bar. Also offering refreshments for travellers and other visitors to the airport is the 200-seat Lancaster restaurant and cocktail lounge, which overlooks International Pier B, and within just two minutes walk the Excelsior Hotel offers 300 bedrooms, a restaurant, a coffee shop and a bar.

The airport is well placed for passengers coming here by both road and rail. It offers easy access to the M56 and to the national motorway network. Greater Manchester Transport buses link the airport to Manchester and to Stockport all the year round, and also make a link to most towns in Greater Manchester during the summer months. Coach services also run to Birmingham, Liverpool, Lancaster, Leeds and Sheffield.

For railway travellers, the nearest station to the airport is Heald Green, which is about two miles away and has two bus services. Frequent trains go to Manchester (Piccadilly) and to Crewe.

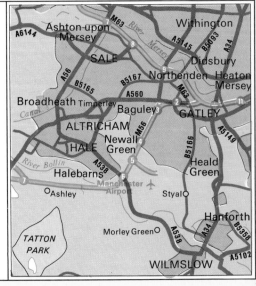